DANIEL XI

DANIEL XI

A HISTORY OF THE WORLD

MICHELLE LYNN

authorHOUSE®

AuthorHouse™
1663 Liberty Drive
Bloomington, IN 47403
www.authorhouse.com
Phone: 1-800-839-8640

Published by AuthorHouse   03/16/2012

ISBN: 978-1-4685-4228-8 (sc)
ISBN: 978-1-4685-4229-5 (hc)
ISBN: 978-1-4685-4230-1 (e)

Library of Congress Control Number: 2012901062

Any people depicted in stock imagery provided by Thinkstock are models, and such images are being used for illustrative purposes only.
Certain stock imagery © Thinkstock.

This book is printed on acid-free paper.

Because of the dynamic nature of the Internet, any web addresses or links contained in this book may have changed since publication and may no longer be valid. The views expressed in this work are solely those of the author and do not necessarily reflect the views of the publisher, and the publisher hereby disclaims any responsibility for them.

CONTENTS

PREFACE

Each chapter is divided into three sections.

➤ At the beginning of each chapter, the text of each verse is shown with some words in bold face type. These words have an actual Hebrew word associated with them. The other words were added by the translators to 'clarify' the meaning. Below this is a summary of the history associated with each verse.

➤ Next, the boxed text of each chapter focuses on the people, places and happenings that are discussed in the summary. This will aid the reader in connecting the verse text with the historical events associated with it.

➤ The final part of the chapter is a way of looking at the verse in an expanded form. Words in the left column are those with a Hebrew word associated with them (the bold face words in the scripture reference). The next column shows bold face words which are taken from the Strong's Exhaustive Concordance and which show the actual Hebrew meaning of the word. Finally, after these bold face words are dictionary definitions which help to expand the sentence.

This expanded view of the verses helps the reader see at a glance the words Daniel used without looking through the lens of a translator.

Enjoy the view as you dive into the depths of this rich chapter and discover that our journey as the human race is no accident, but has been foretold long ago.

A HISTORY OF THE WORLD

DANIEL 11:1

*Also I in the **first year** of **Darius** the **Mede,** even **I, stood** to **confirm** and to **strengthen** him.*

This chapter is a narrative telling what will happen in the latter days (Daniel 10:14). The first verse gives us a starting point, Darius the Mede, and also leaves us with the understanding that the power of God helps the powers of this world stand or fall.

According to the Columbia Encyclopedia, Darius the Mede is a king of the Medes who succeeded to the throne of Babylonia after Belshazzar. Otherwise unknown outside biblical tradition, it is likely that this Darius has been confused with Cyrus the Persian, who succeeded Belshazzar and decreed (539 BC) the return of exiled Jews. He is also mentioned by Herodotus and Josephus.[1]

I disagree with the use of the word 'confused' in the previous passage—Darius is a title rather than a name and Cyrus did have a Median mother—so Darius the Mede is another name or title for Cyrus the Great.

🔲 Daniel 6:28—So **this Daniel prospered** in the **reign** of **Darius,** and in the **reign** of **Cyrus** the **Persian.**

(The words that are not bold type are only added in translation and are not in the original text. All bold type words are defined using Strong's Exhaustive Concordance in Section II of this book.)

Cyrus II—Conqueror who founded the Achaemenian Empire

born c. 585, Media or Persis

died c. 529, Asia

Known as Cyrus the Great

The grandson of Cyrus I (fl. late 7th century BC), he came to power by overthrowing his maternal grandfather, the king of the Medes. The empire he developed was thenceforth centered on Persia and included Media, Ionia, Lydia, Mesopotamia, Syria, and Palestine. Cyrus conquered by diplomacy as well as by force. The subject of a rich legend in Persia and Greece (recorded by Xenophon and others), he was called the father of his people. He appears in the Bible as the liberator of the Jews held captive in Babylon. He died battling nomads in Central Asia. His legacy is the founding not only of an empire but also of a culture and civilization that continued to expand after his death and lasted for two centuries. He exerted a strong influence on the Greeks and Alexander the Great. Awarded heroic qualities in legend, he has long been revered by Persians almost as a religious figure. In 1971 Iran celebrated the 2,500th anniversary of his founding of the monarchy. [2]

Michelle Lynn

DANIEL 11:1

I	*I* - self
first	*first* - being number one in a countable series : beginning a series
year	*year* - 12 months that constitute a measure of age or duration
Darius	*Darejavish* - a title (rather than name) of several Persian kings
Mede	*Madian* - a native of Madai
I	*I* - self
stood	*stand* - to take up or maintain a (specified) posture
confirm	*strengthen* - to increase in power or amount : improve in effectiveness : AUGMENT, INTENSIFY
	fortify - to give physical strength, courage, or endurance to : INVIGORATE, REFRESH
strengthen	*defense* - capability of resisting attack : practice or manner of self-protection

DANIEL 11:2

And **now** will **I shew the truth. Behold,** there shall **stand up yet three kings in Persia;** and the **fourth** shall **be far richer** than they **all:** and by his **strength** through his **riches he** shall **stir up all** against the **realm** of **Grecia.**

Three more Persian kings come to power . . .

Cambyses II 529-522

Smerdis 522

Darius I 522-486

And a fourth is richer and greater than the previous three and is after Greece.

Xerxes I 485-465

As said by Herodotus in his *History,* "For what nation did Xerxes not lead out of Asia against Hellas (Greece)? And what water was not exhausted, being drunk by his host, except only the great rivers? For some supplied ships, and others were appointed to serve in the land army; to some it was appointed to furnish cavalry, and to others vessels to carry horses, while they served in expedition themselves also; others were ordered to furnish ships of war for the bridges, and others again ships with provisions."[3]
Xerxes was murdered in his palace about 465 BC, and thereafter Persia made no further attempts at conquest in Europe.[4]

Michelle Lynn

Xerxes I

born c. 519 BC

died 465 BC, Persepolis

Persian king (486-465 BC) of the Achaemenian dynasty.

Persian Khshayarsha The son of Darius I, he had been governor of Babylon before his succession. He ferociously suppressed rebellions in Egypt (484) and Babylonia (482). To avenge Darius's defeat by the Greeks at the Battle of Marathon, he spent three years raising a massive army and navy. When a storm destroyed the bridges he had built to cross the Hellespont, he had them rebuilt and for seven days oversaw the crossing of his army, numbering 360,000 troops by modern estimates, supported by more than 700 ships. The Persians broke through at the Battle of Thermopylae and pillaged Athens, but then lost their navy at the Battle of Salamis (480). Xerxes returned to Asia, leaving the army behind; it withdrew after its defeat at the Battle of Plataea (479). In Persia he began an extensive building campaign at Persepolis. Drawn unwittingly into palace intrigues, he killed his brother's family at the queen's demand. He was murdered by members of his court. His setback in Greece was regarded as the beginning of the decline of the Achaemenid dynasty. [5]

DANIEL 11:2

Now	at *this time*
I	*I* - self
shew	*predict* - to declare in advance : PROPHESY
thee	*thee* - you
truth	*certainty* - something that is certain
Behold	*lo!* - used to call attention or to express surprise
stand	*stand* - to take up or maintain a (specified) posture
up	*upward* - toward a greater amount or higher number, degree, or rate
yet	*still* - in addition : beyond this
three	*three* - being one more than two in number
kings	*king* - one that holds a supreme or preeminent position in a particular sphere or class
Persia	*Persia* - an Eastern country
fourth	*fourth* - number four in a countable series
be	*become* - to emerge as an entity : grow to manifest a certain essence, nature, development, or significance
far	*great* - PREDOMINANT, OVERRULING
richer	*rich* - possessed of great temporal power : MIGHTY : possessing great wealth : WEALTHY
all	*all* - that is the whole extent or duration of
strength	*vehemence* - INTENSITY, SEVERITY
riches	*accumulate* - to grow or increase in quantity or number
he	*he, she, it* - the person or thing spoken of
stir	*wake* - to arouse consciousness or interest in
up	*upward* - toward a higher position
all	*all* - that is the whole amount or quantity of

Michelle Lynn

realm   *rule* - DOMINION, GOVERNMENT, SWAY

Grecia   *Ionians* - one of the Greek people descended from an early group of Hellenic invaders of Greece

DANIEL 11:3

*And a **mighty king** shall **stand up, that** shall **rule with** great **dominion,** and **do** according to his **will.***

Alexander the Great (356-323 BC) was twenty-two years old at his fathers' death and before him lay a short career of conquest so brilliant that it would leave his name a myth down the ages and provide a setting for the widest expansion of Greek culture.[6] He spread Greek thought and culture over the whole of the Middle East and inspired two centuries of Greek inspired civilization known as the Hellenistic Age.[7]

Alexander was indomitable in his war conquests and only his troops refusal to go any further through India stopped him from reaching the Pacific Ocean.

Alexander the Great

born 356 BC, Pella, Macedonia

died June 13, 323 BC, Babylon

King of Macedonia (336-323) and the greatest military leader of antiquity.

or Alexander III The son of Philip II of Macedonia, he was taught by Aristotle. He soon showed military brilliance, helping win the Battle of Chaeronea at age 18. He succeeded his assassinated father in 336 and promptly took Thessaly and Thrace; he brutally razed Thebes except for its temples and the house of Pindar. Such destruction was to be his standard method, and other Greek states submitted meekly. In 334 he crossed to Persia and defeated a Persian army at the Granicus River. He is said to have cut the Gordian knot in Phrygia (333), by which act, according to legend, he was destined to rule all Asia. At the Battle of Issus in 333, he defeated another army, this one led by the Persian king Darius III, who managed to escape. He then took Syria and Phoenicia, cutting off the Persian fleet from its ports. In 332 he completed a seven-month siege of Tyre, considered his greatest military achievement, and then took Egypt. There he received the pharaohs' double crown, founded Alexandria, and visited the oracle of the god Amon, the basis of his claim to divinity. In control of the eastern Mediterranean coast, in 331 he defeated Darius in a decisive battle at Gaugamela, though Darius again escaped. He next took the province of Babylon. He burnt Xerxes' palace at Persepolis, Persia, in 330, and he envisioned an empire ruled jointly by Macedonians and Persians. He continued eastward, quashing real or imagined conspiracies among his men and taking control to the Oxus and Jaxartes rivers, founding cities (most named Alexandria) to hold the territory. Conquering what is now Tajikistan, he married the princess Roxana and embraced Persian absolutism, adopting Persian dress and enforcing Persian court customs. By 326 he reached the Hyphasis in India, where his weary men mutinied; he turned back, marching and pillaging down the Indus, and reached Susa with much loss of life. He continued to promote his unpopular policy of racial fusion, a seeming attempt to form a Persian-Macedonian master race. When his favourite, Hephaestion (324), died, Alexander gave him a hero's funeral and demanded that divine honors be given at his own funeral. He fell ill at Babylon after long feasting and drinking and died at age 33. He was buried in Alexandria, Egypt. His empire, the greatest that had existed to that time, extended from Thrace to Egypt and from Greece to the Indus valley. [8]

Michelle Lynn

DANIEL 11:3

mighty   *valiant* - marked by, exhibiting, or carried out with courage, persistence, or determination : HEROIC

warrior - a man engaged or experienced in warfare and especially in primitive warfare or the close combat typical of ancient or medieval times

king   *king* - one that holds a supreme or preeminent position in a particular sphere or class

stands   *stand* - to take up or maintain a (specified) posture

up   *upward* - toward a higher position

that   *that* - the person who : persons who

rule   *rule* - to control, direct, or influence the mind, character, or actions of : to exercise authority or power over: GOVERN

with   *with* - by means of : by the use or agency of : THROUGH

dominion *rule* - the exercise of authority or control : DOMINION, GOVERNMENT, SWAY

do   *do* - to bring to pass : carry out

will   *delight* - a high degree of gratification of mind or sense

DANIEL 11:4

And when **he** shall **stand up,** his **kingdom** shall **be broken,
and** shall **be divided** toward the **four winds** of **heaven;** and
not to his **posterity, nor** according to his **dominion which
he ruled: for** his **kingdom** shall be **plucked up,** even **for
others beside** those.

At the time of Alexander's death (323 BC) his territories were divided among his generals. These generals are referred to as the "diadochi" or Successors. This "provided a peaceful setting for the greatest extension of Greek culture and this is why these states are important. It is their contribution to the diffusion and growth of a civilization that constitute their claim on our attention, not the obscure politics and unrewarding struggles of the diadochi."[9]

After the division of Alexander's empire we see the rising of the Roman Empire. " . . . In the end she (Rome) herself stood forth as, potentially, the heir to the world empire of Alexander, and she came closer to achieving it than did any other power in the ancient world."[10] As an empire the Romans made possible the further spread of Hellenization, many of the achievements of Greece were utilized by Rome and, as a result, by those in their empire. The use of baths, literature, comedies, styles of architecture are some of the things interwoven into the Roman Empire. Rome's greatest triumph rested on the bringing of peace and it was the second great Hellenistic age in which men could travel from one end of the Mediterranean to the other without hindrance.[11] In essence, this was a Hellenistic world dominated by the Roman republic.[12]

Michelle Lynn

Roman Republic and Empire

Ancient state that once ruled the Western world.

It centered on the city of Rome from the founding of the republic (509 BC) through the establishment of the empire (27 BC) to the final eclipse of the empire in the west (5th century AD). The republic's government consisted of two consuls, the Senate, and magistrates, originally all patricians, and two popular plebeian assemblies: the military centuriate assembly and the civilian tribal assembly. A written code, the Law of the Twelve Tables (451 BC), became the basis of Roman private law. By the end of the 3rd century BC, Roman territory included all of Italy; by the late republican period it encompassed most of western Europe, northern Africa, and the Near East, organized into provinces. [13]

DANIEL 11:4

he	**this** - a demonstrative pronoun used to point out or designate persons or things for special attention
stand	**stand** - a defensive effort of some duration or degree of success
up	**above** - superior to or surpassing in any respect
kingdom	**rule** - the exercise of authority or control : DOMINION, GOVERNMENT, SWAY
be	**be** - to exist under conditions specified
broken	**burst** - to pass from one place to another especially with great vigor against obstacles or on release from some restraint
be	**be** - to exist under conditions specified
divided	**cut** - to divide into segments
four	**four** - four units or objects
winds	**region** - a particular part of the world or universe
heaven	**sky** - the expanse of space surrounding the earth
not	**not** - in no manner or degree
posterity	**posterity** - the offspring of one progenitor to the furthest generation : DESCENDENTS
nor	**not** - in no manner or degree
dominion	**empire** - an extended territory usually comprising a group of nations, states, or peoples under the control or domination of a single power
which	**which** - a relative pronoun that relates back to the noun
he	**he, she, it** - the thing or person spoken of
ruled	**rule** - to exercise authority or power over : GOVERN
for	**causal** - expressing or indicating cause

Michelle Lynn

kingdom	**rule** - the exercise of authority or control : DOMINION, GOVERNMENT, SWAY
be	**be** - to exist under conditions specified
plucked	**tear away** - to remove (as oneself) reluctantly
up	**from** - used as a function word to indicate the source or original or moving force of something
	the
	top - foremost in order, rank, achievements, value, or precedence
for	**causal** - expressing or indicating cause
others	**next** - nearest or adjacent to (as in place or order)
	other - a different one
beside	**besides** - in addition : over and above

DANIEL 11:5

> And the **king** of the **south** shall **be strong,** and one of
> his **princes;** and **he** shall **be strong above** him, and have
> **dominion;** his **dominion** shall be a **great dominion.**

Ptolemy Soter, one of Alexander's best generals, had at once seized power in Egypt at his master's death and to it he subsequently conveyed the valuable prize of Alexander's body. Ptolemy's descendants were to rule the province for nearly three hundred years until the death of Cleopatra in 30 BC; Ptolemaic Egypt was the longest-lived and richest of the successor states.[14]

Alexandria, which was founded by Alexander, had a library, a college of sorts, and she produced men like Euclid, who systematized geometry and Archimedes, who is famous for the construction of war-machines and Eratosthenes, who measured the size of the earth and Hero, who invented the steam engine and used steam to transmit energy.[15]

Michelle Lynn

Ptolemy I Soter

born 367/366, Macedonia

died 283/282 BC, Egypt

Ruler of Egypt (323-285) and founder of the Ptolemaic dynasty.

A Macedonian general of Alexander the Great, he and the other generals divided the empire after Alexander's death, Ptolemy becoming satrap of Egypt. Alexander's successors were soon at war. Ptolemy was defeated in 306 by Antigonus I Monophthalmus, though he and the others rebuffed Antigonus's attack on Egypt. He earned the name Soter ("Saviour") after defeating Antigonus on Rhodes (304), but Antigonus was not finally crushed until 301 at the Battle of Ipsus. Ptolemy secured and expanded his empire through alliances and marriages. He and his fellow kings won a final war (288-286) against Demetrius of Macedonia, freeing Athens from Macedonian occupation. He obtained control of the League of Islanders (including most of the Aegean islands), which formed the basis of Egypt's maritime supremacy. As king he respected Egyptian culture, blended Greek and Egyptian peoples and religions, and founded the Library and Museum of Alexandria. After his death the Egyptians raised him to the level of a god. He was succeeded by his son, Ptolemy II Philadelphus. [16]

DANIEL 11:5

king   *king* - one that holds a supreme or preeminent position in a particular sphere or class

south   *south* - regions or countries lying to the south of a specified or implied point of orientation

be   *be* - to exist under conditions specified

strong   *obstinate* - not yielding readily : not easily subdued or removed

      strong - able to bear or endure :ROBUST, RUGGED

princes   *head* person - one who stands in relation to others somewhat as the head does to the other members of the body : DIRECTOR, CHIEF

he   *himself* - used to emphasize the noun

be   *be* - to exist under conditions specified

strong   *obstinate* - not yielding readily : not easily subdued or removed

      strong - able to bear or endure : ROBUST, RUGGED

above   *over* - used as a function word to indicate the possession or or enjoyment of authority, power, or jurisdiction in regard to some thing or person

dominion   *rule* - to exercise authority or power over : GOVERN

dominion   *rule* - the exercise of authority or control : DOMINION, SWAY GOVERNMENT

great   *great* - considerable or remarkable in magnitude, power, intensity, degree, or effectiveness

dominion   *rule* - the exercise of authority or control : DOMINION, SWAY GOVERNMENT

      Michelle Lynn

DANIEL 11:6

*And in the **end** of **years** they shall **join** themselves together; for the **king's daughter** of the **south** shall **come** to the **king** of the **north** to **make** an **agreement**: but **she** shall **not retain** the **power** of the **arm; neither** shall **he stand**, nor his **arm**: but **she** shall **be given up**, and **they that brought** her, and **he that begat** her, and **he that strengthened** her in these times.*

Rome and Egypt now join. Cleopatra, ruler of Ptolemaic Egypt, is facing opposition from her brother, who is waging war with her, and she seeks help from Caesar.

Cleopatra becomes the lover of Julius Caesar, who at this time is master of the Roman world. Her target was power: she was determined to restore the glories of the first Ptolemies and to recover as much as possible of their dominions, which had included southern Syria and Palestine. She realized that Caesar was the strong man; the dictator of Rome, and it was therefore on him that she relied.[17] In 44 BC Julius Caesar was assassinated and after his death, she set herself to capture the emotions and vanity of Marc Antony, who was Caesar's second in command.[18]

"Her design of attacking Rome by means of Romans," as one historian put it, "was one of such stupendous audacity that we must suppose that she saw no other way." Her first had been frustrated by Caesars death; she felt now that she could win all by using the far more pliant and apparently equally powerful Antony.[19]

For a time, Octavian (Caesar's adopted heir), Antony and a third figure, Lepidus, divided the Roman world. Octavian took the hardier west, Antony had the more gorgeous east—and Cleopatra, and Lepidus took Carthaginian Africa.[20]

In 32 B.C, Octavian induced the senate to depose Antony from the command of the east and proceeded to attack him. A great naval battle at Actium (31 BC) was decided by the unexpected desertion of Cleopatra with 60 ships in the midst of the fight . . . Antony abandoned his men to follow her.

Octavian besieged Alexandria, and Antony being led to believe that Cleopatra had committed suicide, stabbed himself, but so ineffectually as to die lingeringly, and he was carried off to expire in her presence (30 BC).

Cleopatra had an interview with Octavian, in which she presented herself as a beauty in distress and very lightly clad. But when it became manifest that Octavian lacked the god-like spark, and that his care for her comfort and welfare was dictated chiefly by his desire to exhibit her in a triumphal procession through the streets of Rome, she committed suicide by letting an asp bite her.[21]

As a result of all of this Octavian is now the ruler of Ptolemaic Egypt and sole ruler of Rome.

Michelle Lynn

Cleopatra

born 69 BC

died Aug. 30, 30 BC, Alexandria

Egyptian queen (of Macedonian descent), last ruler of the Ptolemaic dynasty in Egypt.

in full Cleopatra VII Thea Philopator Daughter of Ptolemy XII (b. 112?—d. 51 BC), she ruled with her two brother-husbands, Ptolemy XIII (r. 51-47) and Ptolemy XIV (r. 47-44), both of whom she had killed, and with her son, Ptolemy XV, or Caesarion (r. 44-30). She claimed the latter was fathered by Julius Caesar, who had become her lover after entering Egypt in 48 BC in pursuit of Pompey. She was with Caesar in Rome when he was assassinated (44), after which she returned to Egypt to install her son on the throne. She lured Mark Antony, Caesar's heir apparent, into marriage (36), inviting the wrath of Octavian (later Augustus), whose sister Antony had earlier wed. She schemed against and antagonized Antony's friend Herod the Great, thereby losing his support. At a magnificent celebration in Alexandria after Antony's Parthian campaign (36-34), he bestowed Roman lands on his foreign wife and family. Octavian declared war on Cleopatra and Antony and defeated their joint forces at the Battle of Actium (31). Antony committed suicide and, after a failed attempt to beguile Octavian, so, too, did Cleopatra, possibly by means of an asp. [22]

DANIEL 11:6

end	**after** - following in time or place : AFTERWARD, BEHIND
years	**revolution** of time - the completion of a course (as of years)
they	**they** - those ones
join	**join** - ATTACH, UNITE, COUPLE
for	**causal** - expressing or indicating cause
king's	**king** - one that holds a supreme or preeminent position in a particular sphere or class
daughter	**daughter** - a human female descended from remote ancestors : female descendent : girl or woman of a given lineage
south	**south** - regions or countries lying to the south of a specified or implied point of orientation
	Egypt - of or from Egypt
come	**come** - to move toward or away from something
king	**king** - one that holds a supreme or preeminent position in a particular sphere or class
north	**north** - regions or countries lying to the north of a specified or implied point of orientation
make	**make** - to cause to exist, occur, or appear : bring to pass
agreement	**concord** - agreement by stipulation, compact, or covenant : TREATY ; esp. : one establishing or reestablishing peaceful and amicable relationships between people or nations
she	**he, she, it** - the person or thing spoken of
not	**not** - in no manner or degree : in no way : NOWISE

Michelle Lynn

retain	*maintain* - to keep in a state of repair, efficiency, or validity : preserve from failure or decline
power	*means* - resources (as of force or wealth) available for disposal
arm	*force* - might or greatness especially of a prince or state; often : strength or capacity for waging war
neither	*not* - in no manner or degree : in no way : NOWISE
he	*he, she, it* - the person or thing spoken of
stand	*stand* - to hold one's ground : maintain one's position : resist attack
force	*force* - might or greatness especially of a prince or state; often : strength or capacity for waging war
she	*that* - at which : in which : on which : by which : with which : to which
be	*become* - to come to exist or occur
given	*give* - to transfer from one's authority, custody, or responsibility
up	*upward* - toward a higher position
they	*they* - those ones : he or she : THOSE
that	*causal* - containing or involving cause or a cause : marked by cause and effect
brought	*come* - to arrive at a particular place, end, result, or conclusion
he	*he, she, it* - the person or thing spoken of
that	*who* - the person or persons involved or meant or referred to
begat	*beget* - to procreate as the father : SIRE : to give birth to : BREED : to produce usually as an effect or as a natural outgrowth

he	***he, she, it*** - the person or thing spoken of
that	***who*** - the person or persons involved or meant or referred to
strengthened	***strengthen*** - to give added strength or vigor to
	help - to give assistance or support to : AID
	fortify - to make strong : STRENGTHEN
times	***time*** - a period during which something (as an action, process, or condition) exists or continues

DANIEL 11:7

> But **out** of a **branch** of her **roots** shall one **stand up** in his **estate**, which shall **come with** an **army**, and shall **enter** into the **fortress** of the **king** of the **north** and shall **deal** against them, and shall **prevail.**

The Roman Emperor Constantine became a Christian in 312 AD, and as a result declared Christianity tolerated and the persecution of the Christians stopped. Ultimately, unwittingly, he founded Christian Europe and, therefore, the modern world. One of his decisions only slightly less enduring (the other linking Church and Empire) in its effects was his foundation, "on the command of God," he said, of a city to rival Rome on the site of the old Greek colony of Byzantium at the entrance to Black Sea. It was dedicated in 330 AD as Constantinople.[23]

Byzantium owed its wealth to its position along trade routes, it's law to Rome, and it's language to Greece. It is known as the eastern Roman Empire. The last western (Roman) emperor was deposed by a Germanic warlord, Odoacer, in 476 and formal sovereignty passed to the eastern emperors. Odoacer sent the insignia of the Roman emperor to Constantinople, claiming that he, Odoacer, would rule as the eastern emperor's representative in the West.

Although the barbarians had taken over the Western Roman Empire, they still respected the Empire. As said by a Goth, "I hope to go down to posterity as the restorer of Rome, since it is not possible that I should be its supplanter."[24] Even though the Byzantine intellectual firmly believed that civilization ended with boundaries of his world, he opened it to the barbarians (German,

Hun, Avar, Slav, and Arab), provided that the latter (with his kin) would accept Baptism and render loyalty to the emperor.[25] The Roman Empire centering at Constantinople held out for nearly a thousand years.[26]

Byzantine Empire

Empire, southeastern and southern Europe and western Asia.

It began as the city of Byzantium, which had grown from an ancient Greek colony founded on the European side of the Bosporus. The city was taken in AD 330 by Constantine I, who refounded it as Constantinople. The area at this time was generally termed the Eastern Roman Empire. On the death of Constantine in 395, Theodosius I divided the empire between his two sons. The fall of Rome in 476 ended the western half of the Roman Empire; the eastern half continued as the Byzantine Empire, with Constantinople as its capital. The eastern realm differed from the west in many respects: heir to the civilization of the Hellenistic era, it was more commercial and more urban. Its greatest emperor, Justinian (r. 527-565), reconquered some of western Europe, built the Hagia Sophia, and issued the basic codification of Roman law. After his death the empire weakened. Though its rulers continued to style themselves "Roman" long after Justinian's death, "Byzantine" more accurately describes the medieval empire. The long controversy over iconoclasm within the eastern church prepared it for the break with the Roman church (see Schism of 1054). During the controversy, Arabs and Seljuq Turks increased their power in the area. In the late 11th century, Alexius I Comnenus sought help from Venice and the pope; these allies turned the ensuing Crusades into plundering expeditions. In the Fourth Crusade the Venetians took over Constantinople and established a line of Latin emperors. Recaptured by Byzantine exiles in 1261, the empire was now little more than a large city-state. In the 14th century the Ottoman Turks began to encroach; their extended siege of Constantinople ended in 1453, when the last emperor died fighting on the city walls and the area came under Ottoman control.[27]

DANIEL 11:7

out
   from - used as a function word to indicate the source or original or moving force of something

branch
   shoot - a growth from a main stem or stock : OFFSHOOT

   descendant - something that derives its character directly from a precursor or prototype

roots
   root - a race, family, or progenitor that is the source or beginning of a group or line of descendants

stand
   stand - to take up or maintain a (specified) posture

up
   above - superior to or surpassing in any respect : higher than (as in rank, position, quality, or degree)

estate
   stand - a defensive effort of some duration or degree of success

come
   come - to move toward or away from something : pass from one point toward another nearer or more central : APPROACH

with
   with - by means of : by the use or agency of : THROUGH : as a result of : in consequence of : because of

army
   virtue - moral practice or action : conformity to a standard of right (as divine law or the highest good) : moral ex- cellence : integrity of character : uprightness of conduct RECTITUDE, MORALITY

enter
   come - to move toward or away from something : pass from one point toward another nearer or more central : APPROACH

                  Michelle Lynn

fortress	*fortified* - to give physical strength, courage, or endurance to : INVIGORATE, REFRESH
	defense - capability of resisting attack : practice or manner of self-protection
king	*king* - one that holds a supreme or preeminent position in a particular sphere or class
north	*north* - regions or countries lying to the north of a specified or implied point of orientation
deal	*do* - to bring to pass : carry out
prevail	*strengthen* - to give added strength or vigor to
	help - further the advancement of : PROMOTE

Daniel 11:8

*And shall **also carry captive** into **Egypt** their **gods, with** their **princes,** and **with** their **precious vessels** of **silver** and **gold;** and **he** shall **continue** more **years** than the **king** of the **north.***

It was the coming of Christianity that sounded the death knell of the old Egyptian religion. The ancient temples crumbled, the gods were neglected and finally denounced, their very images on the temple walls defaced or obliterated. Only the ancient language exists (ironically) in the (Christian) Coptic Church.[28]

Constantine despoiled (pagan) temples of their gold to build splendid churches.[29] Theodosius . . . the last ruler of the united (Roman) empire at last forbade the public worship of the ancient gods in 380 AD. What this meant in practice is hard to say. In Egypt it seems to have been the final landmark in the process of overcoming the ancient civilization which had been reached; in principle the closed Christian society of the Middle Ages was now in existence.[30]

Egypt

Country, Middle East.

officially Arab Republic of Egypt formerly United Arab Republic Area: 385,210 sq mi (997,690 sq km). Population (2002 est.): 66,341,000. Capital: Cairo. The people are mainly a homogeneous mix of Hamitic and Semitic lineages. Language: Arabic (official). Religions: Islam (official), mostly Sunnite; Coptic Christianity (minority). Currency: Egyptian pound. Egypt occupies a crossroads between Africa, Europe, and Asia. The majority of its land is in the arid western and eastern deserts, separated by the country's dominant feature, the Nile River. The Nile forms a flat-bottomed valley, generally 5-10 mi (8-16 km) wide, that fans out into the densely populated delta lowlands north of Cairo. The Nile valley (which begins in Upper Egypt) and delta (Lower Egypt), along with scattered oases, support all of Egypt's agriculture and have virtually all of its population. It has a developing, mainly socialist, partly free-enterprise economy based primarily on industry, including petroleum production, and agriculture. It is a republic with one legislative house; its chief of state is the president, while the head of government is the prime minister. It is one of the world's oldest continuous civilizations. Upper and Lower Egypt were united c. 3000 BC, beginning a period of cultural achievement and a line of native rulers that lasted nearly 3,000 years. Egypt's ancient history is divided into the Old, Middle, and New Kingdoms, spanning 31 dynasties and lasting to 332 BC. The Pyramids date from the Old Kingdom, the cult of Osiris and the refinement of sculpture from the Middle Kingdom, and the era of empire and the Exodus of the Jews from the New Kingdom. An Assyrian invasion occurred in the 7th century BC, and the Persian Achaemenids established a dynasty in 525 BC. The invasion by Alexander the Great in 332 BC inaugurated the Macedonian Ptolemaic period and the ascendancy of Alexandria as a center of learning and Hellenistic culture. The Romans held Egypt from 30 BC to AD 395; later it was placed under the control of the Byzantine Empire. After the Roman emperor Constantine granted tolerance to the Christians in 313, a formal Egyptian (Coptic) church emerged. [31]

DANIEL 11:8

also	*also* - in addition : as well : BESIDES, TOO
	yea - more than this : not only so but—used to mark addition or substitution of a more explicit or emphatic phrase and thus interchangeable with nay
carry	*go* - to take a certain course or follow a certain procedure
captive	*captured* - to get control or secure domination of : WIN, GAIN
	exile - forced removal from one's native country : expulsion from home : BANISHMENT
Egypt	*Mitsrajim (Egypt)* - of or from Egypt
gods	*god* - a person or thing that is honored as a god or deified : something held to be of supreme value
with	*with* - used as a function word to indicate accompaniment or companionship
princes molten	*image* - a sculptured or fabricated object of symbolic value : IDOL
with	*with* - used as a function word to indicate accompaniment or companionship
precious	*delight* - something that gives great pleasure or gratification
vessels	*apparatus* - a collection or set of materials, instruments, appliances, or machinery designed for a particular use
silver	*silver* - coin made of silver : silver money : MONEY
gold	*gold* - gold coins : a gold piece : MONEY, RICHES

he	**he, she, it** - the person or thing spoken of
continue	**stand** - to hold ones ground : maintain ones position : resist attack
years	**revolution** of time - the completion of a course (as of years)
king	**king** - one that holds a supreme or preeminent position in a particular sphere or class
north	**north** - regions or countries lying to the north of a specified or implied point of orientation

DANIEL 11:9

*So the **king** of the **south** shall **come** into his **kingdom,** and shall **return into** his own **land.***

In 622 AD, Muhammad founded the religion of Islam. He believed that all other religions had falsified what their prophets had said, and according to tradition, the angel Gabriel told him that he was the prophet chosen to receive God's last message to men.[32]

Muhammad's purpose was the conversion of the "infidels", that is, anyone not worshipping Allah and incredibly, by the time of his death in 632, he was the master of Arabia. His religion had been established and is still in practice today.

Islam teaches that the surest way to paradise is to die fighting in the cause of God, and the Arabs soon began their career of conquest.[33]

Muhammad

born c. 570, Mecca, Arabia

died June 8, 632, Medina

or *Mohammed* The son of a merchant of the ruling tribe, he was orphaned at age six. He married a rich widow, Khadījah, with whom he had six children, including Fatimah, a daughter. According to tradition, in 610 he was visited by the angel Gabriel, who informed Muhammad that he was the messenger of God. His revelations and teachings, recorded in the Qur'an, are the basis of Islam. He began to preach publicly c. 613, urging the rich to give to the poor and calling for the destruction of idols. He gained disciples but also acquired enemies, whose plan to murder Muhammad forced him to flee Mecca for Medina in 622. This flight, known as the Hijrah, marks the beginning of the Islamic era. Muhammad's followers defeated a Meccan force in 624; they suffered reverses in 625 but repelled a Meccan siege of Medina in 627. He won control of Mecca by 629 and of all Arabia by 630. He made his last journey to Mecca in 632, establishing the rites of the hajj, or pilgrimage to Mecca. He died later that year and was buried at Medina. His life, teachings, and miracles have been the subjects of Muslim devotion and reflection ever since. [34]

Michelle Lynn

DANIEL 11:9

king   *king* - one that holds a supreme or preeminent position in a particular sphere or class

south   *south* - regions or countries lying to the south of a specified or implied point of orientation

come   *come* - to arrive at a particular place, end, result, or conclusion

kingdom   *rule* - the exercise of authority or control : DOMINION, GOVERNMENT, SWAY

           dominion - a supremacy in determining and directing the actions of others or in governing politically, socially, or per- sonally : acknowledged ascendancy over human or non-human forces such as assures cogency in commanding or restraining and being obeyed : SOVEREIGNTY

return   *turn* back - to cause to have or take another path or direction : bend or change the course of

into   *towards* - along a course leading to : with a view to gaining : to the end or purpose of

land   *soil* - COUNTRY, LAND

DANIEL 11:10

But his **sons** shall **be stirred up,** and shall **assemble** a **multitude** of great **forces:** and one shall certainly **come,** and **overflow,** and **pass** through: then shall **he return,** and **be stirred up,** even to his **fortress.**

The next generations of Muslims erupted from the (Arabian) peninsula and, picking up recruits as they went, overran the neighboring lands. As they advanced, they were joined by the discontented subjects of the older empires . . . Men of many races joined the Arabs in creating a new empire and a new civilization.[35]

By 732 AD the nation of Islam ruled an empire that stretched from the Pyrenees to the borders of India; larger than the Roman Empire at its height.

The Arab Empire slipped into decline and disintegration as a political unit, as one provincial governor after another threw off his allegiance to the central government.[36]

In the eleventh century the Seljuk Turks broke with irresistible force . . . into the decaying Muslim Empire Islam, which had appeared far-gone in decay, which had been divided religiously and politically, was suddenly discovered to have risen again.[37]

Michelle Lynn

Seljuks

By 1040 the lands of Central Asia would pass from under the control of the Ghaznavids to that of the Seljuks. As the immediate forebears of the Ottomans, who would later come to dominate Asia Minor and the Mediterranean, the Seljuks established the Turks as a unified military force. Until the Seljuk Empire provided cohesion to the Turks of Central Asia, the Turks had existed only in separate, nomadic groups. In 1050, the Seljuk leader, Tughril Beg, was awarded the title of *Sultan* from the Abbasid caliph, and he became the first Muslim ruler to use that title. It later became a common title for a Muslim ruler. [38]

DANIEL 11:10

sons   **nation** - a community of people composed of one or more nationalities and possessing a more or less defined territory and government : a particular group or aggregation (as of men or animals)

be   **become** - grow to manifest a certain essence, nature, development, or significance

stirred   **grate** - FRET, IRRITATE, OFFEND

         irritate - to increase the action of : heighten excitement in : to produce excitation in : STIMULATE

         offend - to strike against : ATTACK, ASSAIL

up   **upward** - toward a greater amount or higher number, degree, or rate

assemble   **gather** - to prepare (as oneself) by mustering strength or force

multitude   **tumult** - a noisy and turbulent popular uprising : DISTURBANCE, RIOT

forces   **force** - might or greatness especially of a prince or state; often : strength or capacity for waging war

         army - a body of persons organized for the advancement of a cause

come   **go** - to take a certain course or follow a certain procedure

overflow   **conquer** - to gain or acquire by force of arms : take possession of by violent means : gain domination over : SUBJUGATE

pass   **cover** - to lie over : spread over : be placed on or often over the whole surface of : ENVELOP, FILM, COAT

         Michelle Lynn

	irritate - to increase the action of : heighten excitement in : to produce excitation in : STIMULATE
	offend - to strike against : ATTACK, ASSAIL
he	*same* - something that has previously been defined or described
return	*again* - another time : once more : ANEW
be	*become* - grow to manifest a certain essence, nature, development, or significance
stirred	*grate* - FRET, IRRITATE, OFFEND
up	*upward* - toward a greater amount or higher number, degree, or rate
fortress	*fortified* - to make strong : STRENGTHEN
	defense - means or method of defending : defensive plan, policy, or structure

DANIEL 11:11

*And the **king** of the **south** shall **be** moved **with choler,** and shall **come forth** and **fight with** him, even **with the king** of the **north:** and **he** shall **set forth** a great **multitude;** but the **multitude** shall **be given** into his **hand.***

The Seljuk Turks, who converted to Islam in 960, began a successful career of conquest. After occupying Syria and Palestine they invaded Asia Minor, where they inflicted on the Byzantines one of the worst defeats in their history at Manzikert in 1071. Significantly the Seljuks called the sultanate (*sultan* means head of state) they had set up there the Sultanate of Rum, for they saw themselves henceforth as the inheritors of the old Roman territories.[39]

The Turks were not as tolerant of Christians as the Arab's had been. They began to trouble Christian pilgrims going to the holy places.

In response to this persecution, Pope Urban II called for a holy war in the Holy Land. He contrasted the sanctity of Jerusalem and the holy places with the plunder and desecration directed against them by the infidel Turks. He vividly described the numerous attacks upon the Christian pilgrims visiting these centers. He also spoke of the military threat to the fellow Christians at Constantinople.

Special preachers like Peter the Hermit and Walter the Penniless carried the message into the more rural and less sophisticated communities. These people, simple peasants, were given a purpose, which was to free the Holy Land from the Muslims.[40]

Michelle Lynn

Seljuks

In the mid-11th century the Seljuks also began their assault on Byzantine-ruled Asia Minor. Initially, raids into Byzantine territory were intended only to deter the Byzantines from concluding an alliance with the Shiite Fatimids in Egypt and Syria, who were the Seljuks' enemies, but the raids soon acquired expansionist zeal. In 1071, the Seljuks achieved a decisive victory against the Byzantines in the Battle of Manzikert, in Armenia. They captured the Byzantine emperor, Romanos Diogenes, and forced him to accept a peace treaty that in effect opened the door for Seljuk expansion into Asia Minor. In 1078, the Seljuks had reached Nicaea, near Constantinople, and the Seljuk sultan, Suleiman, moved his capital there. It was the first permanent Turkish settlement in Asia Minor, and the Turkish presence in the region has continued ever since. The rise of the Islamic Turks at the expense of the Greek Byzantines in Asia Minor is indeed one of the most significant demographic shifts of the medieval period. Numerous battles with the Christians ensued over the next few centuries, with each side trading small parcels of territory after each battle. The Seljuks were also involved in several Crusades, sometimes in allegiance with Western European countries against the Greek Byzantines, and they also faced the wrath of the invading Mongols in the 13th century. [41]

The People's Crusade (1096 AD)

In November 1095, Pope Urban II's call for a crusade to liberate Jerusalem was spread throughout Europe by his priests. Soon swarms of poor knights, peasants, vagrants, beggars, women and children were on the move; a "People's Crusade" of paupers and adventurers all fanatical in their zeal to free the Holy land. They marched well in advance of the armies of the Kings and Princes of Europe, which were slow to muster. The mobs were gathered in five large crusading armies, the principal of which was lead by Peter the Hermit, a priest of Amiens, who quickly emerged as the dynamic leader of the People's Crusade, collecting nearly 15,000 crusaders as he marched overland from Flanders to Cologne.

Walter the Penniless (Sans-Avoir), a pious knight sworn to poverty, had started out with eight knights and a company of Frankish foot soldiers. His band quickly grew to several thousand strong. They were given safe conduct through Hungary, and were encamped outside Semlin, where they were denied a market. Sixteen of his men were sent to buy supplies and resorted to pilferage when they were refused. They were seized and stripped of their arms and goods. Passing on to Belgrade, Walter was again denied a market and Walter's men responded by helping themselves to livestock and pasturage. The Belgrade garrison fell upon Walter's forces and scattered them, burning alive 60 who had taken shelter in a chapel. The survivors escaped to Nish, where the Emperor Alexius I granted them safe passage and a military escort to Constantinople.

Walter's band was followed shortly thereafter by the army of Peter the Hermit. Reaching Semlin, they found the spoils taken from

Walter's companions displayed on the city's walls and resolved to avenge the wrongs done their fellow crusaders. Godfrey, at the head of two hundred Frankish foot soldiers joined by the knight Reinald of Broyes (Rainald of Breis) and his dismounted followers stormed the walls and opened the gates. The Hungarians fled the city through an eastern gate to the banks of the Danube, where they reformed on the summit of a steep hill, approximately 7000 strong. Here they were overwhelmed by the avenging crusaders, who killed an estimated 4000 to the loss of a hundred pilgrims.

Peter and his followers held the city for five days, until he learned that the Hungarian king was approaching with a formidable host. After a difficult crossing of the Sava river, made more trying by a Byzantine unit of Patzinaks/Pechenegs, they marched to Nish. Again denied a market, they marched onward only to be assaulted by the Byzantine garrison of Nish after Peter's Germans set fire to several mills following a dispute with the townsfolk. In the ensueing fight, Peter lost his train (including his treasury) and a quarter of his force before abandoning the battle. The remainder of his army pressed on through Sofia and Philippopolis arriving at Constantinople in August 1096, where they were ordered to encamp at a distance.

Walter and Peter were followed by three armies of crusaders recruited in Lorraine, eastern France, Bavaria and Alemmania, which were collectively dubbed the "German Crusades." Inspired by one of Peter's sermons, Gottschalk gathered a band of 15,000 and set out after the Hermit. His followers arrived peacefully in the kingdom of Hungary, and were favorably received by King Coloman on a bond of peace, but after several days in the Hungarian city, the Germanic crusaders became undisciplined and disorderly.

To restore the peace, Gottschalk and his officers counseled their soldiers to turn over their arms. But once the weapons were under lock and key, the Hungarians set upon Gottschalk's host, slaughtering many and dispersing the rest.

Another large force of approximately 12,000 under the command of Count Emico (Emich) of Leinigen followed the footsteps of Gottschalk southward through the Rhenish lands. Emico was a Swabian noble with the reputation of a robber baron, and his army committed horrific pogroms at Spier, Worms, Cologne and in the Kingdom of Lorraine as they marched southward. Arriving at Mainz, they besieged the city until a ransom was paid, and then stormed it anyway, slaughtering nearly a thousand Jews who had sought sanctuary with Bishop Rothard. They then set forth on the Royal Highway to Wieselburg, an imperial fortress of King Coloman of Hungary, to find the gates closed against them. They breached and stormed the walls, but took fear for some unknown reason, and were overwhelmed in turn. The army of Emico was scattered to the winds, some few finding their way to Constantinople. Emico survived the battle and joined the following of Hugh of Vermandois, arriving in Constantinople in November 1096.

A fifth band under Volkmar (Folcmar) lead crusaders from Saxony south through Bohemia, committing pograms in Magdeburg and Prague. After crossing the border into Hungary, they fell upon the town of Nitra, but were attacked and dispersed by the Hungarian army.

Meanwhile, Peter the Hermit had joined forces with Walter the Penniless outside Constantinople. Their combined army was bolstered by later arriving survivors of the German Crusades

Michelle Lynn

as well as crusaders arriving by ship from Italy. As the crusader encampments became increasingly boisterous, the Emperor Alexius I had the army ferried across the Bosphorus, where they occupied an abandoned military camp at Civetot (Kibotos). The army segregated by nationality into rival camps of Franks and Germans, who then launched a series of local raids against the mostly Christian villages.

Peter counseled the host to wait until more seasoned warriors arrived before proceeding southward against the Turks and Saracens, and then departed to Constantinople to negotiate with the Emperor for regular Byzantine troops to support his army of crusaders. With Peter away, the Franks launched a raid southward as far as Nicaea, the capital of Kilij Arslan, the Seljuk Turk sultan of Asia Minor, who was off with his army suppressing a rebellion in central Anatolia. Returning laden with booty, the Frankish success inspired a similar raid by the German crusaders under Reinald, who moved south and then east to occupy an abandoned castle at Xerigordon as a new base of operations . . . .[42]

DANIEL 11:11

king	**king** - one that holds a supreme or preeminent position in a particular sphere or class
south	**south** - regions or countries lying to the south of a specified or implied point of orientation
be	**be** - to exist under conditions specified
with	**with** - used as a function word to indicate manner of action
choler	**be bitter** - VEHEMENT, RELENTLESS, DETERMINED : exhibiting intense animosity
come	**go** - to move on a course
	out - used as a function word to indicate movement or direction away from the center
forth	**egress** - the act or right of going or coming out (as from a place of confinement)
fight	**battle** - participation in armed conflict : WARFARE
with	**with** - in opposition to : AGAINST
with	**with** - as a result of : in consequence of : because of
king	**king** - one that holds supreme or preeminent position in a particular sphere or class
north	**north** - regions or countries lying to the north of a specified or implied point of orientation
he	**he, she, it** - the person or thing spoken of
set	**stand** - to take up or maintain a (specified) posture
forth	**bring** - to convey, lead, carry, or cause to come along from one place to another, the direction of movement being toward the place from which the action is being regarded

	out - used as a function word to indicate movement away from the center
multitude	*crowd* - an unorganized aggregate of people temporarily united in response to a common stimulus or situation in which the individuality of the participants is submerged
multitude	*crowd* - an unorganized aggregate of people temporarily united in response to a common stimulus or situation in which the individuality of the participants is submerged
be	*become* - to emerge as an entity : grow to manifest a certain essence, nature, development, or significance
given	*give* - to cause to have or receive
hand	*direction* - the way of advancement, furtherance, or cultivation : AIM, PURPOSE, OBJECTIVE

DANIEL 11:12

*And when **he** hath **taken** away the **multitude,** his **heart** shall*
*be **lifted up;** and **he** shall **cast down** many **ten thousands:***
*but **he** shall **not be strengthened** by it.*

Such religious enthusiasm was aroused in the people that they could not be deterred from their expeditions. The first forces to move eastward were great crowds of undisciplined people rather than armies. This was the "peoples crusade". Never before in the whole history of the world had there been such a spectacle as these masses of practically leaderless people moved by an idea.[43]

This great host numbered possibly 50,000, and included entire families with small children. Many were lost or killed on their way through Hungary. The remnants that reached Constantinople were shipped across the Bosporus by Emperor Alexius, but were massacred by the Muslims.[44]

The People's Crusade
Continued from v. 11

. . . . They chose poorly, finding themselves quickly invested by Turks without supplies or access to water. After eight grueling days in which they were reduced to drinking the blood of their horses and their own urine, the Crusaders surrendered. Those who did not convert to Islam were executed on the spot. Reinald choose conversion and was sold into slavery. With Peter still in Constantinople, the army at Civetot worked itself into a fervor and marched southward under the command of Geoffrey Burel to avenge Xerigordon. Not far from Civetot, where the road passed through a wooded valley, Arslan's Turks fell upon the unexpecting crusaders. Heavy bow fire raked the knights in the advance of the army, dismounting them and forcing them back into the ranks. The Turkish cavalry outflanked and overwhelmed the straggling crusader army along its line of march, and then overran the encampment at Civetot. Walter the Penniless was cut down in the fighting. Of an estimated 20,000 crusaders, only 3,000 survived the rout by escaping to a small fortress on the coast, where they were rescued from the sea by Emperor Alexius I. Thus ended the People's Crusades, although Peter the Hermit and a number of its survivors joined forces with the new bands of crusaders arriving from Europe under the command of the great Kings and Princes.[45]

Consequences

Kilij Arslan had won a great victory for Islam. The Turks had been hearing stories of a great army of the Franj (their name for all Latin Europeans) marching against Allah. He had met this fearful army and had annihilated it. To his mind, the Franj were not so fearful after all, but were hardly more than peasants. He was both right and wrong, of course. The army he had beaten was in fact not much of an army, but he had not faced the **real** army yet. His victory near Civetot would cause the Turk to underestimate the next wave of Crusaders when they arrived, with serious consequences. The disaster also had consequences for the Christians. It showed plainly that mere piety and fervor would not be enough to liberate the Holy Sepulchre. There would be no crusade of the common people to the Holy Land, but an organized invasion by armies. And Peter the Hermit would not be its leader. That role would fall to the princes who were beginning to arrive at Constantinople even as the Turks were crushing the People's Crusade.[46]

DANIEL 11:12

he	*this* - the person, thing, or idea that is present or near in place, time, or thought, or that has just been mentioned
taken	*lift* - to raise from a lower to a higher position
multitude	*crowd* - an unorganized aggregate of people temporarily united in response to a common stimulus or situation in which the individuality of the participants is submerged
heart	*heart* - COURAGE, ARDOR, ENTHUSIASM
be	*become* - to come to exist or occur
lifted	*rise* - to go to war: take up arms: launch an attack: make
insurrection	
up	*from* - used as a function word to indicate the source or original or moving force of something the
	top - CHIEF, HEAD, PREEMINENT
he	*he, she, it* - the person or thing spoken of
cast down	*fall* - FELL *fell*: to cut, beat or knock down or bring down: SLAUGHTER
ten thousands	*myriad* - an immense number: an indefinitely large number: a great multitude
he	*he, she, it* - the person or thing spoken of
not	*not* - in no manner or degree: in no way: NOWISE
be	*be* - to exist under conditions specified
strengthened	*stout* - resistant to stress or pressure: TOUGH, RIGID

DANIEL 11:13

> For the **king** of the **north** shall **return,** and shall **set** forth
> a **multitude greater than** the **former,** and shall certainly
> **come after certain years with** a **great army** and **with** much
> **riches.**

The People's Crusade was followed by the first real crusade. It consisted of several separate feudal armies, each under its own leader.[47] They included French, German, Norman and Italian knights. They started moving east in 1096 and after many squabbles among themselves and much loss of life from dysentery and disease, captured Jerusalem in 1099 after a 40-day siege.[48]

When Urban was calling for this war, in order to make the prospect more appealing, he hinted at the possibility of obtaining feudal fiefs, lands, wealth, power, and prestige, all at the expense of the Arabs and Turks.[49]

Michelle Lynn

Crusades

Military expeditions, beginning in the late 11th century, that were organized by Western Christians in response to centuries of Muslim wars of expansion.

Their objectives were to check the spread of Islam, to retake control of the Holy Land, to conquer pagan areas, and to recapture formerly Christian territories. The Crusades were seen by many of their participants as a means of redemption and expiation for sins. Between 1095, when the First Crusade was launched by Pope Urban II at the Council of Clermont, and 1291, when the Latin Christians were finally expelled from their kingdom in Syria, there were numerous expeditions to the Holy Land, to Spain, and even to the Baltic; the Crusades continued for several centuries after 1291, usually as military campaigns intended to halt or slow the advance of Muslim power or to conquer pagan areas. The Crusaders initially enjoyed success, founding a Christian state in Palestine and Syria, but the continued growth of Islamic states ultimately reversed those gains. By the 14th century the Ottoman Turks had established themselves in the Balkans and would penetrate deeper into Europe despite repeated efforts to repulse them. Crusades were also called against heretics (the Albigensian Crusade, 1209-29) and various rivals of the popes, and the Fourth Crusade (1202-04) was diverted against the Byzantine Empire. Crusading declined rapidly during the 16th century with the advent of the Protestant Reformation and the decline of papal authority. The Crusades constitute a controversial chapter in the history of Christianity, and their excesses have been the subject of centuries of historiography. [50]

DANIEL 11:13

for	*causal* - expressing or indicating cause
king	*king* - one that holds a supreme or preeminent position in a particular sphere or class
north	*north* - regions or countries lying to the north of a specified or implied point of orientation
return	*again* - in return or in response: BACK: as a result or con- sequence: another time: ANEW
set	*stand* - to take up or maintain a (specified) posture
multitude	*crowd* - an unorganized aggregate of people temporarily united in response to a common stimulus or situation in which the individuality of the participants is submerged
greater	*abundant* - amply supplied: ABUNDANT
than	*from* - used as a function word to indicate the source of original or moving force of something
	part - a unit (as a number, quantity, or mass) held to constitute with one or more other units something larger: CON- STITUENT, FRACTION, FRAGMENT, MEMBER, PIECE
former	*first* (in place, time, or rank)—being number one in a countable series: beginning a series
come	*go* - move on a course
after	*after* - following in time or place
certain	*time* - measured or measurable duration
years	*year* - a time or era marked in some special way
with	*with* - used as a function word to indicate manner of action

Michelle Lynn

great	*great* - considerable or remarkable in magnitude, power, intensity, degree, or effectiveness
army	*army* - a body of persons organized for the advancement of a cause
with	*with* - used as a function word to indicate a related or supplementary fact or circumstance
riches	*property* - something that is or may be owned or possessed: WEALTH, GOODS
as	*gathered* - to effect the collection of

DANIEL 11:14

*And in **those times** there shall **many stand up against** the **king** of the **south**: also the **robbers** of thy **people** shall **exalt** themselves to **establish** the **vision**; but **they** shall **fall**.*

Many times the Crusaders came against the Islamic forces. The first four crusades are most notable, however, there were many more than four. The first to rescue the Holy Land, the second to recapture the Christian city of Edessa, the third to recapture Jerusalem, the fourth doesn't reach the Holy Land but the crusaders sack and loot Constantinople, to set up a "Latin (Roman) Empire" (as opposed to Greek).[51]

When the Crusaders captured Jerusalem on July 15, 1099, the slaughter was terrible; the blood ran down the streets, until men splashed in blood as they rode.[52] Not only did they kill the Muslim armed forces, but also women and children and Jews. The second crusade began with a massacre of Jews in the Rhineland.[53]

By the time of the third crusade, the magic and wonder had gone out of these movements altogether. The common people had found "them" out. Men went, but only kings and nobles straggled back; and that often only after heavy taxation for a ransom. The idea of the crusades was cheapened by their too frequent and trivial use. Whenever the pope quarreled with anyone now he called for a crusade.[54]

What should have been a great Christian adventure proved to be a story of greed and ambition, and ended in disillusion. 'The Crusaders forsook God,' said a chronicler, 'before God forsook them.'

60   Michelle Lynn

Aftermath and Heritage of the Crusades

After the fall of Acre no further Crusades were undertaken in the Holy Land, although several were preached. Already, however, the term crusade was also being used for other expeditions, sanctioned by the pope, against heathens and heretics. Albert the Bear and Henry the Lion led (1147) a crusade against the Wends in NE Germany; Hermann von Salza in 1226 received crusading privileges for the Teutonic Knights against the Prussians; the pope proclaimed (1228) a crusade against Emperor Frederick II; and several crusades were fought against the Albigenses and the Hussites (see Hussite Wars).

War against the Turks remained the chief problem of Eastern Europe for centuries after 1291. Campaigns akin to crusades were those of John Hunyadi, John of Austria (d. 1578), and John III of Poland. In their consequences, the crusades in Europe were as important as those in the Holy Land. However, although the Crusades in the Holy Land failed in their chief purpose, they exercised an incalculable influence on Western civilization by bringing the West into closer contact with new modes of living and thinking, by stimulating commerce, by giving fresh impetus to literature and invention, and by increasing geographical knowledge. The crusading period advanced the development of national monarchies in Europe, because secular leaders deprived the pope of the power of decision in what was to have been the highest Christian enterprise.

In the Levant the Crusades left a lasting imprint, not least on the Byzantine Empire, which was disastrously weakened. Physical reminders of the Crusades remain in the monumental castles built by the Crusaders, such as that of Al Karak. The chief material beneficiaries of the Crusades were Venice and the other great Mediterranean ports. [55]

DANIEL 11:14

those   **they** - those ones

times   **time** - a period during which something (as an action, process, or condition) exists or continues

many   **abundant** - occurring or existing in great quantity

stand   **stand** - to take up or maintain a (specified) posture

up   **upward** - toward a higher position

against   **against** - in opposition or hostility to

king   **king** - one that holds supreme or preeminent position in a particular sphere or class

south   **south** - regions or countries lying to the north of a specified or implied point of orientation

robbers   **violent** - characterized by extreme force

    tyrant - a person in a position of control who exercises unlawful or improper authority in an arbitrary or oppressive manner

people   **people** - human beings making up a group or assembly: persons linked by a common factor: as: the members of a geographically distinct community: persons who share in common a point of origin or residence, etc.

    tribe - a social group comprising numerous families, clans, or generations together with slaves, dependents, or adopted strangers

exalt   **lift** - to raise in rank, condition, or position

establish   **stand** - to take up or maintain a (specified) posture

vision   **revelation** - an act of revealing or communicating divine truth; esp.: God's disclosure or manifestation of himself or of his will to man

    Michelle Lynn

oracle - a revelation received from the God of Judaism and Christianity: a divine revelation

they   *they* - those ones

fall   *falter* - to hesitate in purpose or action: WAVER, FLINCH: to lose drive, effectiveness, or momentum in some way: WEAKEN, DECLINE, FAIL

DANIEL 11:15

*So the **king** of the **north** shall **come**, and **cast up** a **mount**, and **take** the most **fenced cities** and the **arms** of the **south** shall **not withstand, neither** his **chosen people, neither** shall there **be** any **strength** to **withstand.***

Feudalism was a class system, in which the status that a person held in society depended in large part on the amount of land he controlled. At the top rung of the ladder was the king, who granted land to nobles in exchange for their support.

Central to the system were the castles of major nobles, in militarily defensible positions and garrisoned with a contingent of professional troops for the nobleman's personal protection.[56] The design of European castles changed dramatically after Crusaders returned from the Middle East. The simple stone keep, walls and moat (motte and bailey castles) of earlier centuries were replaced by double rows of thick walls guarded by tall, rounded towers, arranged so that their lines of fire covered all approaches.[57]

As far as Islam, perhaps the biggest impact of the Arab Empire was the cohesiveness it gave to culture. Arabic became the learned, and therefore the common, language from Baghdad to the Alhambra in Spain.[58] The Muslims held Jerusalem until British troops arrived in 1917, during the First World War.[59]

After the Crusades began in 1096 and aroused hostility toward Jews, surviving Jewish communities in central and northern Europe became increasingly isolated from the surrounding culture. Although Jews still exercised a fair degree of control over their religious and cultural affairs, their circumstances did not encourage thinking about much beyond their religious traditions.[60]

Michelle Lynn

MOTTE AND BAILEY CASTLES

Alternative, colloquial, and related terms: Castle; Motte and bailey; Castle mound; Courtyard; Donjon; Earthwork; Earthwork castle; Enclosure; Fort; Mound; Ward Ordnance Survey map term: Motte & Bailey

Definition

A motte and bailey castle comprises a large conical or pyramidal mound of soil or stone (the motte) surrounded by, or adjacent to, one or more embanked enclosures (the bailey). Both may be surrounded by wet or dry ditches and could be further strengthened with palisades, revetments, and/or a tower on top of the motte.

The motte and the bailey of a motte and bailey castle need not have been contemporary in origin. Sometimes a motte could be added to an existing defensive enclosure, while in other cases a bailey was added to an isolated motte. For the purposes of evaluation, isolated mottes are specifically excluded from the definition of motte and bailey castle and are considered as a separate class. Also excluded are defended enclosures without mottes; these, defined as ringworks, are considered as a separate class too.

Motte and bailey castles are usually fairly easy to identify as field monuments, although sometimes large round barrows, windmill mounds, garden landscape features, and isolated mottes have been confused with the mottes of motte and bailey castles. It is possible that some mounds may have been used for more than one of these purposes; the sitting of the mound can be significant as the motte and bailey castles may dominate a road, river crossing, or settlement; the presence of a bailey is conclusive. Close attention to historical documents can be an important factor in recognizing and authenticating motte and bailey castles.

Motte and bailey castles were military strongholds, built as a base for offensive operations, and are found in urban areas and in rural settings.[61]

Early Stone Castles (1150-1250)

As medieval weapons improved, nobles and kings needed to build fortresses that were more secure. This, combined with the skill of stone masonry led to the early stone castles. The change over to stone castles was a gradual process and really increased during the reign of Henry II. Much of the work was simply replacing the timber of the motte-and-bailey to stone. Palisades were replaced by stone walls, wooden towers were replaced by stone gatehouses and the houses within the bailey were transformed into a stone keep. In some keeps, entry was a staircase through a forebuilding to the 2nd floor. The keep housed many things: A chapel, kitchens, a sleeping chamber on the 4th floor and the Great Hall. These earlier castles included 2 baileys: the inner and outer bailey.[62]

Jews—The Late Middle Ages: 1096 to 1492

After the Crusades began in 1096 and aroused hostility toward Jews, surviving Jewish communities in central and northern Europe became increasingly isolated from the surrounding culture. Although Jews still exercised a fair degree of control over their religious and cultural affairs, their circumstances did not encourage thinking about much beyond their religious traditions. Jewish literature focused primarily on the Talmud. Scholars produced new and monumental commentaries on the Babylonian Talmud to make it widely known and understood among European Jews. In addition, after the Crusades mystical trends emerged among European Jews who turned inward and wished for more direct contact with the divine. The most important form of Jewish mysticism, Kabbalah, developed in Spain. Jewish poets also wrote elegies and dirges commemorating the sacrifices of the Jews who were killed in 1096. Jews in Germany developed their own language, which came to be known as Yiddish. Yiddish began as a dialect of the German language spoken at that time but branched off from it and became a distinct Jewish language, written in Hebrew letters. [63]

DANIEL 11:15

king	***king*** - one that holds a supreme or preeminent position in a particular sphere or class
north	***north*** - regions or countries lying to the north of a specified or implied point of orientation
come	***go*** - pass from point to point or station to station
cast	***to spill forth*** - to gather into a heap: PILE
up	***upward*** - toward a higher position
mount	***mound*** - BOUNDARY: an earthwork used as a fortification
	rampart - something that fortifies, defends, or secures against attack or intrusion
take	***cohere*** - to become harmoniously united by common interests or sense of social membership or by emotional ties and especially with the cooperative playing down any individual differences or disagreements
fenced	***castle*** - a retreat or stronghold safe against intrusion or invasion
cities	***city*** - an inhabited place: HAMLET, VILLAGE
arms	***arm*** - power, might, strength, support
south	***south*** - regions or countries lying to the south of a specified or implied point of orientation
not	***not*** - in no manner or degree: in no way: NOWISE
withstand	***stand*** - to take up or maintain a (specified) posture
neither	***non-entity*** - a person who is totally undistinguished or unimpressive in mind, character, or achievement: one of small or mediocre talents: something of no consequence or

Michelle Lynn

significance: something totally lacking in distinction

chosen   *select* - chosen from a number or group by fitness or preference

people   *tribe* - a social group comprising numerous families, clans, or generations together with slaves, dependents, or adopted strangers

neither   *non-entity* - a person who is totally undistinguished or unimpressive in mind, character, or achievement: one of small or mediocre talents: something of no consequence or significance: something totally lacking in distinction

be   *exist* - to have being in any specified condition or place or with respect to any understood limitation

strength   *vigor* - active strength or force of body or mind: capacity for physical, intellectual, or moral exertion

withstand   *stand* - to be in a particular state or situation

DANIEL 11:16

> But **he that cometh against** him shall **do** according to his **own will,** and **none** shall **stand before** him: and **he** shall **stand** in the **glorious land,** which by his **hand** shall **be consumed.**

Urban II (Pope at Rome) used the first crusade to become the diplomatic leader of Europe's lay monarchs; they looked to Rome, not Constantinople. Urban also built up the Church's administrative machine; under him emerged the curia, a Roman bureaucracy that corresponded to the household administrations of the English and French kings. Through it the Papal grip on the Church itself was strengthened.[64]

Prestige, dogma, political skill, administrative pressure, judicial practice and the control of more and more benefices all buttressed the new ascendancy of the papacy in the Church.[65]

The final christening of Europe in the central Middle Ages was a great spectacle. Monastic reform and papal autocracy were wedded to intellectual effort and the deployment of new wealth in architecture to make this the next peak of Christian history after the age of the Fathers . . . Until the twelfth century the major buildings of the Church were unusually monastic; then began the building of the astonishing series of cathedrals, especially in northern France and England, which remains one of the great glories of European art and together with castles, constitutes the major architecture of the Middle Ages.[66]

This from another source: This was the great age of European church building; each city strove to outdo its neighbor by expressing in architecture its religious zeal. Over 1000 cathedrals and churches

Michelle Lynn

were built in France in the 11th century, and at least another 500 in the 12th; and to them (cathedrals and churches) people gave their money and the labor of their hands over many generations.[67]

Among new practices, which were pressed of the Church in the 13th century, was that of frequent and individual confession, a powerful instrument of control in a religiously minded and anxiety-ridden society.[68]

THE MEDIEVAL MASON

It's hard to say too much about Gothic cathedrals. Incredible size combined with a delicacy of balance and detail that you must see to believe. The spire of Strasbourg Cathedral is 466 feet tall, almost as high as the Washington monument. Not until the late nineteenth century did Europe erect anything taller.

Gothic architecture suddenly appeared in the middle of the twelfth century, and it kept evolving for 250 years. Then it abruptly stopped developing toward the end of the 14th century.

The people who created this art weren't formally educated. In the early days, only forty percent of master masons could even write their name on a document. They weren't trained in formal geometry, and it's unlikely they made any calculations. They didn't know Euclid, but they worked magic with a compass and square.

Medieval cathedral builders learned their empirical art through apprenticeship. Master builders held all kinds of jealously guarded tricks of the trade—a vast inventory of knowledge about material selection, personnel management, geometrical proportioning, load distribution, design, liturgy, and Christian tradition.

And make no mistake, those masons saw no clear boundary between things material and things spiritual. Their art flowed from their right brain. It was visual and spatial. They levitated tons of stone into the air to communicate their praise of God, and when they were finished, they embellished the nooks and crannies and high aeries of their buildings with the phantoms of their minds—with cherubs

and they embellished the nooks and crannies and high aeries of their buildings with the phantoms of their minds—with cherubs and gargoyles and wild caricatures of one another.

Of course, working on such a titanic scale in the highest technology of the age, they grew increasingly wealthy, powerful, and proud. They signed their work boldly and dramatically. A twenty-five foot long inscription on the south transept of Notre-Dame Cathedral says:

Master Jean de Chelles commenced this work for the Glory of the Mother of Christ on the second of the Ides of the month of February, 1258.

Even the contemplative labyrinths on cathedral floors led the faithful to a central plaque where they found, not a holy symbol or a saint, but an image of the master mason wielding a compass.

So what became of this marvelous Gothic art? It died out as master builders became educated gentlemen—when they moved into an office and managed the work of others at a distance.[69]

Daniel 11:16

he	**he, she, it** - the person or thing spoken of
that	**who** - the person or persons involved or meant or referred to
cometh	**go** - pass from point to point or station to station
against	**toward** - along a course leading to: with a view to gaining: to the end or purpose of
do	**make** - to cause to exist, occur, or appear: bring to pass: CREATE, CAUSE: to give rise to: favor the growth of
own will	**delight** - the power of affording pleasurable emotion or felicity (something that promotes or is the source of happiness)
none	**non-entity** - something on no consequence or significance: something totally lacking in distinction
	non-entity - this word can also be used as a negative particle
stand	**stand** - to be in a particular state or situation
before	**before** - in greater esteem, significance, or value than: more important than
he	**he, she, it** - the person or thing spoken of
stand	**stand** - to be in a particular state or situation
glorious	**splendor** - sumptuous display, ornament, or ceremonial: gorgeous show: MAGNIFICENCE, POMP, GLORY
	conspicuous - attracting or tending to attract attention by reason on size, brilliance, contrast, station: STRIKING, EMINENT

Michelle Lynn

land   *land* - REALM, DOMAIN

hand   *hand* - CONTROL, DIRECTION, SUPERVISION: right or privilege in controlling or directing

be   *exist* - to have being in any specified condition or place with respect to any understood limitation

consumed   *complete* - show attainment to the total or totality of

DANIEL 11:17

He shall also *set* his *face* to *enter* with the **strength** of his
whole kingdom, and **upright** ones **with** him; thus shall
he do: and *he* shall *give* him the *daughter* of **women,**
corrupting her: but *she* shall **not stand** on his side, **neither
be for** him.

The power and penetration of organized Christianity were
further reinforced by new religious orders.[70] One such order, the
Dominicans (also known as Black Friars), was started by the Spaniard
St. Dominic (1170-1221). Dominic had a passion for the argumentative
conversion of heretics . . . and is quoted as saying "For many years
I have exhorted you in vain, with gentleness, preaching, praying,
and weeping. But according to the proverb of my country, 'Where
blessing can accomplish nothing, blows may avail,' we shall rouse
against you princes and prelates, who, alas! will arm nations and
kingdoms against this land . . . and thus blows will avail where
blessings and gentleness have been powerless." The 13th century
saw the development of a new institution in the church; the
papal Inquisition . . . Pope Innocent III saw in the new order of the
Dominicans a powerful instrument of suppression. The Inquisition
was organized as a standing inquiry under their direction, and with
fire and torment the church set itself, through this instrument, to
assail and weaken the human conscience in which its sole hope of
world dominion resided.[71]

Dogma had developed through the ages as a result of debate
within the Church on such matters as the nature of God and Christ.
Any new ideas that seemed to contradict established teaching in
these matters were denounced as dangerous heresy, and punished

Michelle Lynn

with varying degrees of severity.[72] The word *dogma* comes from a Greek word *dokein* meaning *to seem good*. Dogma means *a doctrine or body of doctrines of theology and religion formally stated and authoritatively proclaimed by a church.*[73]

Before the 13th century the penalty of death had been inflicted but rarely upon heretics and unbelievers. Now in a hundred marketplaces in Europe the dignitaries of the church watched the blackened bodies of its antagonists, for the most part poor and insignificant people, burn and sink pitifully, and their own great mission to mankind burn and sink with them into the dust and ashes.[74]

Inquisition

During the 12th century opinion began to change, in reaction to a resurgence of heresy in an organized form, especially the Albigensianism of southern France. Albigensian doctrine and practice seemed destructive of matrimony and other institutions of society, and after less vigorous efforts by his predecessors, Pope Innocent III organized a Crusade against the group. He issued punitive legislation against them and sent preachers to the area. The various efforts to control heresy were, however, still uncoordinated and relatively ineffective.

The Inquisition properly so called did not come into existence until 1231, with the constitution *Excommunicamus* of Pope Gregory IX. By his action the pope lessened the bishops' responsibility for orthodoxy, placed inquisitors under the special jurisdiction of the papacy, and established severe penalties. The office of inquisitor was entrusted almost exclusively to the Franciscans and, especially, the Dominicans, because of their superior training in theology and their supposed freedom from worldly ambition. In putting the prosecution of heretics under papal direction, Gregory IX acted at least in part out of fear that Holy Roman Emperor Frederick II intended to pursue the task himself and turn it to political purposes. Restricted at first to Germany and Aragón, the new institution was soon extended in effect to the whole church, although it functioned not at all, or in an extremely limited way, in many parts of Europe.

Two inquisitors with equal authority—bestowed directly by the pope—were in charge of each tribunal, aided by assistants,

even princes, the inquisitors were formidable figures. Under these circumstances it is surprising that among their contemporaries the inquisitors generally had a reputation for justice and mercy. Some, nevertheless, were accused of excessive cruelty and other abuses.

The inquisitors established themselves for a definite period of weeks or months at some central place, from which they issued orders demanding that all guilty of heresy present themselves. The inquisitors could themselves bring suit against any suspect person. Lesser penalties were imposed on those who came forward and confessed their heresy than on those who had to be tried and convicted. A period of grace of about a month was allowed for this spontaneous confession; after that, the actual trials began.

If the inquisitors decided to try a person suspected of heresy, the suspect's pastor delivered the summons. Inquisitorial police sought out those persons who refused to obey a summons, and the right of asylum did not apply to heretics. The accused were given a statement of charges against them. For some years the names of accusers were withheld from suspects, but Pope Boniface VIII abrogated that practice. The accused were compelled under oath, however, to answer all charges against them, thus becoming their own accusers. The testimony of two witnesses was generally considered proof of guilt.

The inquisitors usually had a kind of jury, composed of both clergy and laity, to assist them in arriving at a verdict. They were permitted to imprison suspects who were thought to be lying. In

1252 Pope Innocent IV, under the influence of the revival of Roman law, officially sanctioned the use of torture to extract the truth from suspects. Until then, this procedure was alien to the canonical tradition.

The penances and sentences for those who confessed or were found guilty were pronounced together in a public ceremony at the end of all the processes. This was the *sermo generalis* or auto-da-fé. Penances might consist of a pilgrimage, a public scourging, a fine, or the wearing of a cross. The wearing of two tongues of red cloth, sewn onto an outer garment, marked those who had made false accusations. The penalties in serious cases were confiscation of property or imprisonment. The most severe penalty the inquisitors could themselves impose was life imprisonment. Thus, when the inquisitors handed a guilty person over to civil authorities, it was tantamount to a demand for that person's execution.

Although the Inquisition in the beginning directed most attention to the Albigensians and, to a lesser degree, the Waldensians, it later extended its activities to other heterodox groups, such as the Fraticelli, and then to witches and diviners. Once the Albigensians were under control, however, the pace of the Inquisition decidedly slackened, and in the late 14th and 15th centuries relatively little was heard of it. In the later Middle Ages, however, secular princes employed a pattern of repression corresponding to the Inquisition.[75]

he	**he, she, it** - the person or thing spoken of
set	**put** - to bring into or establish in a specified state or condition
face	**face** - SEMBLENCE
	semblance - outward show
enter	**come** - to arrive at a particular place or end by the use or agency of: THROUGH
strength	**might** - the power, authority, or collective resources wielded by an individual, group, or other entity
whole	**whole** - each or all of the
kingdom	**rule** - the exercise of authority or control: DOMINION, GOVERNMENT, SWAY
upright	**straight** - exhibiting no deviation from what is established or accepted as usual, normal, or proper: as: making no exceptions or deviations in one's support of some- thing accepted as right (as principle, policy, or party)
with	**equally** - in the same way: LIKEWISE, SIMILARLY
	with - by the use or agency of
he	**this** - the person, thing, or idea that is present or near in place, time, or thought, or that has just been mentioned
do	**make** - to seem to begin an action: BEGIN: to cause to exist, occur, or appear: bring to pass: CREATE, CAUSE
he	**he, she, it** - the person or thing spoken of
give	**make** - to bring into the power or under the protection or care of someone

daughter	***daughter*** - something derived from it's source or origin as if feminine
women	***woman*** - one possessing in high degree the qualities considered distinctive of womanhood
corrupting	***decay*** - to decline from a prosperous condition: to pass gradually from a comparatively sound or perfect state to one of unsoundness, imperfection or dissolution
she	***he, she, it*** - the person or thing spoken of
not	***not*** - in no manner or degree: in no way: NOWISE
stand	***stand*** - to hold one's ground: maintain one's position
neither	***not*** - in no manner or degree: in no way: NOWISE
be	***exist*** - to have being in any specified condition or place or with respect to any understood limitation
for	***causal*** - expressing or indicating cause

Michelle Lynn

DANIEL 11:18

After this shall *he turn* his *face* unto the *isles,* and shall *take many:* but a *Prince for* his own behalf shall cause the *reproach* offered by him to *cease; without* his own *reproach he* shall cause it to *turn upon* him.

As the church became increasingly powerful and worldly, it drew criticism both from the kings who clashed with it and from purists who called for reform. Rulers and kings began to consolidate their feudal states under centralized control. People began to develop a sense of national, rather than regional, identity. At times supporting—and at times opposing—this trend toward national power was the Roman Catholic Church, which had widespread influence on matters great and small in the Middle Ages.[76]

Pope Boniface VIII (1294-1303) . . . embodied all the pretensions of the papacy at its most political and its most arrogant. He quarreled violently with the kings of England and France and in the Jubilee of 1300 had two swords carried before him to symbolize his possession of temporal as well as spiritual power. Two years later he asserted that a belief in the sovereignty of the pope over every human being was necessary to salvation.[77]

In the 14th century, Philip the Fair of France determined to elect a Pope he could control. A French archbishop was elevated (to Pope) and moved the papal court to Avignon in southern France, where he and his successors lived for 70 years as French puppets. The consequence was the most melancholy 40 years in papal history, with rival Popes hurling anathema's at each other and, in the end, three Popes, each claiming to be the legitimate successor of Peter, while the nations divided their allegiance among them, according to what seemed their political interest. "The miserable truth has to be faced," says the Catholic historian Philip Hughes, "that no pope, on either side, was at all worthy of his office. They were, all of them, little better than partisan leaders of rival factions.[78]

These events are known as the Great Schism. In 1417 the Council of Constance set a single Pope in Rome, but the damage had been done.

The moral authority of the Papacy had not been restored at the Council. Anti-papal feeling was rampant in Europe at this time. Two men worth mention here are John Wyclif (1320-84) and John Hus (1373-1415). Wyclif spoke out against the corruption of the clergy and the unwisdom of the church. He organized a number of poor priests, the Wycliffites, to spread his ideas throughout England; and in order that people should judge between the church and himself he translated the Bible into English. Rome raged against him but he died a free man, although later, by a decree of the Council of Constance, his remains were ordered dug up and burnt.[79] John Hus delivered a series of lectures based on the doctrines of Wyclif, and was burned (1415) for heresy because he wouldn't recant.[80]

As fleeting as seemed the influence of such men, they were the forerunners of the most violent struggle in the annals of the Church, the Reformation.[81] This is discussed in later chapters.

The Decline Of The Medieval Church 1300-1500

In Europe, the fourteenth and fifteenth centuries were marked by the gradual passing of the culture that is thought of as typically "medieval." In the years of the High Middle Ages, European civilization had reached a pinnacle of development.

But after 1300, the nature of civilization during the High Middle Ages began to change. In thought and art, a rigid formalism replaced the creative forces that had given the Middle Ages such unique methods of expression as scholasticism and the Gothic style. Economic and social progress yielded to depression and social strife, with peasant revolts a characteristic symptom of instability.

Church government in Rome experienced a loss of prestige, and a series of challenges weakened its effectiveness after 1300. The church was gravely weakened from within by would-be reformers and dissidents as well as by external factors, chiefly political and economic. By the sixteenth century these forces would be strong enough to bring about the Protestant and Catholic reformations.

Despite the desolation and death brought about by the Hundred Years' War between France and England, the process of nation-making continued during the fourteenth and fifteenth centuries. In western Europe the contrasting political trends clearly evident at the end of the thirteenth century—unification in England, France, and Spain, and fragmentation in Germany and Italy—reached their culmination. In much of Europe by the end of the fifteenth century, the conflicting aims of what are sometimes

The history of the medieval church divides roughly into three periods—dissemination, domination, and disintegration. In the initial period, which lasted from about the fifth through the eleventh centuries, Roman Catholic Christianity spread throughout the West.

The advent of feudalism in the tenth century hindered the development of the church's administrative structure dominated by the papacy; but late in the eleventh century, the church, directed by strong popes, became the most powerful institution in the West. The period of the papacy's greatest power—the twelfth and thirteenth centuries—reached its height with the pontificate of Innocent III, who exerted his influence over kings and princes without challenge. The church then seemed unassailable in its prestige, dignity, and power. Yet that strength soon came under new attack, and during the next two centuries the processes of disintegration were to gain in influence. Papal power was threatened by the growth of nation-states, which challenged the church's temporal power and authority. Joined by some of the local clergy, rulers opposed papal interference in state matters and favored the establishment of general church councils to limit papal power. In addition, the papacy was criticized by reformers, who had seen earlier reform movements and the crusades transformed from their original high-minded purposes to suit the ambitions of the popes, and by the bourgeoisie, whose realistic outlook was fostering growing skepticism, national patriotism, and religious self-reliance. During the fourteenth and fifteenth centuries these challenges to papal authority were effective, and papal influence rapidly declined.

Michelle Lynn

Boniface VIII

A century after the papacy's apex under Innocent III, Pope Boniface VIII (1294-1303) was forced to withdraw his fierce opposition to taxes levied on the great wealth of the church by Edward I in Britain and Philip IV in France. Modeling his actions after Innocent, Boniface threatened to depose the "impious king," as he termed Philip, but he gave way when Philip with the support of the Estates-General prohibited the export of money to Rome.

A final and more humiliating clash with the French king had long-term implications for the papacy. When Boniface boldly declared, in the papal bull, Unam Sanctam (1302), that "subjection to the Roman pontiff is absolutely necessary to salvation for every human creature," Philip demanded that the pope be tried for his "sins" by a general church council. In 1303 Philip's henchmen broke into Boniface's summer home at Anagni to arrest him and take him to France to stand trial. Their kidnapping plot was foiled when the pope was rescued by his friends. Humiliated, Boniface died a month later, perhaps from the shock and physical abuse he suffered during the attack.

The Avignon Papacy

The success of the French monarchy was as complete as if Boniface actually had been dragged before Philip to stand trial. Two years after Boniface's death, a French archbishop was chosen pope. Taking the title of Clement V, he not only excused Philip but praised his Christian zeal in bringing charges against Boniface. Clement never went to Rome, where feuding noble families created turmoil in the city, but moved the papal headquarters to Avignon in southern France, where the papacy remained under French influence from 1305 to 1377. During this period, the so-called Babylonian Captivity of the church, papal prestige suffered enormously. All Christendom believed that Rome was the only suitable capital for the church. Moreover, the English, Germans, and Italians accused the popes and the cardinals, who were also French, of being instruments of the French king. The Avignon papacy added fuel to the fires of those critics who were attacking church corruption, papal temporal claims, and the apparent lack of spiritual dedication. Increasing their demands for income from England, Germany, and Italy, and living in splendor in a newly built fortress-palace, the Avignon popes expanded the papal bureaucracy, added new church taxes, and collected the old taxes more efficiently. Such actions produced denouncements of the wealth of the church and a demand for its reform.

The Great Schism

When the papacy paid attention to popular opinion and returned to Rome in 1377, it seemed for a time that the fortunes of the Roman church would improve. But the reverse proved true. In the papal election held the following year, the College of Cardinals, perhaps influenced by a shouting mob milling around the Vatican, elected an Italian pope. A few months later the French cardinals declared the election invalid and elected a French pope, who returned to Avignon. The church was now in an even worse state than it had been during the Babylonian Captivity. During the Great Schism, as the split of the church into two allegiances was called, there were two popes, each with his college of cardinals and capital city, each claiming universal sovereignty, each sending forth papal administrators and taxing Christians, and each excommunicating the other. The nations of Europe gave allegiance as their individual political interests prompted them. In order to keep that allegiance, the rival popes had to make numerous concessions to their political supporters and largely abandoned the practice of interfering in national politics.

The Great Schism continued after the original rival popes died and each camp elected a replacement instead of working to heal the breach in the church. Religious life suffered, for "Christendom looked upon the scandal helpless and depressed, and yet impotent to remove it. With two sections of Christendom each declaring the other lost, each cursing and denouncing the other, men soberly asked who was saved." ^1

Doubt and confusion caused many to question the legitimacy and true holiness of the church as an institution.

[Footnote 1: A. C. Flick, Decline of the Medieval Church, vol. I (London: Kegan Paul, Trench, Trubner and Co., 1930), p. 293.]

The Conciliar Movement

Positive action came in the form of the Conciliar Movement, a return to the early Christian practice of solving church problems by means of a general council of churches. In 1395 the professors at the University of Paris proposed that a general council, representing the universal church, should meet to heal the schism. A majority of the cardinals of both factions accepted this solution, and in 1409 they met at the council of Pisa, deposed both pontiffs, and elected a new pope. But neither of the two deposed popes would give up his office, and the papal throne now had three claimants. Such an intolerable situation necessitated another church council. In 1414 the Holy Roman emperor assembled at Constance the most impressive church gathering of the period. For the first time voting took place on a purely national basis. Instead of the traditional assembly of bishops, the council included lay representatives and was organized as a convention of "nations" (German, Italian, French, and English, the Spanish entering later). Each nation had one vote.

The nationalistic structure of the council was significant as an indication that the tendency toward such alignments was being recognized by the church's hierarchy. Finally, through the deposition of the various papal claimants and the election of Martin V as pope in 1417, the Great Schism was ended, and a single papacy was restored at Rome.

Failure Of Internal Reform

The Conciliar Movement represented a reforming and democratizing influence in the church, aimed at transforming the papacy into an institution similar to a limited monarchy. But the movement was not to endure, even though the Council of Constance had solemnly decreed that general councils were superior to popes and that they should meet at regular intervals in the future. Taking steps to preserve his position, the pope announced that to appeal to a church council without having first obtained papal consent was heretical. The restoration of a single head of the church, together with the inability of later councils to bring about much-needed reform and with lack of support for such councils by secular rulers, enabled the popes to discredit the Conciliar Movement by 1450. Not until almost a century later, when the Council of Trent convened in 1545, did a great council meet to reform the church. By that time the church had already irreparably lost many countries to Protestantism. Unfortunately, as the popes hesitated to call councils to effect reform, they failed to bring about reform themselves.

The popes busied themselves not with internal problems but with Italian politics and patronage of the arts. "Thus the papacy emerged as something between an Italian city-state and a European power, without forgetting at the same time the claim to be the vice-regent of Christ. The pope often could not make up his own mind whether he was the successor of Peter or of Caesar. Such vacillation had much to do with the rise and success . . . of the Reformation." [2]

[Footnote 2: R. H. Bainton, The Reformation of the Sixteenth Century (Boston:Beacon Press, 1952), p. 15.]

Wycliffe And Hus

Throughout the fourteenth century the cries against church corruption became louder at the same time that heretical thoughts were being publicly voiced. In England Piers Plowman mercilessly ridiculed the corruption, ignorance, and worldliness of the clergy, and a professor at Oxford named John Wycliffe (1320?-1384) attacked not only church abuses but especially church doctrines. Because of his beliefs that the church should be subordinate to the state, that salvation was primarily an individual matter between human beings and God, that transubstantiation as taught by the church was false, and that outward rituals and veneration of relics were idolatrous, Wycliffe has been called the forerunner of the Protestant revolt. He formed bands of "poor priests," called Lollards, who spread his views, and he provided the people with an English translation of the Bible, which he considered the final authority in matters of religion.

Although Wycliffe's demands for reform did not succeed, the Lollards, including the famous John Ball, spread a more radical version of Wycliffe's ideas until the movement was driven underground early in the next century. In Bohemia, where a strong reform movement linked with the resentment of the Czechs toward their German overlords was under way, Wycliffe's doctrines were popularized by Czech students who had heard him at Oxford. In particular, his beliefs influenced John Hus (1369?-1415), an impassioned preacher in Prague and later rector of the university there. Hus' attacks on the abuses of clerical power led him, like Wycliffe, to conclude that the true church was composed of a universal priesthood of believers and that Christ alone was its head.

But Hus, who was more preacher and reformer than theologian, did not accept Wycliffe's denial of the validity of transubstantiation. Alarmed by Hus' growing influence, the church excommunicated him. Summoned to the Council of Constance to stand trial for heresy, Hus was promised safe conduct. But Hus refused to change his views, and the council ordered him burned at the stake.

This action made Hus a martyr to the Czechs, who rebelled against both the German emperor and the Catholic church. In the sixteenth century the remaining Hussites merged with the Lutheran movement in frustration with a church deaf to their protests.[82]

DANIEL 11:18

he	*he, she, it* - the person or thing spoken of
turn	*turn* - to set in another especially contrary direction
face	*before* - as a result of: in consequence of
isles	*land* - REALM, DOMAIN
take	*cohere* - to become harmoniously united by common interests or sense of social membership or by emotional ties and especially with the cooperative playing down any individual differences or disagreements
many	*abundant* - occurring or existing in great quantity
prince	*magistrate* - a public official entrusted with the administration of laws
for	*causal* - containing or involving cause or a cause: marked by cause and effect
reproach	*disgrace* - loss of grace, favor, or honor: the condition of one fallen from grace or honor usually through some in-decorous, dishonest, or immoral action
cease	*desist* - to give over or leave off
without	*not* - NO
reproach	*disgrace* - loss of grace, favor, or honor: the condition of one fallen from grace or honor usually through some in-decorous, dishonest, or immoral action
he	*he, she, it* - the person or thing spoken of
turn	*retreat* - to make a retreat: retire from a position or place: WITHDRAW
upon	*upon* - on the occasion of: at the time of

DANIEL 11:19

Then *he* shall *turn* his *face* toward the *fort* of his own *land:*
but *he* shall *stumble* and *fall,* and *not be found.*

A subtitle in one of my history books reads, 'A rival for the Church as cities grow strong'.[83]

The fourteenth and fifteenth centuries saw the building of numerous Gothic town churches and town halls throughout Europe, which still in many cases serve their original purpose. The power and prosperity of the towns find their best expression in these and in the fortifications, with their strong towers and gateways. The town did many things that in our time are done by the State. Social problems were taken up by the town administration or the corresponding municipal organization. The regulation of trade was the concern of the guilds (these will be discussed in greater depth in a later chapter) in agreement with the council, the care of the poor belonged to the church, while the council looked after the protection of the town walls and the very necessary fire brigades.[84] Lords everywhere sought the support of towns against kings, while kings sought the support of townsmen against over mighty subjects.

The rise of the merchant class (discussed next chapter) was almost a function of the growth of towns; that is to say that merchants were inseparably linked with this most dynamic element in medieval European history. Unwittingly, at least first, towns and cities held within their walls much of the future history of Europe.[85]

During the Middle Ages the papacy had dominated life in most ways, politically and morally. Yet we can see that that is not the case now. Cities and towns were starting to show their superiority over

Michelle Lynn

the feudal world. The papacy had failed to achieve the very noble and splendid idea of a unified and religious world.[86]

All in all the 15th century leaves a sense of withdrawal, an ebbing after a big effort which had lasted nearly two centuries. Yet to leave the medieval Church with that impression uppermost in our minds would be to risk a grave misunderstanding of a society made more different from our own by religion than any other factor. Even when men attacked churchmen, they did so in the name of the standards the Church had itself taught them.[87]

Reasons For Church Decline

The reasons for the church's decline during the fourteenth and fifteenth centuries can be divided into internal and external ones.

By the early sixteenth century, these forces were strong enough to bring about the Reformation.

Valid criticisms of the clergy had come from a variety of sources, and the Conciliar Movement had challenged the supreme power of the papacy itself.

While criticisms increased, the church continued to decline in spiritual leadership.

The worldly concerns of the fourteenth—and fifteenth-century popes—including their deep involvement in Italian politics—pushed the church further and further away from religious concerns.

Among the outside pressures that led to the church's decline, the growing spirit of inquiry resulted in a new critical attitude toward the institutionalization of the church. Further, the newly invented printing press provided the means for the rapid dissemination of ideas.

From a socioeconomic view, the medieval church was slow in adapting itself to the new environment of the towns.

Michelle Lynn

The problems arising from town life too often went unanswered by the church, which failed to provide enough parish priests to keep pace with the growth of urban population.

It is no accident that the towns became centers of heresy.

Finally, the development of nationalism and the growing reluctance of kings to obey any opposing institution, including the church, were evident in the encounters between Boniface VIII and the French ruler Philip IV.[88]

DANIEL 11:19

he	*he, she, it* - the person or thing spoken of
turn	*retreat* - to make a retreat: retire from a position or place: WITHDRAW
face	*before* - as a result of: in consequence of
fort	*fortified* - (past of *fortify*) to make strong: STRENGTHEN: as: to strengthen and secure (as a town) by forts or batteries or by surrounding with fortifications
land	*land* - a portion (as a country, estate, farm, or tract) of the earth's solid surface considered by itself or as belonging to an individual or a people
he	*he, she, it* - the person or thing spoken of
stumble	*falter* - to lose drive, effectiveness, or momentum in some way: WEAKEN, DECLINE, FAIL
fall	*fall* - loss of greatness, power, status, influence, or dominion
not	*not* - in no manner or degree: in no way: NOWISE
be	*be* - to exist under conditions specified
found	*acquire* - to come into possession, control, power, or disposal of often by some uncertain or unspecified means

DANIEL 11:20

*Then shall **stand up** in his **estate** a **raiser** of **taxes** in the **glory** of the **kingdom:** but within **few days** he shall **be destroyed, neither** in **anger, nor** in **battle.***

Now comes a transition that was crucial for the development of the world as it is today. (As is every event in Daniel 11.)

The manorial (feudal) system kept the countryside in balance. Population density was low, and the estates could feed their inhabitants without cutting back forests for farmland. But, as population began to grow and trade began to develop, the need for more arable land increased. Forests were cut down to make way for farms to meet the demand for more food. But the increasingly prosperous population encouraged the development of cities. Peasants left the land to find work in the cities, and the population density in the country dropped again. During this time the manorial (feudal) system began to die out as trade and industry developed, and money once again came into widespread use.[89]

The Middle Ages in Europe ended as powerful new monarchs arose, ruling entire nation states, and supported by the wealth of expanding commercial cities. Kings could hire professional soldiers who would be permanently in their service, instead of the feudal levies who were prompt to go back to their farms after the 40 or 60-day duty that was all that feudalism required. Kings stood for unity, for the enforcement of written laws and for trade and peace. And the business groups and middle classes in the towns were tired of war and anarchy. Since kings needed cash, they turned increasingly to the merchants for it. In the towns modern capitalism was born; it was the money power of the towns that destroyed the feudal world. The past was losing its grip on the present, a new spirit had appeared.[90]

From the 13th century onwards many rulers, usually kings, were able for a variety of reasons to increase their power over those they ruled. Kings were arguing about the frontiers they shared, and this expressed more than just better techniques of surveying. It marked a change in emphasis within government, from a claim to control persons who had a particular relationship to the ruler to one to control people in a certain area. Territorial was replacing personal dependence.[91]

Medieval Merchant Culture

The 13th and 14th centuries saw a tremendous growth in commercial activity, and a consequent restructuring of society, away from the feudal system. Changing attitudes towards trade and the merchant class marked this period. The merchant himself changed in his attitude towards his work, in his duties and abilities, and in his educational background. All of this, combined with the Church's criticism of commerce and usury, created a multi-layered complex of attitudes towards those who made their living by buying and selling goods or dealing with money. Boccaccio reflects these changes in several of his novellas, as he portrays merchants as victims of the times, and also as heroes on the forefront of social change.

The old, feudal model of society was dominated by the concept that there were three divinely ordained orders: knights, clergy, and peasants. Each of these groups had a role to play, either defense of the realm, maintenance of the soul of society, or the growing of essential foodstuffs. The merchant, as a class, was discriminated against for not contributing to these essential duties, but rather for aiming to get rich himself. His pursuit of gain was considered against the laws of God, because he was not a producer of real goods, but rather a resaler, or a usurer. Although medieval society increasingly came to rely upon the merchant's services in distributing and obtaining items not produced locally, he was nonetheless considered a parasite and a sinner, barely tolerated for his questionable contribution to society's output. The objection to the presence of commerce and banking in early medieval times was spearheaded by the clergy, who thundered against the sinful nature of their calling. No sin was worse than that of the usurer, no activity more repugnant to the Lord. But by the time of Boccaccio, the merchant's place in society was much more secure, his numbers had proliferated, his standing in society backed up by land and power, and his services accepted as essential to urban life. They were still hated, especially during certain periods when they were blamed for natural occurrences, thought to be God's punishment for the excesses of greed and usurious activity, but their numbers had grown so large, and their services so essential, that they were not in danger of extinction.

The merchant, during this transitional period, had to contend for respect and honor with the nobility and the knighthood, that traditional order that stood at the head of medieval civic society. The knighthood's pre-eminence had been guaranteed by the vital role they played in the period of feudal wars that accompanied the chaos of early medieval politics. The nobility cultivated a disdain for the petty details of moneymaking and money-saving, which were the domain of the merchant. The nobility prided themselves on their ability to spend, to be showy and magnanimous. These qualities were directly at odds with the careful attention to profit and loss which characterized the commercial man. By Boccaccio's era, however, the merchant class was very rich, often intermarrying with impoverished members of the nobility, and they held positions of power in civic government. But they never completely overcame the general contempt for the way in which they acquired their wealth.

Michelle Lynn

As commercial activity grew and developed in complexity, new methods of tracking and distributing information grew at the same time. Education, no longer solely an avocation of the aspiring clergyman, became the means by which a new generation of merchants increased their ability to think and count. The need for current, up-to-date information about distant parts of Europe and the world required that letters be sent back and forth with increasing volume. Coupled with the need to hear and report news, was the need to record and compute numbers, reflecting more complicated transactions and banking instruments, such as bills of credit, interest rates, and exchange rates. Merchants left a large body of literature of their own, as they wrote about current events, family histories, and economic changes and fluctuations. The mental world of the merchant reflected their difficult and ambivalent place in society. The derision leveled at the merchant by clergy and others had an effect, and often merchants left instructions in their wills to repay those to whom they had lent money and charged interest, or to the poor of the city, in reparation. The traditional role of the merchant in popular literature reflected their lost status, whereby in the *exempla* (short moral tales) they are subjected to a variety of tortures in hell, or dreams, as a result of their evil way of life. In spite of this prejudice, merchants dressed more elaborately, were housed more elegantly, and enjoyed greater entertainment than most of their fellow citizens. They had officially entered medieval society, by Boccaccio's time, and ceased to be merely on the margins. [92]

Capitalism

Many of the institutions of capitalism can be traced back to Greek and Roman times. Things such as trade, moneylending, and insurance were well known practices to them. Unfortunatly, growth of the Roman Empire prevented further development of a private business class. As power over economic growth came back to the people or lords during the Middle Ages, modern capitalism started to evolve. In the late Middle Ages, the medieval economy was based on *manoralism*. This system said that peasants worked on the land that the lord's owned, but everyhing that was produced by them was kept and in return they had to perform services or pay dues to their lord. During this time period, there was no incentive to produce large and productive resources. The end of the medieval manoralism was brought about by a larger demand for goods. Kings competed against lords, and lords competed with peasants for the rights to what was produced. As a result, there was an emergence of merchants and businessmen who accumulated large sums of capital. In addition, there was also a large emergence of banks and the start of corporations. [93]

Michelle Lynn

stand	***stand*** - to be in a particular state or situation
up	***upward*** - toward a higher position: in a direction from a lower to a higher place
estate	***stand*** - a place or port where one stands: STATION, POSITION
raiser	***transition*** - a passage or movement from one state, condition, or place to another: CHANGE
taxes	***tax*** - to exact money from for the support of the government
glory	***honour*** - to show high regard or appreciation for: pay tribute to: EXALT, PRAISE: to confer a distinction upon
kingdom	***rule*** - a generally prevailing condition, quality, state or mode of activity or behavior
few	***united*** - being or living in agreement: HARMONIOUS
days	***day*** - the period of the existence or prominence of a person or thing: AGE
he	***this*** - the person, thing, or idea that is present or near in place, time, or thought, or that has just been mentioned
be	***become*** - grow to manifest a certain essence, nature, development, or significance
destroyed	***burst*** - to pass from a less to a more vigorous, ardent, or glowing state
neither	***not*** - in no manner or degree: in no way: NOWISE
anger	***ire*** - ANGER, WRATH
nor	***not*** - in no manner or degree: in no way: NOWISE
battle	***warfare*** - the process of struggle between competing entities: CONFLICT

Daniel 11:21

*And in his **estate** shall **stand up** a **vile** person, to **whom they** shall **not give** the **honour** of the **kingdom:** but **he** shall **come** in **peaceably,** and **obtain** the **kingdom** by **flatteries.***

The Black Death, the plague, ravaged Europe's population and therefore it's workforce. There was a great shortage of labor and a great shortage of goods, and the rich abbots and monastic cultivators who owned so much of the land, and the nobles and rich merchants . . . made violent statutes to compel men to work without any rise in wages, and to prevent their straying in search of better employment.[94] It is scarcely surprising that an age of such colossal disasters should have been marked by violent social conflicts. Everywhere in Europe the 14th and 15th centuries brought peasant uprisings.[95] John Ball best describes the "disesteem" heaped on the poor and lowly—"Good people, things will never go well in England so long as goods be not in common, and so long as there be villeins and gentlemen. By what right are they whom we call lords greater folk than we? On what grounds have they deserved it? Why do they hold us in serfage? If we all came of the same father and mother, of Adam and Eve, how can they say or prove that they are better than we, if it be not that they make us gain for them by our toil what they spend in their pride? They are clothed in velvet and warm in their furs and their ermines, while we are covered in rags. They have wine and spices and fair bread; and we oat-cake and straw, and water to drink. They have leisure and fine houses; we have pain and labor, the rain and the wind in the fields. And yet it is of us and of our toil that these men hold their estate."[96]

Michelle Lynn

Inside the cities, the nobility lived in spacious palaces, often with defensive towers to protect them from rival families. The middle classes, too, lived in fine houses with their servants. Other (poor) townspeople were crowded into tall, narrow houses with upper stories that jutted out above the ground-floor shops.[97]

Peasants flocked to the cities in search of opportunity and the hope of a fuller life . . . The newcomers took whatever jobs they could get. Women for the most part did domestic work. Failing that, there were few options beyond prostitution. Most men eked out a precarious living as day laborers, but a lucky or industrious few might become apprenticed to a trade, at which point they would enter the world of the medieval guilds.[98]

Increased wealth meant that many people had more leisure; as a result there was increasing demand for the products of craftsmen to beautify the palaces and villas of the leading families.[99] This offers security to craftsmen who can provide what the wealthy want.

The Black Death

How did the Black Death effect European civilization? It affected Europe's population and also its economy. Changes in the size of civilization led to changes in trade, the church, music and art, and many other things.

The Black Death killed off a massive portion of Europe's population. The plague is more effective when it attacks weakened people and Europe at the time was already weakened by exhaustion of the soil due to poor farming, the introduction of more sheep which reduced the land available for corn, and persistent Scottish invasions.

Fleas infected with the Bubonic Plague would jump from rats to travelers, killing millions and infesting the continent with world shaking fear. Normal people were tormented by the threat of death, causing them to change their views on leisure, work, and art. Even children suffered.

Leisure

The Black Death crept slowly into the recreational time of people no matter how much the rich attempted to avoid it or how little time the poor had for recreation. Even the abundant death was used for laughter. Funeral processions were used as jokes. It got to the point where deaths were ignored altogether. Citizens looked for causes and the developmentally delayed, deformed and crazy people outside town were the perfect candidates. Bored? Go toss some stones at the witch and help to stop the plague.

Michelle Lynn

Art

The damage to art is irreparable. As a result of death in the church, written language was almost lost and whole churches were abandoned. Carving was changed. Coffins had pictures of corpses on the lid, usually showing a very flattering likeness of the body inside wearing their best clothes. Some of these dated around 1400 showed bodies with about half of their flesh and shredded garments. A few of the sculptures showed worms and snails munching on the diseased. Painting was effected too.There are a number of paintings containing people socializing with skeletons. These paintings were made on a powerful person's command, and called "danse macabre". Artists abandoned old ways of painting things idolized by the Christian religion. They were so depressed by the death that surrounded them that they began to paint pictures of sad and dead people.

Children

Partially due to the lack of children's skills to provide for themselves, the children suffered. A common nursery rhyme is proof.

Ring a-round the rosy

Pocket full of posies

Ashes, ashes!

We all fall down!

Ring around the rosy: rosary beads give you God's help. A pocket full of posies: used to stop the odor of rotting bodies which was at one point thought to cause the plague, it was also used widely by doctors to protect them from the infected plague patients. Ashes, ashes: the church burned the dead when burying them became to laborious. **We all fall down: dead.** Not only were the children effected physically, but also mentally. Exposure to public nudity, craziness, and (obviously) abundant death was premature. The decease of family members left the children facing death and pain at an early age. Parents even abandoned their children, leaving them to the streets instead of risking the babies giving them the dreaded "pestilence". Children were especially unlucky if they were female. Baby girls would be left to die because parents would favor male children that could carry on the family name.

Effect over Time

After the plague had raised the level of leisure, the people kept it up. This was so injuring to the economy that it has been suggested that Europe is just now recovering from the devastation. The population is also a cause of disruption in the economy because small populations mean few taxes, however the economy improved. If the Black Death had an effect on today's economy, it would be that prices aren't as high as they would have been due to the fact that there was a century where the economy made no progress. Art was also a victim of the Plague because paintings are a lasting record. The art is still an easy thing to find and a good reminder of how the most creative people can panic when there's panic around them. Death inspired artists to stray from religious pictorials.

Soon after the last eruption of the Black Death, the views on children changed. Although carrying on the family name was still considered important, the birth rate dropped. Children were considered "not worth the trouble" to raise. It took four hundred years before Europe's population equaled the pre-Black Death

Michelle Lynn

figures. The demand for agricultural workers gave survivors a new bargaining power. Workers formerly bound to the land could now travel and command higher wages for their services. In addition, people left rural areas and migrated to cities for higher wages. The economic structure of land-based wealth shifted. Portable wealth in the form of money, skills and services emerged. Small towns and cities grew while large estates and manors began to collapse. The very social, economic, and political structure of Europe was forever altered. One tiny insect, a flea, toppled feudalism and changed the course of history in Europe. [100]

John Ball and the Peasants' Revolt

John Ball lived during the turbulent 14th century in English. A poor man and an itinerant, he was made a peasant priest by John Wyclif although Ball opposed some of the church's tenets. As these dissensions existed between factions within the church and between the mobility and the peasantry, the governmental control was being tossed about in the royal courts and claims to land was causing destructive wars. Wars between countries led to wars between social classes and death became characteristic of these years. An added mortal destructive force came from the presence of the Black Death which hit England first in 1348-49, and returned in 1362 and 1369. Although John Ball's birth date is questionable, his death came as a result of his participation in the Peasant's Revolt in 1381-82.

Edward III became king of England at the age of fifteen in 1327 at the disposition of his father Edward II; in 1328 Edward III was married and had his first son, Edward the Black Prince, in 1330. Until this time, the government was primarily in the hands of his mother Isabella and Roger de Mortimer; however, in 1330 Edward took control of the government forcing his mother to retire and killing Mortimer. Attempting to solidify the English areas only led to trouble and in 1337 a series of wars (called the Hundred Years Wars from 1337-1453) began, which existed throughout Edwards' reign and after.

The Black Death hit England in 1348-49 and killed nearly a third of the population.

Labor became scarce and wages rose sharply. In 1351, Parliament passed a statute controlling wages which caused unrest in the peasantry. Another plague struck in 1362 and again in 1369. Added frustration came when landlords began "asserting their ancient manorial rights." In 1375 a truce was signed with France, but unrest still prevailed. Poor health and eventual death of his son and the strength of his brother John of Gaunt led to Edward's death in 1376.

John Ball was excommunicated in 1376 for his advocacy of "ecclesiastical poverty and social equality" for priests in direct opposition to the church's ideas and he was imprisoned at Maidstone by John of Gaunt. The next year Edward II died and Richard became king in 1377 at the age of 10, but John of Gaunt was in control and there was much parlaying for power among the lords in court. finally rebellion of the peasants occurred in 1380 when the poll tax was increased and the peasants rebelled.

The Peasant's Revolt of 1381 began at Essex and quickly spread to Kent, where Wat Tyler was chosen leader. As they captured Canterbury and went on to London, their numbers increased as they freed many from prisons, including John Ball, who, being a priest, was an important addition to their cause. His enthusiasm in their cause tried unsuccessfully to talk with the king (who was being controlled by others, chiefly John of Gaunt), which resulted into a mob of peasants storming many royal houses and burning Savoy Palace, the residence of John of Gaunt. On June 14, 1381, Richard II met with the rebels at Miles End and agreed to "abolish serfdom, feudal service, market monopolies, and restrictions on buying and selling."

But this was short-lived because some of the rebels, led by Tyler, continued their plundering, captured the Tower of London, killing the archbishop of Canterbury and other officials. Tyler presented more demands but this time was challenged to a duel by the mayor of London; Tyler was mortally wounded and the peasants were quickly dispersed. Angry over the continued destruction and killing after their initial agreement, Richard revoked the earlier grants. John ball was taken to St. Albans, "where he was hanged, drawn, and quartered." [101]

The following lists many occupations that prevailed during the Middle Ages. Even though the individuals who held the positions have long since disappeared, often leaving no record of their existence, their legacy is still very visible in modern surnames.

Almoners: ensured the poor received alms.

Atilliator: skilled castle worker who made crossbows.

Baliff: in charge of allotting jobs to the peasants, building repair, and repair of tools used by the peasants.

Barber: someone who cut hair. Also served as dentists, surgeons and blood-letters.

Blacksmith: forged and sharpened tools and weapons, beat out dents in armor, made hinges for doors, and window grills. Also referred to as Smiths.

Bottler: in charge of the buttery or bottlery.

Butler: cared for the cellar and was in charge of large butts and little butts (bottles) of wine and beer. Under him a staff of people might consist of brewers, tapsters, cellarers, dispensers, cupbearers and dapifer.

Carder: someone who brushed cloth during its manufacture.

Carpenter: built flooring, roofing, siege engines, furniture, panelling for rooms, and scaffoling for building.

Carters: workmen who brought wood and stone to the site of a castle under construction.

Castellan: resident owner or person in charge of a castle (custodian).

Chamberlain: responsible for the great chamber and for the personal finances of the castellan.

Chaplain:	provided spirtual welfare for laborers and the castle garrison. The duties might also include supervising building operations, clerk, and keeping accounts. He also tended to the chapel.
Clerk:	a person who checked material costs, wages, and kept accounts.
Constable:	a person who took care (the governor or warden) of a castle in the absence of the owner. This was sometimes bestowed upon a great baron as an honor and some royal castles had hereditary constables.
Cook:	roasted, broiled, and baked food in the fireplaces and ovens.
Cottars:	the lowest of the peasantry. Worked as swine-herds, prison guards, and did odd jobs.
Ditcher:	worker who dug moats, vaults, foundations and mines.
Dyer:	someone who dyed cloth in huge heated vats during its manufacture.
Ewerer:	worker who brought and heated water for the nobles.
Falconer:	highly skilled expert responsible for the care and training of hawks for the sport of falconry.

Glaziers: a person who cut and shaped glass.

Gong Farmer: a latrine pit emptier.

Herald: knights assistant and an expert advisor on heraldry.

Keeper of the Wardrobe: in charge of the tailors and laundress.

Knight: a professional soldier. This was achieved only after long and arduous training which began in infancy.

Laird: minor baron or small landlord.

Marshal: officer in charge of a household's horses, carts, wagons, and containers. His staff included farriers, grooms, carters, smiths and clerks. He also oversaw the transporting of goods.

Master Mason: responsible for the designing and overseeing the building of a structure.

Messengers: servants of the lord who carried receipts, letters, and commodities.

Miner: skilled professional who dug tunnels for the purpose of undermining a castle.

Minstrels: part of of the castle staff who provided entertainment in the form of singing and playing musical instruments.

Reeve:	supervised the work on lord's property. He checked that everyone began and stopped work on time, and insured nothing was stolen. Senior officer of a borough.
Sapper:	an unskilled person who dug a mine or approach tunnel.
Scullions:	responsible for washing and cleaning in the kitchen.
Shearmen:	a person who trimmed the cloth during its manufacture.
Shoemaker:	a craftsman who made shoes. Known also as Cordwainers.
Spinster:	a name given to a woman who earned her living spinning yarn. Later this was expanded and any unmarried woman was called a spinster.
Steward:	took care of the estate and domestic administration. Supervised the household and events in the great hall. Also referred to as a Seneschal.
Squire:	attained at the age of 14 while training as a knight. He would be assigned to a knight to carry and care for the weapons and horse.

Watchmen: an official at the castle responsible for security. Assited by lookouts (the garrison).

Weaver: someone who cleaned and compacted cloth, in association with the Walker and Fuller.

Woodworkers: tradesmen called Board-hewers who worked in the forest, producing joists and beams.

Other medieval jobs included:

tanners, soap makers, cask makers, cloth makers, candle makers (chandlers), gold and silver smiths, laundresses, bakers, grooms, pages, huntsmen, doctors, painters, plasterers, and painters, potters, brick and tile makers, glass makers, shipwrights, sailors, butchers, fishmongers, farmers, herdsmen, millers, the clergy, parish priests, members of the monastic orders, innkeepers, roadmenders, woodwards (for the forests), slingers.

Other Domestic jobs inside the castle or manor:

Personal attendants—ladies-in-waiting, chamber maids, doctor. The myriad of people involved in the preparation and serving of meals—brewers, poulterer, fruiterers, slaughterers, dispensers, cooks and the cupbearers (who had the dubious privilege of tasting drinks for impurities!). [102]

estate	*stand* - a place or post where one stands: STATION, POSITION
stand	*stand* - to be in a particular state or situation
up	*upper* - higher in rank or order: superior in position
vile	*disesteem* - to consciously lack esteem for :
	esteem - hold in high regard
whom	*against* - with respect to: relating to :TOWARD
they	*they* - those ones
not	*not* - in no manner or degree: in no way: NOWISE
give	*make* - REACH, ATTAIN, ACHIEVE
honour	*grandeur* - greatness of power or position
kingdom	*rule* - a generally prevailing condition, quality, state or mode of activity or behavior
he	*same* - something that has previously been defined or described
come	*go* - to reach a certain point: ATTAIN, EXTEND
peaceably	*security* - freedom from fear, anxiety, or care: freedom from un- certainty or doubt: CONFIDENCE, ASSURANCE: sureness of technique: basis for confidence: GUARANTEE: FIRMNESS: DEPENDABILITY, STABILITY
they	*they* - PEOPLE: unspecified persons and especially those responsible for a particular act, practice, or decision
obtain	*help* - to be of use to: BENEFIT: to further the advancement of: PROMOTE
kingdom	*rule* - a generally prevailing condition, quality, state or mode of activity or behavior

flatteries **blandishments** - speech, action, or device that flatters and tends to coax or cajole: ALLUREMENT

Michelle Lynn

DANIEL 11:22

*And **with** the **arms** of a **flood** shall **they be overflown** from **before** him, and shall **be broken**; **yea, also** the **prince** of the **covenant**.*

As the towns grew larger the merchants found it necessary to cooperate. They began to make rules about trade that was carried on inside their own towns. These associations of merchants were called *guilds*, from a word that meant *payment*. A guild made its members pay a fee for belonging to it. At first these guilds were for merchants only but it was not long before the workers imitated the merchants and formed their own associations. Many different guilds sprang up. There were guilds for each kind of worker: weavers, dyers, carpenters, potters, blacksmiths, goldsmiths, silversmiths, coppersmiths, tailors, butchers, bakers, candle-makers, locksmiths, harness-makers, druggists, stonemasons, oil dealers, and many others.[103]

Guilds were 'closed shops', and only guild members could trade within a town or engage in a craft. Entry into a guild was governed by strict rules. A would-be member had first to serve a lengthy apprenticeship under a master craftsman, but before he could set up in business on his own he had to spend a further spell as a journeyman under a master, then pass an examination. This often entailed the production of a 'masterpiece', the original meaning of which was an example of work that proved a journeyman's mastery of his craft.[104]

Medeival Guilds

The guilds were an important part of city and town life. Guilds were exclusive, regimented organizations; created in part to preserve the rights and privileges of their members; and separate and distinct from the civic governments, but since the functions and purposes of guild and civic government overlapped, it was not always easy to tell them apart, especially since many well-to-do guildsmen were prominent in civic government.

Two kinds of guilds were especially important to civic life— merchant guilds and craft guilds.

Merchant Guilds
The merchant guilds were probably the first to appear and constituted the nucleus for civic organization. As early as the 10th c. merchants formed organizations for mutual protection of their horses, wagons, and goods when traveling. Often a merchant guild would found a town by obtaining a charter.

Craft Guilds
The craft guilds came about by increased specialization of industry. A group of artisans engaged in the same occupation, e.g., bakers, cobblers, stone masons, carpenters, etc. would associate themselves together for protection and mutual aid. As these craft associations became more important than the older merchant guilds, their leaders began to demand a share in civic leadership. Soon no one within a town could practice a craft without belonging to the appropriate guild associations. The purpose of the guilds was to maintain a monopoly of a particular craft especially against outsiders. For example, the harness makers would get together

and figure out what the owners of business needed from that trade then allow as many masters to set up shop as the business could support.

Consumer and Worker Protection
In protecting its own members, the guilds protected the consumer as well. Many craft regulations prevented poor workmanship. Each article had to be examined by a board of the guild and stamped as approved. Because of lack of artificial light, work at night was prohibited. In Florence the number of dyers was specified by the guild. In one place it was forbidden to see pigs fattened by a barber-surgeon lest the pig had been fattened on rich peoples' blood. Metalware plating was tantamount to fraud and, therefore, was forbidden.

To regulate competition between members the guild forbade advertising.

All prices were regulated. Craftsmen could take work outside where it could be seen. Price-cutting was strictly forbidden. To preserve its monopoly a guild forbade the sale of foreign artisans' work within a city.

The most important processes used in manufacturing were guarded. In Florence a worker who possessed any essential trade secrets and for some reason fled to a foreign territory must be tracked down and killed lest he divulge the information.

Monopoly existed within individual guilds through the limitation of the number of masters. No member was ever allowed to corner the market by purchasing a large supply of a product or commodity so as to be able to fix the price.

Services Performed by Guilds

Guilds performed other services for their members as well. They provided funeral expenses for poorer members and aid to survivors; provided dowries for poor girls; covered members with a type of health insurance and provisions for care of the sick; built chapels; donated windows to local churches or cathedrals; frequently helped in the actual construction of the churches; watched over the morals of the members who indulged in gambling and usury; and were important for their contribution to emergence of Western lay education. In earlier times, the only schools in existence had been the monastic or cathedral schools.

Guilds and Community Interrelationships

The members of the guild were called *confraternities*, brothers helping one another. From the political viewpoint, the guild was neither sovereign nor unrelated to society outside the guild and town organization. As a collective unit, the guild might be a vassal to a bishop, lord or king, as in Paris. The extent of vassalage depended on the degree of independence of the town where it was located. There was a close connection between the guild and the city authorities: The City Council could intervene in event of trouble between guilds. Council could establish the hours of work, fix prices, establish weights and measures. Guild officials were frequently appointed to serve in civic government because guilds usually voted as a unit, raised troops for the civic militia, and paid taxes as a group. Each guild was required to perform public services. They took turns policing the streets and constructed public buildings and walls to defend the town or city.

A perceived higher social status could be achieved through guild membership. The guildsmen of *The Canterbury Tales* had wives who liked to be called "Ma Dame" by their inferiors.

By the 13th c. to become a guild man one had to go through 3 stages: lowest was apprentice, next was journeyman, and top-ranking stage was master. The same structure is present in labor unions and colleges today.

Apprentice—usually a male teenager who went to live with a master and his family; his parents paid to have him taken on. He probably occupied the attic of their 3 story home. The shop where he would learn his trade was located on the ground floor. The second story was the masters' living area. The third story housed the journeyman who was there to learn also.

The apprentice was subject to the master. During his apprenticeship he was not allowed to marry. This learning period might vary from 2-7 years depending on the craft. His training included the rudiments of the trade. The apprentice then progressed to journeyman.

Journeyman or day worker—entitled to earn a salary. The next hurdle was to produce a masterpiece that would satisfy the master of the guild so that he could assume the title of master craftsmen and would thus get membership in the guild. This was not easy to accomplish because the journeyman had to work on his own time to produce this masterpiece—Sunday was the only day he did not work sun-up to sun-down. He must use his own tools and raw materials which required a capital outlay that he might not have been able to accomplish as a wage earner. Then if he did produce the required work, the state of the economy guided the vote of acceptance—it was not desriable to have too many masters in a guild and when the economy was tight. The masters would not admit anyone to their ranks to strain the economy.

Master—Once the masterpiece was completed and the guild voted to accept the journeyman as a master, he could become one.[105]

DANIEL 11:22

with	**with** - used as a function word to indicate manner of action
arms	**force** - strength or energy especially of an exceptional degree: active power: VIGOR
flood	**deluge** - an irresistible rush of something (as in overwhelming numbers, quantity, or volume)
they	**they** - those ones
be	**become** - to come to exist or occur
overflown	**conquer** - to gain mastery over
before	**before** - as a result of: in consequence of
be	**become** - to come to exist or occur
broken	**burst** - to give or receive sudden or unexpected release or expression
yea	**even** - without disagreement: in accord
prince	**commander** - one in an official position of command or control
covenant	**compact** - an agreement, understanding, or covenant between two or more parties

Michelle Lynn

DANIEL 11:23

*And after the **league** made **with** him **he** shall **work** deceitfully: **for he** shall **come up**, and shall **become strong** with a **small people.***

New ideals were born and fostered in the 14th century among the multitude of city-states in central and northern Italy. Florence was the leading city of the Renaissance, and its leading family, the Medici, lavished the profits they made from banking on making the city renowned throughout Europe.[106]

Renaissance, a word which means *a new birth*, is a name given to this period of history because of a new birth, or revival, of the ancient learning of the Greeks and Romans. People not only revived the ancient learning, but also made progress in their own arts and literature and science.[107]

New ideas led to a challenging of medieval conceptions in all fields. Man might still be a sinner, as the Church taught—but he was capable of greatness, and interesting for his own sake. Men ceased to be anonymous, and instead became proud of themselves and their achievements.[108] Artists were no longer humble and anonymous servants of the Church, but individuals proud of their achievements and reputation.[109] Though artists' settings were often still religious, the feeling behind their paintings or sculptures was increasingly humanist (explained in more detail in a later chapter) and secular.[110] Schools of the Middle Ages were Church schools, schools of religion. This changed during the Renaissance. Schools saw it as part of their task to train men for public life, and professional and humanistic studies flourished in universities.[111] This "rebirth" spread from Italy over the rest of Europe bringing new learning and challenging accepted ideas.

THE RENAISSANCE

The Beginnings of the Renaissance

The Renaissance defined—By the term Renaissance ("New Birth"), used in its narrower sense, is meant that new enthusiasm for classical literature, learning, and art which sprang up in Italy towards the close of the Middle Ages, and which during the course of the fifteenth and sixteenth centuries gave a new culture to Europe. [By many writers the term is employed in a still narrower sense than this, being used to designate merely the revival of classical art; but this is to depreciate the most important phase of a *many-sided development*. The Renaissance was essentially an intellectual movement. It is this intellectual quality which gives it so large a place in universal history]

Using the word in a somewhat broader sense, we may define the Renaissance as the reentrance into the world of that secular, inquiring, self-reliant spirit which characterized the life and culture of classical antiquity. This is simply to say that under the influence of the intellectual revival the men of Western Europe came to think and feel, to look upon life and the outer world, as did the men of ancient Greece and Rome; and this again is merely to say that they ceased to think and feel as mediaeval men and began to think and feel as modern men.

Town Life and Lay Culture—The spirit of the new life was nourished especially by the air of the great cities. In speaking of mediaeval town life we noticed how within the towns there was early developed alife like that of modern times. The atmosphere of these bustling, trafficking cities called into existence apractical commercial spirit, a many-sided, independent, secular life which in many respects was directly opposed to medieval teachings and ideals.

This intellectual and social movement within the mediaeval towns, especially in the great city-republics of Italy, was related most intimately, as we shall see in a moment, to that great revival of the fourteenth and fifteenth centuries to which the term Renaissance is distinctively applied.

THE RENAISSANCE IN ITALY

Inciting Causes of the Movement—Just as the Reformation went forth from Germany and the Political Revolution from France, so did the Renaissance go forth from Italy. And this was not an accident. The Renaissance had its real beginnings in Italy for the reason that all those agencies which were slowly transforming the mediaeval into the modern world were here more active and effective in their workings than elsewhere.

Foremost among these agencies must be placed the influence of the Italian cities. We have already seen how city life was more perfectly developed in Italy than in the other countries of Western Europe. In the air of the great Italian city-republics there was nourished a strong, self-reliant, secular, myriad-sided life. It was a political, intellectual, and artistic life like that of the cities of ancient Greece. Florence, for example, became a second Athens, and in the eager air of that city individual talent and faculty were developed as of old in the atmosphere of the Attic capital. " In Florence," says Symonds, " hadbeen produced such glorious human beings as the world has rarely seen . . . . The whole population formed an aristocracy of genius."

In a word, life in Italy earlier than elsewhere lost its mediaeval characteristics and assumed those of the modern type. We may truly say that the Renaissance was cradled in the cities of mediaeval Italy. The Italians, to use again the words of Symonds, were " the firstborn among the sons of modern Europe."

The Paganism of the Italian Renaissance—There was a religious and moral, or, as usually expressed, an irreligious and immoral, side to the classical revival in Italy which cannot be passed wholly unnoticed even in so brief an account of the movement as the present sketch.

In the first place, the study of the pagan poets and philosophers produced the exact result predicted by a certain party in the Church. It proved hurtful to religious faith. Men became pagans in their feelings and in their way of thinking. Italian scholars and Italian society almost ceased to be Christian in any true sense of the word.

With the New Learning came also those vices and immoralities that characterized the decline of classical civilization. Italy was corrupted by the new influences that flowed in upon her, just as Rome was corrupted by Grecian luxury and sensuality in the days of the failing republic. Much of the literature of the time is even more grossly immoral in tone than the literature of the age of classical decadence.[112]

Michelle Lynn

DANIEL 11:23

league	*join* - to put or bring into close contact, association, or relationship: ATTACH, UNITE, COUPLE
with	*with* - by means of: by the use or agency of: THROUGH: as a result of: in consequence of: because of
he	*this* - the person, thing, or idea that is present or near in place, time, or thought, or that has just been mentioned
work	*do* - to take place: go on: HAPPEN
	make - favor the growth or occurrence of
deceitfully	*fraud* - an act of deluding: DELUSION
for	*causal* - containing or involving cause or a cause ; marked by cause and effect
he	*this* - the person, thing, or idea that is present or near in place, time, or thought, or that has just been mentioned
come	*ascend* - to go up or upward from a lower level or degree: RISE
up	*upward* - toward a greater amount or higher number, degree, or rate
become	*be* - to exist under conditions specified
strong	*powerful* - having great prestige or effect: INFLUENTIAL, STIMULATING
with	*with* - by means of: by the use or agency of: THROUGH
small	*few* - consisting of or amounting to a small number: not many
people	*nation* - a community of people composed of one or more nationalities and possessing a more or less defined territory and government

Daniel 11:24

*He shall **enter peaceably** even **upon** the **fattest** places of the province; and **he** shall **do that which** his **fathers** have **not done**, nor his **fathers' fathers**; he shall **scatter** among them the **prey**, and **spoil**, and **riches**: yea, and **he** shall **forecast** his **devices against** the **strong holds**, even **for a time.***

As trade became very active due to the establishment of trade routes, the people of one land were becoming acquainted with the people and products of other lands. Weavers in Ghent made cloth out of wool from England and sold the cloth to merchants in Venice. Silk from Venice was sold in London. Furs from Russia found their way to Paris.[113] Commercial law—the law that controls buying and selling—has its roots here. A merchant from Italy might think that the French measure for cloth was wrong. A German merchant might complain that he did not understand how heavy a certain weight was supposed to be. Other disputes might be about what the money from far-off places was really worth. Many trading fairs had courts to decide just such disputes.[114]

Along with this wealth the banking industry came to be. The currencies of Italy's merchant cities were among the most stable in medieval Europe. The banking industry first thrived there, developing such techniques of modern business as double-entry bookkeeping and prices based on supply and demand.[115]

Powerful families emerged, their wealth based less on the ownership of feudal estates than on the proceeds of investing money at risk. The bank owned by the Medici family in Florence, for instance, had branches at Milan, Naples, Pisa, Venice, Geneva, Lyons and Avignon, Bruges and London. Such banks could transfer credit over the whole of Europe, and they became essential to popes and kings. Increased wealth meant that many people had more leisure; as a result there was increasing demand for the products of craftsmen to beautify the great palaces and villages of the leading families.[116]

Renaissance Banking

Banking in the Renaissance was very different in the way it was thought of and functioned. Now-a-days, banks are closed-in buildings that are run extremely precisely, and the workers pay close attention to detail. Heavy security is mandatory and banks are held with very high esteem. In the Renaissance, however, banks were usually just stalls in the market place with men sitting behind them. As bank comes from the Latin word that means "bench," it's not very surprising that banks were little more than that. When they "open shop," they simply open their accounts books, gold coins, and a scale to weigh coins taken in. Banks in the Renaissance were definitely not as formal as they are now.

During this era, merchants would travel from place, and usually needed money on their journeys. Thievery was definitely a problem, though; highway men would take all of their money and they would be left stranded! Intelligent bankers solved this problem. They set up different banks along the routes that merchants commonly used and instead of making merchants carry lots of money around with them, they could instead make transactions from banks along the way. The bank that a merchant used in his home country would be notified when its client borrowed or put in money and he would pay back money later. This started connections between foreign banks and created an all-in-all safer way to travel.

Even though banks were commonly used by merchants and other rather wealthy people, many did not trust bankers. The main reason bankers were not trusted was because the establishment was very corrupt. Instead of receiving their income based on the customers' transactions, some men would take money that clients put into the bank. Bankers were often the center of gossip at public events—not all very complimentary, either.

Today, everyone pays some tribute to banks, and most establishments are trusted. They are run by a very strict code of conduct and security is tight. In the beginning of this system, however, banking was much more a luxury, and seen as less than truthful, though undoubtedly invaluable to merchants. Like many practices started in the period of "rebirth," the Renaissance, banking started from very humble beginnings in comparison to what it is today.[117]

DANIEL 11:24

he	***this*** - the person, thing, or idea that is present or near in place, time, or thought, or that has just been mentioned
enter	***go*** - to reach a certain point: ATTAIN, EXTEND
peaceably	***security*** - basis for confidence: GUARANTEE: FIRM- NESS: DEPENDABILITY, STABILITY
upon	***over*** - used as a function word to indicate the possession or enjoyment of authority, power, or jurisdiction in regard to some thing or person
fattest	***fat*** - well furnished, filled, or stocked: ABUNDANT: PROSPEROUS, WEALTHY
province	***district*** - a territorial division (as of a nation, state, county, or city) marked off or defined for administrative, electoral, judicial, or other purposes
he	***it*** - ITSELF
do	***do*** - bring to pass: carry out: to perform (as an action) by oneself or before another: EXECUTE
that	***that—***
which	***which—***
fathers	***father*** - a male ancestor more remote than a parent: FOREFATHER, ANCESTOR
not	***not*** - in no manner or degree: in no way: NOWISE
done	***do*** - bring to pass: carry out: to perform (as an action) by oneself or before another: EXECUTE
fathers'	***father*** - a male ancestor more remote than a parent: FOREFATHER, ANCESTOR

Michelle Lynn

father	*father* - a male ancestor more remote than a parent: FOREFATHER, ANCESTOR
he	*he, she, it* - the person or thing spoken of
scatter	*disperse* - to cause to break up and go in different ways: send or drive into different places: SCATTER
prey	*booty* - REWARD, PRIZE, GAIN
spoil	*booty* - REWARD, PRIZE, GAIN
riches	*property* - something that is or may be owned or possessed: WEALTH, GOODS: specif.: a piece of real estate: the exclusive right to possess, enjoy, and dispose of a thing: a valuable right or interest primarily a source or element of wealth: OWNERSHIP
he	*same* - something that has previously been defined or described
forecast	*plait* - to unite by or as if by interweaving
devices	*contrivance* - the act or faculty of contriving: inventive ability: skill at devising: INGENUITY
against	*upon* - having a powerful influence on
strong holds	*fortified* city - past of *fortify* - to strengthen and secure (as a town) by forts or batteries or by surrounding with fortifications
for	*causal* - marked by cause and effect
time	*time* - a period during which something (as an action, process, or condition) exists or continues

DANIEL 11:25

And *he* shall **stir up** his **power** and his **courage against** the **king** of the **south with** a **great army:** and the **king** of the **south** shall **be stirred up** to **battle with** a *very* **great** and **mighty army;** but *he* shall **not stand: for they** shall **forecast devices against** him.

The Ottoman Empire, which was to become the greatest of all Muslim states, in magnificence, territorial extent and duration, was founded at the end of the 13th century by Osman, son of Ertughrul, the leader of a band of Turks who had migrated into Asia Minor from central Asia.

Most of them were only recently converted to Islam, and they displayed enormous energy in fighting the 'infidels' of the Byzantine Empire . . . The Turks were, in principle, in a state of permanent warfare with their Christian neighbors.[118]

Under Islamic influence, the Turks acquired their greatest fighting tradition, that of the gazi warrior. Well-trained and highly skilled, gazi warriors fought to conquer the infidel, acquiring land and riches in the process. While the gazi warriors fought for Islam, the greatest military asset of the Ottoman Empire was the standing paid army of Christian soldiers, the *janissaries.* The janissaries were Christian captives from conquered territories. Educated in the Islamic faith and trained as soldiers the janissaries were forced to provide annual tribute in the form of military service.[119]

It was in 1453, under the Ottoman Sultan Muhammad II, that Constantinople at last fell to the Moslems. He attacked it from the European side, and with a great power of artillery. The Greek Emperor was killed, and there was much looting and massacre. The

Michelle Lynn

Great Church of Saint Sophia, which Justinian the Great had built (532), was plundered of its treasures and turned at once into a mosque. This event sent a wave of excitement throughout Europe, and an attempt was made to organize a crusade; but the days of the crusades were past.[120]

Moving farther into Europe, the conquering Turks occupied Athens in 1456; and over the next 11 years the remainder of the Balkans—Serbia, Bosnia, and Albania—came under Ottoman rule.[121]

The End of Europe's Middle Ages

Ottoman Turks

Although the Ottoman Empire is not considered a European kingdom *per se*, Ottoman expansion had a profound impact on a continent already stunned by the calamities of the fourteenth and fifteenth centuries and the Ottoman Turks must, therefore, be considered in any study of Europe in the late Middle Ages. The ease with which the Ottoman Empire achieved military victories led Western Europeans to fear that ongoing Ottoman success would collapse the political and social infrastructure of the West and bring about the downfall of Christendom. Such a momentous threat could not be ignored and the Europeans mounted crusades against the Ottomans in 1366, 1396, and 1444, but to no avail. The Ottomans continued to conquer new territories.

One of a number of Turkish tribes that migrated from the central Asian steppe, the Ottomans were initially a nomadic people who followed a primitive shamanistic religion. Contact with various settled peoples led to the introduction of Islam and under Islamic influence, the Turks acquired their greatest fighting tradition, that of the gazi warrior. Well trained and highly skilled, gazi warriors fought to conquer the infidel, acquiring land and riches in the process.

While the gazi warriors fought for Islam, the greatest military asset of the Ottoman Empire was the standing paid army of Christian soldiers, the janissaries. Originally created in 1330 by Orhan (d.1359), the janissaries were Christian captives from conquered territories. Educated in the Islamic faith and trained as soldiers, the janissaries were forced to provide annual tribute in the form of military service. To counter the challenges of the gazi nobility, Murad I (1319-1389) transformed the new military force into the elite personal army of the Sultan. They were rewarded for their loyalty with grants of newly acquired land and janissaries quickly rose to fill the most important administrative offices of the Ottoman Empire.

The Ottoman Empire

During the early history of the Ottoman Empire, political factions within Byzantium employed the Ottoman Turks and the janissaries as mercenaries in their own struggles for imperial supremacy. In the 1340's, a usurper's request for Ottoman assistance in a revolt against the emperor provided the excuse for an Ottoman invasion of Thrace on the northern frontier of the Byzantine Empire. The conquest of Thrace gave the Ottomans a foothold in Europe from which future campaigns into the Balkans and Greece were launched and Adrianople became the Ottoman capital in 1366.

Over the next century, the Ottomans developed an empire that took in Anatolia and increasingly larger sections of Byzantine territories in Eastern Europe and Asia Minor.

Ottoman expansion into Europe was well underway in the late fourteenth century. Gallipoli was conquered in 1354 and at the Battle of Nicopolis in 1394, the Ottomans crushed a vast crusading army, taking many European leaders hostage. The disaster was so great that the first survivors to return to France were imprisoned as liars. But Nicopolis was only the beginning. The appearance of the Tatars under Tamarlane early in the fifteenth century temporarily delayed Turkish advances but the Ottomans soon resumed attacks on

Byzantium and Eastern Europe. A Hungarian-Polish army was decimated at Varna in 1444 by Murad II (c.1403-1451) and Ottoman conquests were virtually unchecked during the reign of his son, Mehmed II the Conqueror (1432-1481).

Constantinople itself was captured in 1453, sending a shock wave across Europe. With the fall of Byzantium, a wave of Byzantine refugees fled to the Latin West, carrying with them the classical and Hellenistic knowledge that provided additional impetus to the burgeoning humanism of the Renaissance.

Athens fell in 1456 and Belgrade narrowly escaped capture when a peasant army led by the Hungarian Janos Hunyadi held off a siege in the same year. Nevertheless, Serbia, Bosnia, Wallachia, and the Khanate of Crimea were all under Ottoman control by 1478. The Turks commanded the Black Sea and the northern Aegean and many prime trade routes had been closed to European shipping. The Islamic threat loomed even larger when an Ottoman beachhead was established at Otranto in Italy in 1480. Although the Turkish presence in Italy was short-lived, it appeared as if Rome itself must soon fall into Islamic hands. In 1529, the Ottomans had moved up the Danube and besieged Vienna. The siege was unsuccessful and the Turks began to retreat. Although the Ottomans continued to instill fear well into the sixteenth century, internal struggles began to deteriorate the once overwhelming military supremacy of the Ottoman Empire. The outcome of battles was no longer a foregone conclusion and Europeans began to score victories against the Turks.[122]

he	*he, she, it* - the person or thing spoken of
stir	*wake* - to bring to motion, action, or life ; STIR, EXCITE: to arouse consciousness or interest in: ALERT
up	*upward* - marked by an increase: RISING
power	*vigor* - active strength or force of body or mind: capacity for physical, intellectual, or moral exertion: effective energy or power: intensity of action or effect: FORCE, ENERGY
courage	*heart* - COURAGE, ARDOR, ENTHUSIAM
against	*against* - in opposition or hostility to: not in conformity with: contrary to
king	*king* - one that holds a supreme or preeminent position in a particular sphere or class
south	*south* - regions or countries lying to the south of a specified or implied point of orientation
with	*with* - used as a function word to indicate manner of action
great	*older* - persisting from an earlier time: CHRONIC
army	*army* - a body of persons organized for the advancement of a cause
king	*king* - one that holds a supreme or preeminent position in a particular sphere or class
south	*south* - regions or countries lying to the south of a specified or implied point of orientation
be	*be* - to exist under conditions specified
stirred	*grate* - FRET, IRRITATE, OFFEND *irritate* - to increase the action of: heighten excitement in: to produce excitation in: STIMULATE

	offend - to strike against: ATTACK: ASSAIL
up	*upward* - marked by an increase: RISING
battle	*warfare* - military operations between enemies: armed contest: HOSTILITIES, WAR
with	*with* - by means of: by the use or agency of: THROUGH
great	*great* - considerable or remarkable in magnitude, power, intensity, degree, or effectiveness: LOUD: HEAVY, FORCEFUL: INTENSE: FAR-REACHING: big in scope: EXTREME, MARKED
mighty	*powerful* - having a great force or potency: STRONG, COMPELLING
army	*army* - a body of persons organized for the advancement of a cause
he	*he, she, it* - the person or thing spoken of
not	*not* - in no manner or degree: in no way: NOWISE
stand	*stand* - to hold one's ground: maintain one's position: resist attack
for	*causal* - containing or involving cause or a cause: marked by cause and effect
they	*they* - PEOPLE: unspecified persons and especially those responsible for a particular act, practice, or decision
forecast	*weave* - to produce by elaborately combining available materials or elements: CONTRIVE *contrive* - to fabricate as a work of art or ingenuity: DESIGN, INVENT
devices	*machine* - a structure or constructed thing whether material or immaterial: ERECTION, HANDIWORK
against	*over* - used as a function word to indicate a relation of superiority advantage or preference to another

Michelle Lynn

DANIEL 11:26

*Yea, **they that feed** of the **portion** of his **meat** shall **destroy** him, and his **army** shall **overflow**: and **many** shall **fall** down **slain.***

Humanism—a term freely applied to a variety of beliefs, methods, and philosophies that place central emphasis on the human realm. Most frequently, however, the term is used with reference to a system of education and mode of inquiry that developed in northern Italy during the 14th century and later spread through Europe and England. Alternately known as "Renaissance humanism", this program was so broadly and profoundly influential that it is one of the chief reasons why the Renaissance is viewed as a distinct historical period. Indeed though the word *Renaissance* is of more recent coinage, the fundamental idea of that period as one of renewal and reawakening is humanistic in origin.[123]

This philosophy put greater emphasis on the human than on the divine. Humanists agreed with the Greek philosopher Protagoras, who wrote, "man is the measure of all things."

In the 16th century this (humanistic) process of searching and questioning led to a spiritual crisis on the Continent known as the Reformation.[124]

Humanism

Humanism is the term generally applied to the predominant social philosophy and intellectual and literary currents of the period from 1400 to 1650. The return to favor of the pagan classics stimulated the philosophy of secularism, the appreciation of worldly pleasures, and above all intensified the assertion of personal independence and individual expression. Zeal for the classics was a result as well as a cause of the growing secular view of life. Expansion of trade, growth of prosperity and luxury, and widening social contacts generated interest in worldly pleasures, in spite of formal allegiance to ascetic Christian doctrine. Men thus affected—the humanists—welcomed classical writers who revealed similar social values and secular attitudes.

Historians are pretty much agreed on the general outlines of those mental attitudes and scholarly interests which are assembled under the rubric of humanism. The most fundamental point of agreement is that the humanist mentality stood at a point midway between medieval supernaturalism and the modern scientific and critical attitude. Medievalists see humanism as the terminal product of the Middle Ages. Modern historians are perhaps more apt to view humanism as the germinal period of modernism.

Perhaps the most we can assume is that the man of the Renaissance lived, as it were, between two worlds. *The world of the medieval Christian matrix, in which the significance of every phenomenon was ultimately determined through uniform points of view, no longer existed for him. On the other hand, he had not yet found in a system of scientific concepts and social principles stability and security for his life. In other words, Renaissance man may indeed have found himself suspended between faith and reason.*

As the grip of medieval supernaturalism began to diminish, secular and human interests became more prominent. The facts of individual experience in the here and now became more interesting than the shadowy afterlife. Reliance upon faith and God weakened. *Fortuna* (chance) gradually replaced *Providence* as the universal frame of reference. The present world became an end in itself instead of simply preparation of a world to come. Indeed, as the age of Renaissance humanism wore on, the distinction between this world (the City of Man) and the next (the City of God) tended to disappear.

Beauty was believed to afford at least some glimpse of a transcendental existence. This goes far to explain the humanist cult of beauty and makes plain that humanism was, above everything else, fundamentally an aesthetic movement.

Human experience, man himself, tended to become the practical measure of all things. The ideal life was no longer a monastic escape from society, but a full participation in rich and varied human relationships.

The dominating element in the finest classical culture was aesthetic rather than supernatural or scientific. In the later Middle Ages urban intellectuals were well on the road to the recovery of an aesthetic and secular view of life even before the full tide of the classical revival was felt. It was only natural, then, that pagan literature, with its emotional and intellectual affinity to the new world view, shouldaccelerate the existing drift toward secularism and stimulate the cult of humanity, the worship of beauty, and especially the aristocratic attitude.

Humanism embodied the mystical and aesthetic temper of a pre-scientific age. It did not free the mind from subservience to ancient authority. If the humanists revered Aristotle less than the Schoolmen did, they worshipped Neoplatonism, the Cabala, and Cicero more. They shifted authorities rather then dismissed them. Even Aristotle, the greatest of Scholastic authorities, did not lack humanist admirers. The great libraries assembled by wealthy patrons of literature like Cosimo de' Medici, Pope Nicholas V, and the Duke of Urbino, devoted much space to the Church Fathers and the Scholastic philosophers. The humanists did, however, read their authorities for aesthetic pleasure as well as moral uplift.

The intellectuals of antiquity, in contrast to the Christians, were relatively unconcerned about the supernatural world and the eternal destiny of the soul. They were primarily interested in a happy, adequate, and efficient life here on earth. Hellenic philosophy was designed to teach man how to live successfully rather than how to die with the assurance of ultimate salvation. This pagan attitude had been lost for about one thousand years, when Europe followed the warning of Augustine against becoming too engrossed in earthly affairs, lest assurance of successful entry into the New Jerusalem be jeopardized. Humanism directly and indirectly revived the pagan scale of virtues.

When men like Petrarch and his fellow humanists read pagan literature, they were infected with the secular outlook of the Greeks and Romans. Even rather pious humanists became enamored of what Augustine branded the City of Man. Petrarch, a devout Christian, worshipped the pagan eclecticism of Cicero. Erasmus suggested that "Whatever is pious and conduces to good manners ought not to be called profane," he wrote.

> The first place must indeed be given to the authority of the Scriptures; but, nevertheless, I sometimes find some things said or written by the ancients, nay, even by the heathens, nay, by the poets themselves, so chastely, so holily, and so divinely, that I cannot persuade myself but that, when they wrote them, they were divinely inspired, and perhaps the spirit of Christ diffuses itself farther than we imagine; and that there are more saints than we have in our catalogue. To confess freely among friends, I can't read Cicero on Old Age, on Friendship, his Offices, or his Tusculan Questions, without kissing the book, without veneration towards the divine soul. And, on the contrary, when I read some of our modern authors, treating of Politics, Economics, and Ethics, good God! how cold they are in comparison with these! Nay, how do they seem to be insensible of what they write themselves! So that I had rather lose Scotus and twenty more such as he (fancy twenty subtle doctors!) than one Cicero or Plutarch. Not that I am wholly against them either; but, because, by the reading of the one, I find myself become better, whereas I rise from the other, I know not how coldly affected to virtue, but most violently inclined to cavil and contention.

The leading intellectual trait of the era as the recovery, to a certain degree, of the secular and humane philosophy of Greece and Rome. Another humanist trend which cannot be ignored was the rebirth of individualism, which, developed by Greece and Rome to a remarkable degree, had been suppressed by the rise of a caste system in the later Roman Empire, by the Church and by feudalism in the Middle Ages. The Church asserted that rampant individualism was identical with arrogance, rebellion, and sin. Medieval Christianity restricted individual expression, fostered self-abnegation and self-annihilation, and demanded implicit faith and unquestioning obedience. Furthermore, the Church officially ignored man and nature.

In other ways medieval civilization suppressed the ego. In the feudal regime the isolated individual had little standing. He acquired status and protection mainly as a member of a definite group, whether lordly or servile. The manorial system revolved around the community rather than the individual. When the cities threw off the yoke of feudalism, they promised collective and corporate liberty rather than individual freedom. In commercial relations group life was paramount, both in the town guilds and the peasant villages on manorial estates. Everything was regulated by law and custom. The individual who attempted to challenge authority and tradition, in matters of thought or action, was either discouraged or crushed.

The period from the 14th century to the 17th worked in favor of the general emancipation of the individual. The city-states of northern Italy had come into contact with the diverse customs of the East, and gradually permitted expression in matters of taste and dress. The writings of Dante, and particularly the doctrines of Petrarch and humanists like Machiavelli, emphasized the virtues of intellectual freedom and individual expression. In the essays of Montaigne the individualistic view of life received perhaps the most persuasive and eloquent statement in the history of literature and philosophy.

Individualism and the instinct of curiosity were vigorously cultivated. Honest doubt began to replace unreasoning faith. The skeptical viewpoint proposed by Abelard reached high development and wide acceptance among the humanists. Finally, the spirit of individualism to a certain degree incited the Protestant revolt, which, in theory at least, embodied a thorough application of the principle of individualism in religion.

It need not be supposed that the emancipation of the ego was wholly beneficial to the human race. Yet, that aspect of humanism which combated the sovereignty of tyrant, feudal lord, class, corporation, and tradition, has, for better or worse, had a tremendous influence upon the subsequent history of Europe. Indeed, it was during the humanist era that the freedom of individual expression and opposition to authority was first brought to the surface and became an integral part of the western intellectual tradition.[125]

DANIEL 11:26

they	**they** - those ones
that	**who** - the person or persons involved or meant or referred to
feed	**eat** - to take in in order to obtain some benefit: to accept unquestioningly: believe uncritically
portion	meat **dainty** - something that arouses favor or excites pleasure: something choice or pleasing
destroy	**burst** - to pass from a less to a more vigorous, ardent, or glowing state
army	**force** - power or capacity to sway, convince, or impose obligation: VALIDITY, EFFECT
overflow	**gallop** - a rapid rate or pace
many	**abundant** - occurring or existing in great quantity
fall	**fall** - to suffer ruin, defeat, or failure: fail utterly
slain	**polluted** - made unclean or impure: morally corrupt or defiled: physically tainted

☒ Revelation 18:14 And the fruits that thy soul lusted after are departed from thee, and all things which were dainty and goodly are departed from thee, and thou shalt find them no more at all.

Michelle Lynn

DANIEL 11:27

*And **both** these **kings' hearts** shall **be** to do **mischief,** and
they shall **speak lies at one table;** but it shall **not prosper:**
for yet the **end** shall **be at** the time **appointed.***

Reformation . . . division.

Wyclif and Hus have already been discussed as having protested
the corruption of the Church, but the man who truly touched off
the religious Reformation in Europe was a practicing Catholic and a
university professor at Wittenburg, Germany, named Martin Luther.
He became convinced that salvation was a gift direct from God that
could not be bought or sold and did not require the intercession
of a church official. On October 31, 1517, he nailed to the door of
the Wittenburg castle church a list of 95 theses that questioned the
granting of indulgences. Luther intended merely to spur an academic
debate on the subject. Instead he touched off a religious revolt,
a massive protest against the church's policies which came to be
known as Protestantism. Protestantism broke into numerous sects
as different interpretations were applied to biblical passages.[126]

Like the Christian church during this historical period, the
other major religion to influence Europe—Islam—was also divided
by ideology.[127] The nation of Islam was divided into two major
divisions—the Shiites and the Sunnis. Sunni Muslims carried out wars
against Christians in the name of Allah but also turned east against
the Shiites of Iran, whom they considered heretical Muslims.[128]

As a result of the Reformation, the driving force of Christianity
was squelched—not completely wiped out, of course, but definitely
not as influential as it had once been.

The Reformation

Religious purists in the agrarian hinterland of the West objected strongly to the new secular or materialist spirit growing up with the Renaissance. One of these was the German professor-priest Martin Luther who in 1517 issued a challenge to the church over this new interest in worldly affairs. He wanted the church to return to the pure (spiritual) ways of the early church—and back away from all this recent interest in power and wealth—which was rapidly corrupting it. Also, he wanted faith initiatives to be returned to the individual believer. Priesthood belonged to the believer—not to the religious hierarchy. To press home this challenge, Luther translated the Bible into German—to give the common people access to all priestly authority: the Word of God.

Irritated, the church told him to cease his challenge. But he refused to yield. When princely political interests came to his aid—his rebellion exploded. The "Lutheran" movement began spreading across the north of Germany. It would soon overtake Scandinavia. Medieval Europe, or what was left of it, began rapidly to fall into a state of civil war.

But the challenge to the church came from another direction as well: from the newly rising European urban middle class. This was a prosperous, free-thinking and literate group. Eventually their position seemed to be galvanized around the teachings of the Genevan reformer, Calvin. Taking essentially the same position as Luther, Calvin began to assemble protestant scholars and teachers who would take the movement back to their home provinces. During the second half of the 1500s his "Reformed" movement was well planted in the towns and cities of England, Scotland,

Netherlands, France, Western Germany, Bohemia, Hungary—and even parts of Poland and Spain (where it later got eradicated by the Catholic counter-reformation).

John Wycliff (1320-1384)

At Oxford university, John Wycliff by 1370 stirred up controversy in teaching the freedom of religious conscience of the individual believer, who stood in faith directly before God. He attacked a multitude of practices and features of the church—especially its wealth.

Wycliff's followers, contemptuously called "Lollards," from a Dutch word of derision meaning "mumblers" (originally directed at the Beguines), preached reform in England. Also, Wycliff's movement made much of the Bible available to the masses in its English translation from the Vulgate. Wycliff's Lollard movement was eventually suppressed—but so was the intellectual ferment of Oxford university where his teachings had been widely accepted.

The Reform Councils and the Council of Pisa (1409)

The institutional church was trying to unify and reform itself—and at the same time bring independent voices of reform under submission—through the conciliar movement, a series of church councils called to unify the papacy and reform the church.

The Council of Pisa, in order to end the embarrassment of having two contending popes claiming to be the sole head of the Catholic church, deposed the two contenders, Gregory XII and Benedict XIII. This reform was undertaken even by the cardinals of both popes—

who elected a new pope, Alexander V. But when the two popes refused to step down, there were then three contending popes!

John Huss (1374-1415)

Wycliff's teachings reached Bohemia after his death and were picked up by John Huss, at the University of Prague, in the early 1400s. Huss translated Wycliff's works into Czech and gave life to the reform ideals to the people. This stirred fear in the hearts of church officialdom. In 1414 Huss was called (under the Emperor's promise of safe conduct) to the Council of Constance to explain himself. But he was arrested by the Council and burned at the stake in 1415—sparking revolt in Bohemia. Attempts to put down what had become a popular national revolt failed; finally a compromise was reached with the Hussites.

The Council of Basel (1431-1449)

The council initially made progress toward reconciliation with the Hussites. It defied a papal order to move to Bologna, claiming superior authority to that of the pope (Eugenius IV: 1431-1447). But its subsequent efforts at reform of the ecclesiastical hierarchy caused it to overstep its true power—and Eugenius used this to his own advantage. Also, the pressing problems of the Turks and the need for closer relations with the Eastern church, provided the occasion for the pope to split the council's power bringing a portion of the council to Ferrara while the remainder carried on in Basel. Its decision in 1439 to elect a pope in opposition to Eugenius undermined most of the council's residual authority. In the meanwhile, the papacy in Rome emerged as an ever-stricter defender of its ecclesiastical authority.

Girolamo Savonarola (1452-1498)

Savonarola was an apocalyptic Dominican monk-preacher who was both a very popular figure among the poorer classes of Florence and a thorn in the side of the Florentine aristocracy. He led a grand effort to clean up the morals of Florentine society. But the populace was turned against his influence and he was hanged in 1498.

A Sense of Growing Decadence in the Church

The profound corruption of the church—from popes down to parish priests—was a source of major frustration to the faithful—who had a profound sense of God's judgment over His people, the Christian community. Judgment would fall on this New Israel as surely as it did the Old Israel.

A Growth of Independent Personal Judgment

Combined with this sense of frustration with the church was a growing independent-mindedness on the part of a new humanist intelligentsia. The church no longer held a monopoly over the thinking of scholars and teachers. The new printing presses had put in their hands a wider range of reading that had ever been available previously. Some of it was pagan, most of it was Christian. But in any case it opened up a world that was not automatically sifted through the scrutiny of the religious hierarchy.

Oddly, one of the most unsettling elements of this new literature were the Hebrew and Greek manuscripts of the Old and New Testaments that became widely available. The new Biblical scholarship that this engendered not only pointed out (minor) flaws in the Latin Vulgate—but gave the new scholars a sense of personal judgment superior to that of the official church. The age of the individual conscience was being born!

The church could no longer expect automatically to command the thinking of its Christian subjects. Within the context of this independent and very critical mood—at least on the part of a new breed of humanist scholars—"business-as-usual" on the part of the church was bound to create a massive reaction.

A Major Shift in the Traditional Political Order of Medieval Christendom

For centuries, the whole of the medieval Christian order had been a single piece—understood to be ordained and supported by the will of God. It was the widely understood principle that all the social orders, from kings and popes down to the vast multitudes of peasants, all had their respective "place" in that medieval political, economic, social, cultural, religious, spiritual order—such places determined by God's natural ordering of all people. A person was placed into that order by the logic of his or her birth—and that by the will of God. It was God that determined who would be born a king, who would be born a peasant. This being God's righteous decree, there was little further thought that could be given to a rearranging this larger medieval social or political order.

True, kings and bishops, who both belonged to the upper aristocratic orders, had been battling among themselves since the 1100s for dominance over this larger medieval social order. But such disputes did not involve the masses of European peasant farmers. Theysimply awaited the outcome of such struggles to see how marriages, political alliances, wars would move them from the domain of one lord (priestly or princely) to another. They themselves had no say in such matters. Their job was to till the soil and pay the lord their feudal dues. They always prayed that God would set over them a fair or just lord. But they themselves had no voice in the matter of who ruled over the land that they worked with their labors.

The Rising Urban Power Base of the Renaissance

However the rise during the 1300s and 1400s of European commercial wealth—in competition with the traditional wealth of rural landholdings—was bound to upset this arrangement. Bankers, merchants, industrialists—who congregated along key trade centers—did not fit easily into this older social order. Though certainly their guilds and unions attempted to formalize their wealth, in fact their wealth was dynamic and always subject to a rapid shift in fortunes. The success of their labors was related to the wisdom of investment decisions that they made. To prosper, they needed a free hand—and a mind open to new and ever changing opportunities.

During the 1400s this group sat uneasily under the traditional rule of medieval church and crown. Medieval feudal dues in the form of agricultural and military service owed the lord were cumbersome and at times counterproductive to the larger success of this new urban entrepreneurial class.

It was inevitable that these towns would become centers of resistance against the medieval land-based social system. Indeed, in case after case these rising towns and cities were able to receive from the traditional local princely or priestly lord new charters which granted them (that is, the commercial elite or oligarchy that ran these towns) a tremendous degree of self-goverment—in exchange for the payment of taxes in currency. This was because money was becoming more important than land in undergirding the military might of a local ruler—and the princely and priestly rulers in fact preferred monetary payments over land service from their vassals. While land assessments and service obligations might feed their courts and fill their armies with men-at-arms—only money could buy them the new luxuries—and the new military technologies—that traditional land-based service could not.

Reconstructing a Moral-Legal Order around This Newly Rising Order

But the independence of these towns—in keeping with their real power—did not provide the air of legitimacy that they needed to feel secure in their liberties within the newly rising order. At any time these urban charters might be revoked by the local prince or bishop by any whim or fancy (or suspicion). There really was no "right" of their own that the towns could hold up to these lords in order to demand equitable treatment. At least not until the Protestant Reformation in the 1500s gave them the sense that they had the right to accept or reject political authority in accordance with what their own consciences dictated. There was no power on earth, only God alone, who had the right to judge them in the matters of conscience, even political conscience.

The 95 Theses

The explosion finally came around the matter of the financing of the lavish building program of Saint Peter's Basilica in Rome. As an untended spokesman for this critical mindset, in 1517 Martin Luther posted his 95 theses on the door of the Wittenburg castle church protesting, for theological reasons, the sale of indulgences to finance the pope's schemes.

Behind this defiant action was a long personal pilgrimage of Luther, one based on an deep desire to unburden himself of a profound sense of guilt and personal condemnation before God's judgment. For Luther, a personal breakthrough occurred as the message sank into the head of this Augustinian professor concerning Paul's teaching (Galatians and Romans) about divine Grace and forgiveness received through the simple faith of the believer—and not through the the side of the Roman church.

Luther, now excommunicated but still under the protection of Frederick and widely popular in Germany, was called by the Emperor to an Imperial Council at Worms to give account of his views. Here Luther stood firm in his views against the Roman church. Under an Imperial guarantee of his freedom, Luther was able to get away from the Council before the guarantee was retracted. From then on for the rest of his life, Luther remained in seculsion—publishing works against the papacy and bringing forth his German translation of the Bible.

In the meanwhile the Emperor found himself preoccupied by an on-going war with France over control of various cities and principalities in Italy. Thus the Emperor was seriously distracted in his effort to quiet Luther. Then the Turkish threat to the Emperor's Austrian holdings rose up again. Luther was relatively safe.

The Peasant War

Meanwhile the spiritual rebellion of Luther against Rome soon spread as a mood of political rebellion of the German commoner against princely authority. The autonomy of the individual religious conscience gave over easily to the idea of the autonomy of the individual political conscience. But in this, Luther proved to be no rebel. In fact, he stood strongly on the side of the princes against the German rebels (Karlstadt and Müntzer) who took up the political cause of the German commoner against their rulers. In the peasant rebellion of 1524-1525, Luther came down harshly against the peasants. The peasants and their leaders were put down cruelly (6,000 peasants lost their lives alone in the one-day battle of Frankenhausen).

The result of the Peasant War was to move real power over to the various German princes. Thus in Germany, the rule of the church was not a matter either of local congregational power—nor of the power of popes and bishops. Rather, it was the ruling prince in each of the many principalities that made up Germany who determined each in his own territory its particular Christian character. Some remained loyal to some (the southern German princes), some followed the Lutheran line (the northern German princes). But in any case it was the local princes who made that determination. The dependence of church on state was thus set as the characteristic feature of German Christianity—a feature lasting down into the 20th century.

Furthermore, because of Luther's deep conservatism and the limitation of his vision of reform solely to the context of an ongoing, though theologically reformed, agrarian medieval religious order, Luther's movement remained confined to a highly *rural*, still medieval north-central Europe—and had almost no impact in any of the rapidly developing European urban areas.

Michelle Lynn

Ulrich Zwingli

In Zurich, Switzerland, meanwhile, a young priest was being drawn toward Luther's reform movement. In 1522 Ulrich Zwingli began to make his moves to establish Scripture as the sole religious authority for the Christian. He opposed the Lenten Fast, citing the lack of Scriptural warrant for the practice—a position which was supported by the Zurich civil government.

The bishop of Constance tried to suppress this innovation—but lost out to the Zurich government, which moved to take control of ecclesiastical matters within its jurisdiction. Zwingli supported this shift in authority—claiming that the civil government, under the Lordship of Christ and guided in its work by the dictates of Scripture, was the legitimate voice or conscience of the believing community.

Meanwhile the Reformation began to spread to other parts of Switzerland: most notably to the cities of Basel (where Oecolampadius had been leading the reform movement), Constance and Bern. It also made its way down the Rhine River to Strasburg—where under the leadership of Zell, Capito and Bucer the reform movement there took on the more thoroughgoing Swiss character (as distinct from the more conservative Lutheran variety).

But the conservative rural cantons of Switzerland remained firmly opposed to the Zwinglian reforms. Relations grew bitter and hostilities resulted—with Zwingli himself being wounded and then put to death in a losing battle against the rural cantons in 1531. The more gentle-natured Heinrich Bullinger took over the Zurich reform movement.

The Split within the Protestant Ranks

Meanwhile, the reform movement was beginning to move in different and opposing theological directions. For Luther the reform movement was more narrowly related to the matter of a sinner's personal justification before God. Luther showed little interest in making broader changes within Christianity beyond the throwing off of Roman spiritual authority—with its traditions of works-righteousness. Substantial changes in worship, for instance, were of lesser interest to Luther. Also the episcopal form of church government (rule by bishops) was kept by Luther—though with the understanding that the bishops were answerable to the local princes—not to Rome.

But to Zwingli and the Swiss reformers (identified as the Reformed party) there were strong interests in restructuring the organization and practices of the church around its original constitutional base: Scripture. There was a stripping away of every feature of Christianity that could not be supported by Scriptural warrant.

This was in keeping with Zwingli's humanist background—and its focus on the Greek and Hebrew origins of the church, and the sense that everything that was a departure from this classical age was a perversion of an original purity undergirding the church.

This would not probably have kept Luther and Zwingli from working closely together—except that one portion of Zwingli's reforms were violently opposed by Luther: Zwingli's treatment of the celebration of the Lord's supper. Zwingli (for whom the sermon, not the celebration of the eucharist, was the central point of Christian worship) interpreted Christ's words concerning his presence in the wine andbread as purely symbolic. To Luther, this was a shocking diminution of the power of the real presence of Christ in the elements of the eucharist. The gap was, in both their minds, unbridgeable by the mid 1520s. Others of both parties tried to effect a compromise. But Luther, even after Zwingli's death, would not hear of compromise. Lutheranism and the Reformed faith split permanently.

John Calvin

In the meantime in France, John Calvin (1509 to 1564), as a young jurist, was trying to convince the French king, Francis I, to give sympathy to the reform movement. In 1536 he published his *Institutes of the Christian Religion*.

This not only failed to convince the king, but also identified Calvin as a voice of religious dissent, not tolerated in France. Calvin was forced to flee France. In coming to Geneva, Switzerland, the protestant reformer Farel prevailed upon Calvin to stay in the city and help him with the reformed movement which was growing rapidly there. But for Calvin, this proved to be a stormy proposition. Geneva was an unruly city, and Calvin's natural bent toward orderliness and discipline made him many enemies in the city. In the spring of 1538 Calvin and Farel were banished from Geneva. He fled to Strasbourg, where the Reform movement was well established.

But in 1541, the old group partisan to Calvin urgently requested his return to Geneva. Calvin somewhat reluctantly decided to make his return—but on his terms. Upon his return, Calvin organized (accepting many compromises with the city Council) the religious life of the city around his new *Ordinances*—the foundation of Reformed polity. Geneva in turn became identified under Calvin's leadership as the model Christian city, the "New Jerusalem" of Protestantism.

Calvin was an *urban* European, steeped in the bourgeois mindset of the rising European urban "middle class." Calvin's interest in reform of the crumbling medieval moral-legal order involved importantly a vision of the new urban order as central to a purified Christianity. And his interest in reform did not limit itself merely to matters of religious doctrine—as was the case for Luther.

Calvin truly was interested in a comprehensive reordering of every aspect of post-medieval life: political, economic, and social as well as theological.

Importantly, he gave a theological rationale for the independent-mindedness of the urban commercial class—arming them with Scriptural justification for going their own way within God's creation. Indeed, he encouraged them to establish purified political-economic-social orders as a way of purging Christendom of its corruption and of bringing glory to God in Jesus Christ. He made their soul-searching independent-mindedness a matter of the greatest importance in their standing before God. They not only had the right to be accountable to God alone as sovereign over them—they had the Christian duty to see that this was the case. The supposition was that any earthly lord who positioned himself between them and God was going to be problematic in their "purified" relationship with God and their covenantal life in the purified Christian commonwealth.

The followers of Calvin attempted to convince the rich and powerful kings of Europe that their movement had no treasonous instincts—and that they planned to be good citizens in the realms where they lived. The kings were not convinced. And rightly so. Everything about Calvinism pointed to the idea of these people being accountable to no earthly ruler but to God alone.

Switzerland, which was the birthplace of Calvin's Reformed Movement was well recognized for its mindedness and refusal to acknowledge the rule of any princely lord over the land. No, Calvin's Reformed Movement, or "Calvinism" was destined to bring a clash with traditional princely and priestly rulers who claimed to rule by "divine rights." That was exactly what the Calvinists claimed for their own "self-rule": self-rule by divine right—even by divine imperative. There was no way these two mind-sets were going to work cooperatively.

John Knox

We must at this point mention one of these "Calvinists": John Knox, the great Protestant reformer of Scotland.

Knox not only helped direct Scotland to Calvinist Protantism in the mid 1500s, but also left a powerful political legacy within the Calvinist or Reformed branch of Protestantism, a political legacy we call "Presbyterianism." Knox's Presbyterianism not only determnimed the organization of the Church of Scotland but also layed the foundations for the growth of *representative democracy* in the American middle colonies (from New Jersey to South Carolina) in the 1600s and 1700s.

As with many Protestant reformers, Knox began as a Catholic priest, highly discontent with the moral and spiritual corruption that had overtaken the Mother Church. He was attracted to the Lutheran teachings of the early Scottish reformer, George Wishart; was appalled when in 1546 the Catholic cardinal had Wishart burned at the stake as a heretic; and then joined the group of rebels who moved to overthrow the hand of the Catholic church over Scotland. This put him in opposition to the pro-Frenchparty that ruled Scotland—

and when French troops in 1547 crushed this Protestant rebellion in Scotland, Knox was led off to captivity as a French galley slave. His release was finally secured by the pro-Protestant English King Edward VI, leading Knox to come to England to be a Protestant pastor and then chaplain to the King.

But when Edward died in 1553 and Catholic Mary Tudor ("Bloody Mary") came to the throne, Knox left England and made his way eventually to Geneva Switzerland where he joined a community of English expatriates living and studying under the direction of the great Genevan reformer, John Calvin. Knox took a great liking to both Calvin and his teachings and subsequently became a major voice in the English/Scottish reform movement not only in Geneva, but through letters, to a growing Protestant movement back in Scotland.

He returned briefly to Scotland in 1555, became pastor of the English church in Geneva, and then finally in 1559 he returned definitively to Scotland to take over the spiritual leadership of the Protestant rebellion against the French-Catholic regent of Scotland, Mary of Guise. Seeing that things were not going well in Scotland for the Protestant party, Queen Elizabeth of England came to their aid against the French in Scotland. But when Mary of Guise died suddenly in 1560, the French Catholic cause in Scotland was dead. Scotland was now won for Protestantism.

At this point Knox and his supporters began to reshape the Scottish church—not only theologically along the lines of Calvin's Reformed Faith born in Geneva, but also politically in a way that was Knox's special contribution to the Protestant cause. Knox took the idea of representative government characteristic of Calvin's reformed churches (communities lead by elected elders or"presbyters"), and applied it locally, regionally and nationally in total reversal of the top-down or hierarchical fashion of Catholic or "episcopalian" government. Thus local councils ("Presbyteries"), regional councils ("Synods") and national councils ("General Assemblies") that presided over the faithful were made up of representatives not of the political rulers over the church but of the people themselves. Thus was born "Presbyterian" or representative church government—the source of inspiration for the new Democratic or Republican forms of government that led eventually to the Constitution of 1789 underpinning the new American Republic.

Despite success in the Protestant takeover of the church Scotland, the continuing existence of a Catholic monarchy in Scotland under Mary of Guise's daughter, Mary Queen of Scots, made life still highly problematic for Protestant Scotland—and for John Knox personally as the two locked wills in on-going battle. But eventually Mary's poor diplomacy proved to be her undoing and in 1567 she was forced to flee to England, where Elizabeth put her under house arrest, where she remained for the rest of her life.

In any case Knox, worn out and sickly, died from his labors in 1572. But his work in Scotland was carried forth faithfully by others, notably Andrew Melville.

The papal party finally realized the seriousness of the challenge to its moral authority—and finally in 1546 called a Council at Trent to answer the Protestant charges of ecclesiastical corruption and theological deviation. Rigid discipline was reimposed over the priests who remained loyal to Rome. Luther's teaching on divine grace and justification alone by faith was condemned. A campaign was readied to wipe out any "heretics" not ready to return to Roman discipline. The war was thus on.

The Roman church, championed by the most powerful ruling family in Europe (the Spanish Habsburgs)—well-financed from their plunder of South and Central America—fought back—cruelly, trying to stamp out the fires of the Protestant revolt. They succeeded in many places—and might have been fully successful had not the Muslim Turks attacked Vienna—the Eastern center of Habsburg power—during the height of this struggle. With the Habsburgs thus distracted, Protestantism dug in. [129]

Islamic Discord

Despite military success of their territorial expansion, there remained problems of organisation and government within the Ottoman Empire. Murad II attempted to limit the influence of the nobility and the gazi by elevating faithful former slaves and janissaries to administrative positions. These administrators came to provide an alternative voice to that of the nobility and, as a result, Murad II and successive Sultans were able to play one faction against the other, a feature that came to typify the Ottoman Empire. The power of the janissaries often overrode a weak sultan and the elite military force occasionally acted as 'king-makers.'

Another weakness was that primogeniture was not used in Islam and the transference of power from a deceased sultan to his son was frequently disputed. If a Sultan died without a male heir or if he left several sons, succession was violently contested. In the early period, to prevent ongoing rivalries, all male relatives of a newly crowned Sultan were put to death. Later, however, the potential rivals were merely imprisoned for life. Some historians consider that this policy of imprisonment contributed to the decline of the Ottoman Empire as mentally unstable and politically inexperienced Sultans were rescued from prison and placed upon the throne.

Nevertheless, despite frequent disputes over succession, the Ottoman Empire managed to produce effective leaders in the late Middle Ages and a comprehensive government policy developed. [130]

The Ottoman Empire was Islam's most successful expansion of territory even though the religion itself had fractured into warring sects and bitter rivalries with each claiming the ultimate truths in "the ways of the Prophet". By 1683 the Ottomans had suffered a series of defeats on both land and sea and the final, unsuccessful attempt to capture Vienna set the stage for the collapse of any further territorial ambitions and Islam shrunk into various sheikhdoms, emir dominated principalities, and roving tribes of nomads.[131]

Daniel 11:27

both   **two** - the two: the one and the other

kings   **king** - one that holds a supreme or preeminent position in a particular sphere or class

hearts   **heart** - the center or decisive part of something: the determining aspect

be   **be** - to exist under conditions specified

mischief   **wickedness** - wicked character or conduct: VICE

     wicked - being or acting contrary to moral or divine law: SINFUL, BAD

they   **they** - those ones

speak   **speak** - to give proof or evidence of: INDICATE, SUGGEST

lies   **lie** - to create a false or misleading impression: convey an untruth

at   **against** - not in conformity with: contrary to

one   **united** - being or living in agreement: HARMONIOUS

table   **table** - a flat slab (as of wood or stone): TABLET: a set of laws inscribed on tablets: TABLET: an indelible record

     indelible - that cannot be removed, washed away, or erased: that cannot be effaced or obliterated: PERMANENT, LASTING

not   **not** - used as a generalized negative function word to express an unspecified degree of comparative difference varying from almost identical to almost opposite

prosper   **push** forward - to promote or carry out with vigor: urge or press the advancement, adoption, or practice of: to press forward against

	obstacles or opposition or with energy: advance persistently or courageously
for	*causal* - expressing or indicating cause: CAUSATIVE
yet	*still* - to or at a greater distance: FARTHER: in addition: beyond this: to a greater extent
end	*extremity* - a culminating point (as of emotion or pain): HEIGHT, APEX, CLIMAX
be	*be* - to exist under conditions specified
at	*over* - on the occasion of: at the time of
appointed	fixed *time* - a point or period when something occurs: the moment of an event, process, or condition: OCCASION

DANIEL 11:28

*Then shall **he return** into his **land with great riches;** and his heart shall **be against** the **holy covenant;** and **he** shall **do** exploits, and **return** to his own **land.***

In the 15th century, economics, religion, and the very nature of the Renaissance prompted mariners to venture into the unknown and begin one of the greatest periods of exploration the world has ever known.

With Muslim armies pressuring Eastern Europe, Christians were worried about the spread of Islam. Some thought they might outflank the Muslim Empire by sailing around the great land to the south—Africa—and attacking Islam from a different direction. In addition, they wanted to win souls for Christ.

Trade also spurred exploration. Through the Crusades and overland commerce, Europe had acquired an appetite for Eastern goods—silks, jewels, and spices. Spices from the Orient were used in cosmetics, medicines, and especially in meat, to preserve it by smoking and then curing.[132]

A quote from H.G. Wells, "It is rather a delicate matter to decide whether the Western European was pushing out into the Atlantic or whether he was being pushed out into it by the Turk."[133]

Michelle Lynn

Portuguese Explorers

Portugal led the European world in sea exploration during the fifteenth century. The golden age of discovery for Portugal lasted almost a century until the Dutch eventually seized trade routes from them. During the height of their years of exploration, the Portuguese were attempting to find a route around Africa into the Indian Ocean and eventually trade with India and the Far East.

In the fourteenth century, Portugal managed to drive the Moors out. Muslims (Moors) had controlled the better part orf Portugal and Spain for centuries. In 1415, the Portuguese captured the Moorish city of Ceuta on the northern coast of Africa. From this time forward, Portugal continued to expand its influence on the western coast of Africa in order to outflank the Moors and spread Christianity.

During this timeframe, stories about a Christian king named <u>Prestor John</u> were circulating throughout Europe. Portuguese leaders hoped to find this legendary king to gain his support; but he did not exist.

Since overland routes to Asia were blocked by <u>Ottoman Turks</u>, Portuguese mariners began their slow and persistent progress down the coast of Africa in search for gold and trade routes to the east.

Prince Henry the Navigator

The man chiefly responsible for Portugal's age of exploration was Prince Henry the Navigator, the third son of King Joao I (John) and his English wife, Queen Philippa of Lancaster. Henry was born in 1394.

As a youth, he participated in the capture of Ceuta. In 1419, his father made him governor of Portugal's southernmost coasts. From 1419 until his death in [1460], Prince Henry sent expedition after expedition down the west coast of Africa to outflank the Muslim hold on trade routes and to establish colonies. These expeditions moved slowly due to the mariners' belief that waters at the equator were at the boiling point, that human skin turned black, and that sea monsters would engulf ships.

It wasn't until 27 years after Henry's death that Bartolomeu Dias braved these "dangers" and rounded the Cape of Good Hope in [1487]. Henry was keenly interested in and studied navigation and mapmaking. He established a naval observatory for the teaching of navigation, astronomy, and cartography about [1450]. Unfortunately, Portugal began slaving operations along the west coast of Africa. Sailors could offer glass beads and colored cloth in exchange for tribal captives. In 1452, Pope Nicolas V issued his papal bull allowing the enslavement of "pagans and infidels."

Prince Henry's interest in the slaves was mainly to convert them to Christianity.

Vasco da Gama

Portugal's slow progress down the west coast of Africa in search for a route to the east finally came to fruition with Vasco da Gama (1469—1524). He followed Bartolomeu Dias' route to the Cape of Good Hope in [1497] to 1498 and continued sailing into unknownwaters along the eastern coast of the African continent. He eventually located a route to India, but had to contend with Arab strongholds.

In 1502, da Gama returned with 14 heavily armed ships and managed to defeat the Arab fleet. By 1511, the Portuguese mastered the Spice routes and had access to the Spice Islands. In 1513, Portuguese trade extended to China and Japan. [134]

The Ottoman 'Discovery' of the Indian Ocean in the Sixteenth Century:
The Age of Exploration from an Islamic Perspective

Vasco da Gama's successful voyage around the Cape of Good Hope in 1497 and the foundation of the Portuguese *Estado da India* in the following decades has long been identified as a development of enormous global significance, marking as it did the beginning of direct and continuous contact between the civilizations of Western Europe and the Indian Ocean. Much less well known to modern scholarship, by contrast, is the rival and contemporaneous expansion of the Ottoman Empire into the lands of the Indian Ocean littoral, a process which began with Sultan Selim I's conquest of Egypt in 1517, and which would continue throughout the rest of the sixteenth century. Because the Ottoman state and the merchant communities of the Indian Ocean shared the same religion, most modern scholars have simply assume that they enjoyed a kind of *de facto* familiarity with one another as well. In reality, the early sixteenth century Ottomans were in many ways even less aware of the geography, history and civilization of the Indian Ocean than were their contemporary Portuguese rivals. The subsequent development of direct contact between the Ottoman Empire and the Muslim principalities and trading communities of the Indian Ocean thus represents a kind of Ottoman 'discovery' of an entirely new part of the globe, and one which corresponds in many ways to the much better documented European discoveries of the same period.

Like its Western counterpart, the Ottoman discovery of the Indian Ocean included economic, military and diplomatic components that are all subjects in need of further in-depth research. Specifically, this paper argues that the growth of Ottoman intellectual interest in the Indian Ocean during the course of the sixteenth century closely mirrors, both qualitatively and chronologically, developments in Europe at the same time. Before addressing this issue directly, however, let us briefly compare the state of Medieval Western and Islamic geographical knowledge of the Indian Ocean before the voyages of exploration, and consider how the Ottomans fit into this overall picture.

First Contact:
The Conquests of Selim the Grim and the Beginnings of Ottoman Exploration:

Just as it did for contemporary Europeans, the Ottomans' discovery of the Indian Ocean began at the start of the sixteenth century, and was made possible by a series of unprecedented military successes. In this process, the primary protagonist was undoubtedly Sultan Selim I who, in addition to orchestrating the crucially important conquest of Egypt in 1517, was also an avid collector of maps and geographical texts. Like his grandfather Mehmet II, Selim sponsored local scholars while at the same time actively seeking out the latest productions from Western Europe, and seems to have been particularly interested in works relating to the world outside the familiar confines of the Mediterranean basin.

In the space of just a few decades, the Ottoman's had moved from a state of almost total ignorance about the world of the Indian

Ocean to a comfortable familiarity that was the product of both extensive first-hand experience and sustained intellectual commitment. This development, which mirrored Western experiences during the same period, suggests that the Age of Exploration cannot be properly understood by focusing only on the narrow story of Europe's engagement with the outside world. Intellectually speaking, "discovery" was a process whose limits far exceeded the boundaries of Western Civilization. [135]

Daniel 11:28

he	**he, she, it** - the person or thing spoken of
return	**turn** - to direct one's course
land	**earth** - a particular region of the world: COUNTRY, LAND
with	**with** - used as a function word to indicate a related or supplementary fact or circumstance
great	**great** - considerable or remarkable in magnitude, power, intensity degree, or effectiveness
riches	**property** - something that is or may be owned or possessed: WEALTH, GOODS: specifically: a piece of real estate
heart	**heart** - an essential part: the part that determines the real nature of something or gives significance to the other parts: the determining aspect
be	**be** - have a (specified) qualification or characteristic
against	**upon** - having a powerful influence on: lying heavily on
holy	**sacred** - holy or hallowed especially by association with the divine or consecrated: worthy of religious veneration
covenant	**compact** - an agreement, understanding, or covenant between two or more parties
he	**this** - the person, thing, or idea that is present or near in place, time, or thought, or that has just been mentioned
do	**do** - to be the cause of: bring about as a result: EFFECT
return	**turn** - to direct one's course
land	**earth** - a particular region of the world: COUNTRY, LAND

Michelle Lynn

DANIEL 11:29

*At the time **appointed he** shall **return,** and **come** toward the*
*south; but it shall **not be** as the **former,** or as the **latter.***

It was not until the battle of Lepanto, in 1571—the battle in which Cervantes, the author of *Don Quixote*, lost his left arm—that Christendom, to use his words, "broke the pride of the Osmans (Ottomans) and undeceived the world which had regarded the Turkish fleet as invincible."[136]

Christopher Columbus (1451-1506), born in Genoa, was convinced that the world was round and that he could reach China by sailing west. On October 12, 1492, two months after leaving Spain, Columbus landed in the Bahama Islands, the first land to be sighted in the New World.[137]

The center of interest for European history, shifts now from the Alps and the Mediterranean Sea to the Atlantic.[138]

Christopher Columbus,

born between Aug. 26 and Oct. 31?, 1451, Genoa

died May 20, 1506, Valladolid, Spain

Genoese navigator and explorer whose transatlantic voyages opened the way for European exploration, exploitation, and colonization of the Americas.

Italian Cristoforo Colombo; Spanish Cristóbal Colón He began his career as a young seaman in the Portuguese merchant marine. In 1492 he obtained the sponsorship of the Spanish monarchs Ferdinand V and Isabella I for an attempt to reach Asia by sailing westward over what was presumed to be open sea. On his first voyage he set sail in August 1492 with three ships—the Santa María, the Niña, and the Pinta—and land was sighted in the Bahamas on October 12. He sailed along the northern coast of Hispaniola and returned to Spain in 1493. He made a second voyage (1493-96) with at least 17 ships and founded La Isabela (in what is now the Dominican Republic), the first European town in the New World. This voyage also began Spain's effort to promote Christian evangelization. On his third voyage (1498-1500) he reached South America and the Orinoco River delta. Allegations of his poor administration led to his being returned to Spain in chains. On his fourth voyage (1502-04) he returned to South America and sailed along the coasts of present-day Honduras and Panama. He was unable to attain his goals of nobility and great wealth. His character and achievements have long been debated, but scholars generally agree that he was an intrepid and brilliant navigator.[139]

DANIEL 11:29

appointed   a *fixed* time - to set or place definitely: STATION,
              SETTLE: to assign precisely: settle on:
              DETERMINE, DEFINE: ASSIGN, PLACE
he   *he, she, it*—the person or thing spoken of
return   *turn* - to direct one's course
come   *go* - to reach a certain point: ATTAIN, EXTEND
south   *south* - regions or countries lying to the south of a
              specified or implied point of orientation
not   *not* - in no manner or degree: in no way: NOWISE
be   *become* - to emerge as an entity: grow to manifest a
              certain essence, nature, development, or
              significance
former   *first* - foremost in rank, importance, or worth: CHIEF
latter   *western* - situated in or lying toward the west; coming
              from the west

DANIEL 11:30

*For the **ships** of **Chittim** shall **come against** him: therefore he shall **be grieved**, and **return**, and have **indignation** against the **holy covenant**: so shall **he do: he** shall even **return**, and have **intelligence with** them **that forsake** the holy covenant.*

Throughout the 1500s the Spanish concentrated on conquering Central and South America.[140] The Europeans were here to stay.

The Aztecs, once the greed and treachery of the Spaniards had made their human origins all too clear, fought as if the war was just another tribal conflict, in which the defeated nation lost its political freedom but was allowed to keep its gods and customs. The Spaniards were fighting a more total kind of war in which there was no room for religious toleration. The confrontation between Europe and America was inevitable, and the Spanish triumph established 16th-century European ways in place of native Indian culture.[141] The New World natives, separated from technological advancements that had occurred in Europe and Asia, were no match for armor, fearsome horses, and superior weapons. Diseases such as measles, smallpox, and typhus devastated local populations. Malaria moved from Africa to South America. Whole peoples—for example, the Caribs of the Caribbean—were virtually wiped out by disease, war, slavery, and interbreeding.[142] At a meeting in the Spanish town of Tordesillas in 1494, the Portuguese and Spanish kings signed a treaty dividing the non-Christian world between them by a line passing through the mid-Atlantic from north to south, to the exclusion of all other nations. Rising nations such as England rejected the claim, however, and in 1497 John Cabot, a Genoese who adopted British

Michelle Lynn

nationality, took possession of Newfoundland for England.[143] Henry Hudson, a Dutch explorer, explored the bays and rivers of Long Island Sound, so giving the Dutch the basis of their claim to the area around New York.[144]

All of this is taking place at the time of the Reformation. Not only was the Reformation affecting the common people, it had seeped into the ruling class. In England, Henry VIII, who saw himself to the end as a good Catholic, wanted an annulment of his first marriage to Catherine of Aragon, who seemed unable to give him a male heir. When the pope refused, Henry broke with Rome, married Anne Boleyn, mother of the future Elizabeth, and set up the Church of England, with himself as the head.[145]

In 1555, the Treaty of Augsburg declared that the religion of the ruler should determine the religion of his people, so that every Protestant prince in Europe became his own 'pope'.[146]

European Exploration and Settlement in the New World

Date	Explorer	Representing	Event
c. 1000	Leif Eriksson	Norse	Likely first European to Newfoundland
1418	(Prince Henry the Navigator)	Portugal	Offers training in navigation & cartography
1431	Gonzalo Cabral	Portugal	Discovered Azores
1440s	various	Portugal	Exploration along west African coast; slave trade
1453	(Fall of Constantinople)		Muslim closure of eastward routes may have spurred westward push.
1487-88	Bartholomeu Dias	Portugal	Reached Cape of Good Hope
1492	Christopher Columbus	Spain	First voyage
1494	(Treaty of Tordesillas)		Division of New World between Spain and Portugal
1497	John Cabot	England	To Newfoundland; English claim to North America
1497-98	Vasco da Gama	Portugal	Rounds Africa to India
1497+	Amerigo Vespucci	Spain Portugal	West Indies and South America
1500-01	Pedro Álvarez Cabral	Portugal	Brazil
1513	Ponce de Léon	Spain	Florida
1513	Vasco Núñez de Balboa	Spain	Crossed Panama to Pacific Ocean

1519-22	Ferdinand Magellan	Spain	Circumnavigation of world completed by crew
1519+	Hernán Cortés	Spain	Conquered Aztecs in Mexico
1524-25	Giovanni da Verrazzano	France	Searched for Northwest Passage
1526	Lucas Vazquez Ayllon	Spain	Temporary settlement in in the Carolinas
1528-36	Álvar Núñez Cabeza de Vaca	Spain	From Gulf of Mexico into Texas
1532+	Francisco Pizarro	Spain	Conquered Incas in Peru
1535	Jacques Cartier	France	Gulf of St. Lawrence; established French claim to North America
1539-42	Hernando De Soto	Spain	Southeastern U.S. and Mississippi River
1540	Francisco Coronado	Spain	Northern Mexico and southwestern U.S.
1542	Juan Rodriquez Cabrillo	Spain	California
1565	Don Pedro Menendez de Aviles	Spain	St. Augustine founded
1576-78	Sir Martin Frobisher	England	Search for Northwest Passage
1577-80	Sir Francis Drake	England	First English circumnavigation

1585+		England	Roanoke "Lost Colony"
1598+	Juan de Oñate	Spain	Settlement in New Mexico
1602	Bartholomew Gosnold	England	Explored New England coast
1603-15	Samuel de Champlain	France	Quebec, Great Lakes and Lake Champlain
1607		England	Jamestown founded
1609+	Henry Hudson Netherlands	England	Dutch claim to New York area; explored Hudson Bay
1620		England	Pilgrims arrive at Cape Cod
1630		England	Puritans arrive at Massachusetts Bay
1673	Louis Joliet Jacques Marquette	France	Explored upper Mississippi Basin
1679	Sieur de La Salle	France	Explored upper Mississippi and Lake Michigan areas
1698+	Sieur de Bienville	France	Founded New Orleans; explored Mississippi Valley
1699+	Sieur d'Iberville	France	First to enter Mississippi River from Gulf of Mexico [147]

How Did Native Americans Respond to Christianity?
by Thomas S. Giles

An enterprising European official sailed to the Central American mainland in 1514. He hoped to settle large numbers of Spaniards there, to find gold, and to convert natives. He and his men adopted a simple approach.

They traveled by night, stopping at midnight outside a chosen village. Before they entered, they declared loudly: "Princes and Indians, there is one God, one pope, and one king of Castile, who is lord of this country. Come at once and render
him obedience, or we will make war on you, kill you, and put you into slavery."

Of course, Europeans introduced their faith in other ways. Many missionaries lived in poverty among native peoples and presented the Christian message gently.

How did the indigenous peoples respond to these widely varied missionary efforts? What did they think of the Europeans' faith—and its emissaries?

The accounts below offer firsthand glimpses into three common responses.

Holding to the Ancient Faith

When native Americans were confronted with Christianity, some incorporated elements of Christianity into their own beliefs, creating a new, syncretistic system. Others resisted the faith of their conquerors and held fast to traditional beliefs. Among the Incas of Peru, for example, baptism was considered subjection to the invader; some Incan chiefs killed those who accepted the rite.

Opposition, however, did not always take violent forms. Soon after the fall of his people's capitol (Tenochtitlan), an Aztec priest spoke in response to the evangelistic efforts of Franciscan missionaries:

> Our revered lords, sirs, dear ones, take rest from the toil of the road, . . .
> Out of the clouds, out of the mist, out of the ocean's midst you have appeared.
> The Omneity [God] takes form in you, in your eye, in your ear, in your lips.
> The speaker of the world sent you because of us. Here we are, amazed by this.
> You brought his book with you, his script, heaven's word, the word of god . . . .
> You say that we don't know the Omneity of heaven and earth. You say that our
> gods are not original. That's news to us and it drives us crazy. It's shock and a
> scandal, for our ancestors came to earth and they spoke quite differently.
> They gave us their law and they believed, they served, and they taught the
> honor among gods; they taught the whole service. That's why we eat earth
> before them; that's why we draw our blood and do penance; that's why we
> burn copal [a tree resin] and kill the living . . . .

We don't believe, nor do we mock. We may offend you, . . .
for here stand
the citizens, the officials, the chiefs, the trustees and rulers
of this entire
world. It is enough that we have done penance, that we are
ruined, that we
are forbidden and stripped of power.
To remain here is to be imprisoned . . . . This is all we have
to reply, Senores.

This Aztec priest had seen his capitol destroyed and his empire crushed. He was forced to accept a military conquest, but he refused to accept a spiritual one. For generations this religious leader and his people had honored and served their gods. They would not readily renounce that faith.

Rejecting "Christian" behavior

It was not always the natives' disbelief that impeded their conversion to Christianity. In many instances, they were open to learning more about the Spaniards' God. They were even willing to accept the Christian faith. However, a number of other factors often stood in the way.

By far, the greatest impediment to successful evangelization was the brutality of the European settlers. In many instances, the conquistadors employed violence to force natives to accept baptism. But often this brutality only provoked dogged resistance and outright rejection of the soldiers' beliefs.

In a letter in 1601, Brother Juan de Escalona laments, "We cannot preach the gospel now, for it is despised by these people [the natives of modern day New Mexico] on account of our great offenses and the harm we have done to them."

Countless Indians lost their lives through slaughter, mass suicides, and European diseases. Those who managed to survive times of war were subjected to cruel mistreatment in mines. Or they were placed under the encomienda system, a form of virtual slavery.

A Mayan objected to the behavior of the Spaniards: *"The true God, the true Dios came, but this was the origin too of affliction for us: the origin of tax, of our giving them alms; of trial through the grabbing of petty cacao money, of trial by blowgun; stomping the people; violent removal; forced debt, debt created by false testimony; petty litigation, harassment, violent removal; the collaboration with the Spaniards on the part of the*

priests, . . . and all the while the mistreated were further maltreated . . . . But it will happen that tears will come to the eyes of God the Father. The justicia of God the Father will settle on the whole world."

In some cases, the Spaniards brutality provoked Indians to seek revenge. On the frontier, in areas of what are now the United States (Florida, Georgia, the Carolinas, and Virginia), many missionary friars were killed as soon as they lacked the protection of Spanish arms.

Don Gonzalo, a 70-year-old Nicaraguan Indian, writes his opinion of Spaniards he had known: *"Ultimately, it turns out that one must conclude that Christians are by no means good . . . . Where are the goodones? To be sure, I myself have certainly not yet known any good ones, only bad ones."*

It comes as no surprise that many Indians rejected Christianity not for Christianity's sake, but for the examples of those who called themselves Christian.

Accepting Christianity

What about those Indians who responded positively to the Christian faith?

Many Europeans came to the New World motivated by a sincere desire to spread their faith. Missionaries to the Americas—especially the earliest ones—often demonstrated boundless zeal, high morals, and great courage. Their charity—particularly in contrast to the conquistadors' inhumanity—greatly encouraged acceptance of Christianity.

One church official asked Indians the reason why they liked the one group of friars better than the others. The Indians replied, *"Because these go about poorly dressed and barefoot just like us; they eat what we eat; they settle among us; and their intercourse with us is gentle."*

In their efforts to expose the native Brazilians to Christianity, the Portuguese authorities and the Jesuit fathers brought them from the interior to the coastal region and concentrated them in mission villages. The following letter, written by an anonymous Jesuit missionary, describes this work: *"From far away, they [the Indians] send requests for priests to indoctrinate them because they want friendship with Christians and to change their habits for ours. In this way four large settlements are already constructed for them . . . . Those of Sao Paulo, the first settlement built, are all Christians—that is, the children up to 14 years of age—and every day more are* baptized because those that are born again bring others for baptism, and there are more than two hundred of these."

Even some of the most violent conquistadores came to the New World with at least modest concern for winning souls. Despite the unspeakable violence they witnessed during the conquests, some Indians accepted the faith of their conquerors—ironically because it was the faith of their conquerors. It seemed clear that the Christian God had defeated their gods. Many natives willingly accepted baptism, hoping to garner the favor of the more powerful Christian God.

As Hernando Cortes and his men marched toward the Aztec capitol (Tenochtitlan, present-day Mexico City), they were welcomed by the people of Texcoco, who had long resented Aztec domination. Below is an indigenous account, preserved in the Codex Ramirez, of the conversion of Prince Ixtlilxochitl of Texcoco.

"At the request of Ixtlilxochitl, Cortes and his men ate the gifts of food that had been brought out from Texcoco. Then they walked to the city with their new friends, and all the people welcome them. The Indians knelt down and adored them as sons of the Sun, their gods . . . The Spaniards entered the city and were lodged in the royal palace.

"Cortes was very grateful for the attentions shown him by Ixtlilxochitl and his brothers, he wished to repay their kindness by teaching them the law of God, with the help of his interpreter, Aguilar. The brothers and a number of the other lords gathered to hear him, and he told them that the emperor of the Christians had sent him here, so far away, in order that he might instruct them in the law of Christ. He explained the mystery of the Creation and the Fall, the mystery of the Trinity and the Incarnation, and the mystery of the Passion and the Resurrection. Then he drew out a crucifix and held it up. The Christians all knelt, and Ixtlilxochitl and the other lords knelt with them.

"Cortes also explained the mystery of baptism. He concluded the lesson by telling them how the Emperor Charles grieved that they were not in God's grace, and how the emperor had sent him among them only to save their souls. He begged them to become willing vassals of the emperor, because that was the will of the pope, in whose name he spoke.

"When Cortes asked for their reply, Ixtlilxochitl burst into tears and answered that he and his brothers understood the mysteries very well. Giving thanks to God that his soul had been illumined, he said that he wished to become a Christian and to serve the emperor . . . . The Spaniards wept with joy to see their devotion.

"The prince then asked to be baptized. Cortes and the priest accompanying him said that first they must learn more of the Christian religion, but that persons would be sent to instruct them. Ixtlilxochitl expressed his gratitude, but begged to receive the sacrament at once because he now hated idolatry and revered the mysteries of the true faith.

"Although a few of the Spaniards objected, Cortes decided that Ixtlilxochitl should be baptized immediately. Cortes himself served as godfather, and the prince was given the name Hernando, because that was his sponsor's name . . . . The other Christians became godfathers to the other princes, and the baptisms were performed with the greatest solemnity. If it had been possible, more than twenty thousand persons would have been baptizedthat very day, and a great number of them did receive the sacrament."

Making crucial decisions

As these accounts demonstrate, Christianity was not simply thrust on an uncritical indigenous population. Native Americans viewed Christianity through a variety of experiences. They compared it to their own beliefs and saw it practiced by the people who brought it to their world. They then made crucial decisions whether to accept the new faith.

Many Indians did accept it. The fact that native Americans came to know the Christian God is testimony to more than the immense firepower of the conquistadores. It shows also the power of a faith that was able to reach people despite tremendous obstacles—not the least of which were produced by Christians themselves. [148]

Henry VIII (1509-47 AD)

Henry VIII, born in 1491, was the second son of Henry VII and Elizabeth of York. The significance of Henry's reign is, at times, overshadowed by his six marriages: dispensing with these forthwith enables a deeper search into the major themes of the reign. He married Catherine of Aragon (widow of his brother, Arthur) in 1509, divorcing her in 1533; the union produced one daughter, Mary. Henry married the pregnant Anne Boleyn in 1533; she gave him another daughter, Elizabeth, but was executed for infidelity (a treasonous charge in the king's consort) in May 1536. He married Jane Seymour by the end of the same month, who died giving birth to Henry's lone male heir, Edward, in October 1536. Early in 1540, Henry arranged a marriage with Anne of Cleves, after viewing Hans Holbein's beautiful portrait of the German princess. In person, alas, Henry found her homely and the marriage was never consummated. In July 1540, he married theadulterous Catherine Howard—

she was executed for infidelity in March 1542. Catherine Parr became his wife in 1543, providing for the needs of both Henry and his children until his death in 1547.

The court life initiated by his father evolved into a cornerstone of Tudor government in the reign of Henry VIII. After his father's staunch, stolid rule, the energetic, youthful and handsome king avoided governing in person, much preferring to journey the countryside hunting and reviewing his subjects. Matters of state were left in the hands of others, most notably Thomas Wolsey, Archbishop of York. Cardinal Wolsey virtually ruled England until his failure to secure the papal annulment that Henry needed to marry Anne Boleyn in 1533. Wolsey was quite capable as Lord Chancellor, but his own interests were served more than that of the king: as powerful as he was, he still was subject to Henry's favor—losing Henry's confidence proved to be his downfall. The early part of Henry's reign, however, saw the young king invade France, defeat Scottish forces at the Battle of Foldden Field (in which James IV of Scotland was slain), and write a treatise denouncing Martin Luther's Reformist ideals, for which the pope awarded Henry the title "Defender of the Faith".

The 1530's witnessed Henry's growing involvement in government, and a series of events which greatly altered England, as well as the whole of Western Christendom: the separation of the Church of England from Roman Catholicism. The separation was actually a by-product of Henry's obsession with producing a male heir; Catherine of Aragon failed to produce a male and the need to maintain dynastic legitimacy forced Henry to seek an annulment from the pope in order to marry Anne Boleyn. Wolsey tried repeatedly to secure a legal annulmentfrom Pope Clement VII, but Clement was beholden to the Charles V, Holy Roman Emperor and nephew of Catherine. Henry summoned the Reformation Parliament in 1529, which passed 137 statutes in seven years and exercised an influence in political and ecclesiastic affairs which was unknown to feudal parliaments. Religious reform movements had already taken hold in England, but on a small scale: the Lollards had been in existence since the mid-fourteenth century and the ideas of Luther and Zwingli circulated within intellectual groups, but continental Protestantism had yet to find favor with the English people. The break from Rome was accomplished through law, not social outcry; Henry, as Supreme Head of the Church of England, acknowledged this by slight alterations in worship ritual instead of a wholesale reworking of religious dogma. England moved into an era of "conformity of mind" with the new royal supremacy (much akin to the absolutism of France's Louis XIV): by 1536, all ecclesiastical and government officials were required to publicly approve of the break with Rome and take an oath of loyalty. The king moved away from the medieval idea of ruler as chief lawmaker and overseer of civil behavior, to the modern idea of ruler as the ideological icon of the state.

The remainder of Henry's reign was anticlimactic. Anne Boleyn lasted only three years before her execution; she was replaced by Jane Seymour, who laid Henry's dynastic problems to rest with the birth of Edward VI.

Fragmented noble factions involved in the Wars of the Roses found themselves reduced to vying for the king's favor in court. Reformist factions won the king's confidence and vastly benefiting from Henry's dissolution of the monasteries, as monastic lands and revenues went either to the crown or the nobility. The royal staff continued the rise in status that began under Henry VII, eventually to rival thepower of the nobility. Two men, in particular, were prominent figures through the latter stages of Henry's reign: Thomas Cromwell and Thomas Cranmer. Cromwell, an efficient administrator, succeeded Wolsey as Lord Chancellor, creating new governmental departments for the varying types of revenue and establishing parish priest's duty of recording births, baptisms, marriages and deaths. Cranmer, Archbishop of Canterbury, dealt with and guided changes in ecclesiastical policy and oversaw the dissolution of the monasteries.

Henry VIII built upon the innovations instituted by his father. The break with Rome, coupled with an increase in governmental bureaucracy, led to the royal supremacy that would last until the execution of Charles I and the establishment of the Commonwealth one hundred years after Henry's death. Henry was beloved by his subjects, facing only one major insurrection, the Pilgrimage of Grace, enacted by the northernmost counties in retaliation to the break with Rome and the poor economic state of the region. History remembers Henry in much the same way as Piero Pasqualigo, a Venetian ambassador: " . . . he is in every respect a most accomplished prince."[149]

Daniel 11:30

for   *causal* - expressing or indicating cause: marked by cause and effect

ships   *ship* - any large vessel as a

              fixture - a familiar, invariably present, or permanent item, element, or feature in some particular setting

Chittim   *islander* - a native or inhabitant of an island

              island - a tract of land cut off on two or more sides by water: PENINSULA: something resembling an island by its isolated, surrounded, or sequestered position

come   *go* - to move on a course

against   *over* - used as a function word to indicate the possession or enjoyment of authority, power, or jurisdiction in regard to thing or person: used as a function word to indicate a relation of superiority, advantage, or preference to another

he   *he, she, it* - the person or thing spoken of

be   *be* - to exist under conditions specified

grieved   *deject* - to lower especially in rank or condition

return   *turn* - pass from one state to another: CHANGE

indignation *foam* - RAGE

              rage - to be intense or overwhelming: to prevail uncontrollably: spread with destructive effect

against   *above* - higher than (as in rank, position, quality, or degree

holy   *sacred* - holy or hallowed especially by association with the divine or consecrated

                                       Michelle Lynn

covenant	***compact*** - an agreement, understanding, or covenant between two or more parties
he	***this*** - the person, thing or idea that is present or near in place, time, or thought, or that has just been mentioned
do	***do*** - to perform (as an action) by oneself or before another: EXECUTE
he	***he, she, it*** - the person or thing spoken of
return	***turn*** - to become changed, altered, or transformed (as in nature, character, or appearance): pass from one state to another: CHANGE
intelligence	***separate*** - make a distinction between
with	***with*** - at the moment or time of
that	***who*** - the person or persons involved or meant or referred to
forsake	***loosen*** - free from or lessen the tightness, firmness, or fixedness of
holy	***sacred*** - holy or hallowed especially by association with the divine or consecrated
covenant	***compact*** - an agreement, understanding, or covenant between two or more parties

DANIEL 11:31

> And **arms** shall **stand** on his **part**, and **they** shall **pollute**
> the **sanctuary** of **strength**, and shall **take away** the **daily**
> sacrifice, and **they** shall **place** the **abomination that** maketh
> **desolate.**

Europe's merchant class grew rapidly in the 15th and 16th centuries as new trade routes to the East were opened, and the Spaniards brought back enormous wealth from their new territories in Central America. The major cities of Europe became money markets. Foremost among them was Antwerp, where Quentin Massys in about 1500 painted . . . a telling picture of *The Moneychanger and his Wife*; the wife has been distracted from her study of a religious book by the gleam of gold and silver coins.[150]

Mammon—(confidence, i.e. figuratively *wealth*, personified); *mammonas*, i.e. *avarice* (deified).[151]

Confidence in wealth and self was replacing faith in God.

Matthew 6:24—No man can serve two masters: for either he will hate the one, and love the other; or else he will hold to the one, and despise the other. Ye cannot serve God and mammon.

Daniel 9:27 And he shall confirm the covenant with many for one week: and in the midst of the week he shall cause the sacrifice and oblation to cease, and for the overspreading of abominations he shall make it desolate, even until the consummation, and that determined shall be poured upon the desolate.

Proverbs 6:16-19—These six things the Lord hates, yes, seven are an abomination to Him: A proud look, a lying tongue, and hands that shed innocent blood. An heart that deviseth wicked imaginations, feet that be swift in running to mischief, and one who sows discord among the brethren.

Matthew 12:25—But Jesus knew their thoughts, and said to them: "Every kingdom divided against itself is brought to desolation, and every city or house divided against itself will not stand.

- 1 Corinthians 3:16-18—Know ye not that ye are the temple of God, and that the Spirit of God dwelleth in you? If any man defile the temple of God, him shall God destroy; for the temple of God is holy, which temple ye are. Let no man decieve himself. If any man among you seemeth to be wise in this world, let him become a fool, that he may be wise.

- Romans 12:1-3 I beseech you therefore brethren, by the mercies of God that you present your bodies a living sacrifice, holy, acceptable unto God, which is your reasonable service. And be not conformed to this world, but be ye transformed by the renewing of your mind, that ye may prove what is that good, and acceptable, and perfect will of God. For I say, through grace given unto me, to every man that is among you, not to think of himself more highly than he ought to think; but to think soberly, according as God has dealt to every man the measure of faith.

- Hebrews 13:15-16 By him therefore let us offer the sacrifice of praise to God continually, that is, the fruit of our lips, giving thanks to his name. But to do good and to communicate forget not: for with such sacrifices God is well pleased.

For a complete study on the *abomination of desolation* see page 353.

DANIEL 11:31

arms	*arm* - POWER, MIGHT
	power - a position of ascendancy: ability to compel obedience
stand	*stand* - to be in a particular state or situation
part	*allotment* - something that is assigned by or as if by lot or by destiny
they	*they* - PEOPLE: unspecified persons and especially those responsible for a particular act, practice, or decision
pollute	*profane* - to debase by a wrong, unworthy, or vulgar use: ABUSE, DEFILE, VULGARIZE
sanctuary	*consecrated* place or thing - set apart, dedicate, devote to the service or worship of God
strength	*fortified past of fortify* - to make strong: STRENGTHEN
take	to *turn* off - pass from one state to another: CHANGE
daily	*regular* - harmonious in form, structure or arrangement
they	*they* - those ones
place	*put* - to bring into or establish in a specified state or condition
	make - to give rise to: favor the growth or occurrence of
abomination	*idol* - something or someone on which the affections are strongly and often excessively set: an object of passionate devotion: a person or thing greatly loved or adored
that	*causal* - expressing or indicating cause
desolate	*stun* - to overcome with pleasure or beauty
	devastate - to lay waste: RAVAGE, OVERPOWER, OVERWHELM

Daniel 11:32

And such as **do wickedly** against the **covenant** shall **he corrupt** by **flatteries:** but the **people that do know** their God shall **be strong,** and **do** exploits.

• Matthew 24:4-5—And Jesus answered and said unto them, Take heed that no man deceive you. For many shall come in my name, saying, I am Christ; and deceive many.

■ Romans 16:17-18—Now I beseech you, brethren, mark them which cause divisions and offenses contrary to the doctrine which ye have learned; and avoid them. For they that are such serve not our Lord Jesus Christ, but their own belly; and by good words and fair speeches deceive the hearts of the simple.

• 2 Timothy 3:12-14 Yea, and all that will live godly in Christ Jesus shall suffer persecution. But evil men and seducers shall wax worse and worse, deceiving, and being deceived. But continue thou in the things which thou hast learned and hast been assured of, knowing of whom thou hast learned them;

DANIEL 11:32

do	**do** - CAUSE
wickedly	**violate** - to fail to keep: BREAK, DISREGARD: PROFANE, DESECRATE :
covenant	**compact** - an agreement, understanding, or covenant between two or more parties
he	**he, she, it** - the person or thing spoken of
corrupt	**soil** - to stain or defile morally: CORRUPT, POLLUTE
flatteries	**flattery** - something that flatters or is felt flatteringly: a pleasing self-deception
people	**flock** - all Christians in their relation to Christ
that	**who** - the person or persons involved or meant or referred to
do	**do** - EXECUTE
know	**know** - to have perception, cognition, or understanding of especially to an extensive or complete extent: to recognize the quality of: see clearly the character of: DISCERN
God	**God** - the holy, infinite, and eternal spiritual reality presented in the Bible as the creator, sustainer, judge, righteous sovereign, and redeemer of the universe who acts with power in history in carrying out his purposes
be	**exist** as - to continue to be: maintain being
strong	**strong** - able to bear or endure: ROBUST, RUGGED: able to withstand stress or violence: having or exhibiting moral or intellectual force, endurance, or vigor
do	**do** - go on

DANIEL 11:33

And **they that understand** among the **people** shall **instruct many:** yet **they** shall **fall** by the **sword,** and by **flame,** by **captivity,** and by **spoil,** many **days.**

The sword—The Reformation produced over a century of international religious wars;

The Wars of Religion

The latter half of the sixteenth century and the beginning of the seventeenth century brought about one of the most passionate and calamitious series of wars that Europe had ever experienced. The early Reformation had been, in hindsight, remarkably free from bloodshed; the honeymoon, however, lasted only a short while. It was inevitable that the growing division between Christian churches in Europe would lead to a series of armed conflicts for over a century. Protestants and Catholics would shed each other's blood in prodigious amounts in national wars and in civil wars. These struggles would eventually shatter the European monarchical traditions themselves. The monarchy, which had always seemed an impregnable political institution, was challenged by Protestants unhappy with the rule of Catholic kings. The final result of these struggles would be the overthrow and execution of Charles I in England in the middle of the seventeenth century, an historical earthquake that permanently changed the face of Europe.

Michelle Lynn

France

The first major set of wars fought over the new churches was a series of civil wars fought in France. In 1559 Francis II became king of France at the ripe old age of fifteen. Understanding that the monarch was weak, three major noble families began to struggle for control of France: the Guises (pronounced, geez) in eastern France, the Bourbons in southern France, and the Montmorency-Chatillons in central France. Of the three, the Guises were both the most powerful and the most fanatical about Catholicism; they would eventually gain control of the young monarch and, for all practical purposes, rule the state of France. The Bourbons and the Montmorency-Chatillons were mostly Catholics who—for political reasons—supported the Protestant cause.

The French Protestants were called **Huguenots** (pronounced, hoo-guh-no), and members of both the Bourbon and Montmorency-Chatillon families were major leaders in the Huguenot movement. The Huguenots represented only a very small part of the French population; in 1560, only seven or eight percent of the French people were Huguenots.

They were, however, concentrated in politically important geographical regions; as a result, they were disproportionately powerful in the affairs of France. It is important to understand that the rivalry between the Guises and the other two families was primarily a political rivalry; this political rivalry, however, would be swept up in the spiritual conflict between the Catholic church and the new reformed churches.

Francis II died in 1560 after only one year as king. At his death, his younger brother, Charles IX (ruled 1560-1574) assumed the throne.

Because he was too young to serve as king, his mother, **Catherine de Medicis** became regent (a regent is the ruler of a kingdom when the king is incapable of exercising that rule). Catherine was a brilliant and powerful political thinker; she understood right off that the Guises were a threat to her and to her son. In order to tilt the political balance away from the powerful Guise family, she cultivated the Bourbons and the Montmorency-Chatillons. In the process, however, she also had to cultivate the support of the Huguenots who were closely allied to those two families. Until this time, it was illegal for Huguenots to worship publicly (although there were over 2000 Huguenot churches in 1561). In 1562, Catherine took a great leap forward in religious toleration by allowing Huguenots to hold public worship *outside* the boundaries of towns. They were also allowed to hold church assemblies. Catherine was a Catholic and wanted France to remain Catholic; she did not, however, want the Guises to be calling all the shots. The only way to chip away at the political power of the Guises was to increase the political power of the other major families and their Protestant allies.

The Guises, for their part, understood what this religious tolerance was all about and quickly clamped down on it. In March, 1562, an army led by the Duke of Guise attacked a Protestant church service at Vassy in the province of Champagne and slaughtered everybody they could get their hands on: men, women, and children—all of whom were unarmed. Thus began the French Wars of Religion which were to last for almost forty years and destroy thousands of innocent lives.

For all her brilliance, Catherine was placed in an impossible position. She did not want any noble family to exercise control over France; she simply wanted power to be more balanced. She also did not want a Protestant France. So the only strategy open to her was to play both sides, which she did with enormous shrewdness.

This balancing game came to an end, however, when Catherine helped the Guise family plot the assassination of Gaspard de Coligny, a Montmorency-Chatillon family member who was one of the major leaders of the French Huguenots. The assassination failed; Coligny was shot but not killed. The balancing game was over: the Huguenots and Coligny were furious at both Catherine and the Guises. Fearing a Huguenot uprising, Catherine convinced Charles IX that the Huguenots were plotting his overthrow under the leadership of Coligny.

On August 24, 1572, the day before St. Bartholomew's Day, royal forces hunted down and executed over three thousand Huguenots, including Coligny, in Paris. Within three days, royal and Guise armies had hunted down and executed over twenty thousand Huguenots in the single most bloody and systematic extermination of non-combatants in European history until World War II.

The **St. Bartholomew Massacre** was a turning point in both French history and the history of the European Christian church. Protestants no longer viewed Catholicism as a misguided church, but as the force of the devil itself. No longer were Protestants fighting for a reformed church, but they suddenly saw themselves fighting for survival against a Catholic church whose cruelty and violence seemed to know no bounds. Throughout Europe, Protestant movements slowly transformed into militant movements.

In 1576, Henry III ascended to the throne; he was the youngest brother of Francis II and Charles IX. By this point, France had become a basket case. On the one hand, the Guises had formed a Catholic

League, which was violent and fanatical. On the other hand, the Huguenots were filled with a passion for vengeance. Like his mother, Henry tried to stay in the middle of the conflict. Unlike his mother, he had immense popular support for this middle course; the St. Bartholomew Massacre had deeply troubled moderate Catholics and the growing conflict upset moderate Huguenots. These moderates were called **politiques** ("politicians"), since their central interest was the political and social stability of France rather than their religious beliefs.

The Catholic League was aided by Philip II of Spain who dedicated his monarchy to overthrowing the Protestant churches of other countries. By the mid-1580's, the Catholic League was in control of France and, after Henry III attempted to attack the League in 1588, the League drove him from Paris and embarked on a systematic massacre of non-combatants that rivalled the earlier St. Bartholomew's Massacre.

In exile, Henry III struck up an alliance with his Huguenot cousin, Henry of Navarre. Henry of Navarre was a *politique* ; he believed that the peace and security of France was far more important than imposing his religious views. Before the two Henrys could attack Paris, however, Henry III was stabbed to death by a fanatical, fury-driven Dominican friar in 1589. Since Henry III had no children, Henry of Navarre, as next in line to the throne, became King of France as Henry IV (ruled 1589-1610).

Henry understood that the only way that France would find peace is if it were ruled by a tolerant *Catholic* king, so on July 25, 1593, he rejected his Protestant faith and officially became Catholic. On April 13, 1598, Henry IV ended the long and tiring religious wars in Franceby proclaiming the **Edict of Nantes**. This Edict granted to

Huguenots the right to worship publically, to occupy public office, to assemble, to gain admission to schools and universities, and to administer their own towns.

Spain

The year 1556 saw the accession of perhaps the most important monarch of the sixteenth century: Philip II of Spain (ruled 1556-1598). Of all the monarchs of Europe, Philip was the most zealous defender of his religious faith and his energies in pursuit of this defense greatly changed the face of Europe.

In the first half of his reign, he was instrumental in stopping the Turkish incursions into Europe. Philip's military power lay in his navy, which was the most powerful and imposing navy of the sixteenth century. Allied with Venice, his navy defeated the Turkish navy in the Gulf of Corinth near Greece and effectively halted the Turkish invasions of Europe. After this spectacular triumph, Philip then turned his efforts from routing the Muslims to routing the Protestants in Europe.

He first turned his sights to the Netherlands, a rich and prosperous merchant country that was ruled over by Spain. The Netherlands, however, had strong pockets of Calvinist resistance and the country slowly turned on its Spanish rulers.

Philip responded by sending the Duke of Alba with an army to quell the revolt in 1567. Alba imposed a tribunal, the Council of Troubles, to question and sentence heretics (Protestants). The Dutch called this council the "Council of Blood," for it managed to publically execute thousands of people before Alba was forced from the Netherlands.

Alba and his reign of terror did not quell the Protestant revolt in the Netherlands, but rather strengthened it. The central oppositional leader, William, the Prince of Orange (ruled 1533-1584), became a hero for the whole of the Netherlands and in 1576 the Catholic provinces in the south allied themselves with the Protestant provinces in the north to revolt against Spain. The purpose of this alliance, called the **Pacification of Ghent**, was to enforce Netherlandish autonomy. The southern provinces, however, did not remain long in this alliance. In 1579, they made a separate peace with Spain (these southern provinces eventually became the country of Belgium) and the northern provinces formed a new alliance, the Union of Utrecht. Because Spain was overextended all over Europe, the northern provinces gradually drove the Spanish out until 1593 when the last Spanish soldier left Dutch soil. Still, the northern provinces were not recognized by Spain as an autonomous country until 1648 in the articles of the Peace of Westphalia.

Philip did not, however, want to interfere with the English, for England always seemed poised for a return to Catholicism. Elizabeth I of England also wanted to avoid any confrontation with Spain, so the war between the Spanish and the English was one of those unfortunate accidents of history—unfortunate, that is, for Spain.

In spite of Philip's reluctance to engage militarily with England, Elizabeth slowly ate away at Philip's patience. She had signed a mutual defense treaty with France after Spain had defeated the Turks. Fearful of the Spanish navy, she recognized that only an alliance with another country could protect England from Spain's powerful navy. In the late 1570's, Elizabeth allowed English ships to pirate and ransack Spanish ships sailing to and from theNew World.

In 1585, just as the Protestant provinces of the Netherlands were beginning to drive the Spanish from their country, Elizabeth sent English soldiers to the Netherlands to aid in the revolt.

Philip finally decided to invade England after the execution of the Catholic Mary, Queen of Scots. He was in part encouraged in this move by the Pope's excommunication of Elizabeth several years earlier; the excommunication of a monarch made it incumbent on all practicing Catholics to use any opportunity they could to assassinate or overthrow the monarch. Philip gathered together his navy and on May 30, 1588, he sent a mighty armada of over 130 ships to invade England. The Armada contained over 25,000 soldiers and the ships gathered for the invasion in the English Channel south of England.

The English, however, were ready. Because of their treaty with the French, the invasion barges which were meant to transport soldiers from the Spanish galleons to the English coastline were not allowed to leave the coast of France. When fierce channel winds scattered the Spanish fleet to the east, English and Dutch warships were able to destroy the fleet ship by ship. What few ships remained struggled around the north of England and down along the western coast, where several ships foundered.

In practical terms, the defeat of the Armada was a temporary setback for Spain. The 1590's saw impressive military victories for the Spanish. However, the defeat of the Armada was a tremendous psychological victory for European Protestants. Spain represented the only powerful military force that threatened the spread of Protestantism; when even the mighty Spanish navy could be defeated by an outnumbered English and Dutch fleet, Protestants everywhere were reinvigorated in their struggles against Spain and the Roman church. By the end of the seventeeth century, Spain was no longer a major player in the power politics of Europe.

The Thirty Years War—1618-1648

With the exception of the English civil war, the last major war of religion was the **Thirty Years War**. It is fair to say, however, that this war was as much about politics as it was about religion. Germany, which was called the Holy Roman Empire and extended from the North Sea to the Mediterranean, was not a unified state, but rather a loose collection of a huge number of autonomous city-states or province-states—three hundred and sixty autonomous states to be exact. Each was a more or less sovereign state that levied taxes and tariffs, had its own armies, made its own money, and even enforced its own borders. Religious differences fueled the fires of the political and economic rivalries between these separate states. About half the states were predominantly Protestant while the other half were predominately Catholic.

The Treaty of Augsburg recognized Lutheranism, but it did not recognize Calvinism. However, Calvinism made great strides throughout these territories in the latter half of the sixteenth century. In 1559 **Frederick III** became the Elector of the Palatinate (north of Bavaria) *and* converted to Calvinism. This new Calvinist state would become a force to reckon with when it allied with England, the Netherlands, and France against the Spanish in 1609.

To the south of the Palatinate, Bavaria was unwaveringly Catholic with a powerful Jesuit presence. Just as the Palatinate was fanatical about the spread of Calvinism and Protestantism, so Bavaria was fanatical about the spread of Catholicism and the Counter-Reformation.

When Frederick IV, Elector of the Palatine, formed a defensive league with England, France, and the Netherlands in 1609, Maximillian, Duke of Bavaria, formed a Catholic League.

In 1618, the relationship between these two regions erupted into war; this war would outdo all the other previous religious wars in terms of extent and destructiveness. The Thirty Years War was, perhaps, the first World War fought in Europe, for nearly every state in Europe became involved in the war in some way or another. The sheer amount of casualties and human destruction made this war the most calamitious and disastrous war of European history before the nineteenth century.

After thirty years of untiring bloodshed, the war came to an end with the **Treaty of Westphalia** in 1648. The Treaty was not really an innovation; it simply reaffirmed the Treaty of Augsburg and allowed each state within the Holy Roman Empire to decide its own religion. The only important innovation of the treaty was the recognition of Calvinism. *Richard Hooker*[152]

Flame—Renaissance Humanism

Renaissance—A Definition

Renaissance is French and translates to re-birth. The expression is applied to describe the art history of the period from c 1350 till c 1600, and in a wider sense history of that period in all aspects. The philosophers of that period are better known under the expression Humanists.

The Black Plague of 1347, which killed roughly a third of Europe's population, was widely perceived as God's punishment for humankind's sins. Both early renaissance writers and theologians, the mystics, quickly recognized the church was to blame—the popes resided in Avignon instead of in Rome (the Babylonian Captivity of the church). Feudal society also was in a crisis.

The mystics, writers, artists and scientists all realized the crisis and that new ways out had to be sought. One such way was to turn back to the classics—refugees from Greece (Constantinople fell to the Turks in 1453) settled in Italy and elsewhere in the west, translated Greek literature. Artists in Florence tried to achieve the level of classic Greek art.

There was a general feeling that things had to be looked at from a new perspective, that the old ways, for which the philosophy of scholasticism and church policy largely were to blame, were wrong. Humanists created the expression the **dark ages** for the time in which the studies of classic Greek knowledge was discouraged and facts known to the Hellenistic Greeks were negated. Renaissance intellectuals, in fact, felt, by the study of classic Greek literature, reborn. [153]

Captivity—Exile into other lands (whether by force or choice).

History of the Mayflower Pilgrims

The Pilgrims were a group of English people who came to America seeking religious freedom during the reign of King James I. After twoattempts to leave England and move to Holland, a Separatist group was finally relocated to Amsterdam where they stayed for about one year. From there the group moved to the town of Leiden, Holland, where they remained for about ten years, able to worship as they wished under lenient Dutch law.

Fearing their children were losing their English heritage and religious beliefs, a small group from the Leiden churches made plans to settle in Northern Virginia—as New England was known at the time. In August 1620 the group sailed for Southampton, England, where other English colonists who hoped to make a new life in America met them.

They planned to make the crossing to America in two ships, the Speedwell and Mayflower. However, after many problems the Speedwell was forced to return to England where the group was reorganized. In their second attempt to cross the Atlantic, they boarded the Mayflower in September 1620 bound for the New World. They arrived as winter was settling in and endured significant hardships as they struggled to establish a successful colony at Plymouth.

In time their colony flourished and lead the way to establishing religious freedom and creating the foundations of the democracy Americans enjoy today. Their celebration of the first Thanksgiving has grown to become a festive national holiday. [154]

Spoil—

The New Middle Class

As the fortunes of merchants, bankers, and tradespeople improved, they had more than enough money to meet their basic needs for food, clothing, and shelter. They began to desire larger, more luxurious homes, fine art for these residences, sumptuous clothing to show off their wealth in public, and exotic delicacies to eat. These desires of the middle class stimulated the economy.

The middle-class population also had leisure time to spend on education and entertainment. In fact, education was essential for many middle-class professions. Bankers and accountants needed to understand arithmetic. Those trading with other countries needed a knowledge of foreign currencies and languages. Reading was essential for anyone who needed to understand a contract. In their leisure time, middle-class men and women enjoyed such pastimes as reading for pleasure, learning to play musical instruments, and studying a variety of topics unrelated to their businesses.

The Resurgence of the City

Many Italian coastal cities became centers for trade and commerce, and for the wealth and education that ensued. One of the cities that exemplified these new trends was Florence. Unlike several other important cities of Italy that had noble families as their most prominent citizens (Mantua and Ferrara, for example), the leading citizens of Florence, the Medici family, made their wealth as business people. In all respects the Medicis had the appearance of nobility. They lived in beautiful homes, employed great artists, and engaged in intellectual pursuits for both business and pleasure.[155]

DANIEL 11:33

they	**they** - those ones
that	**who** - the person or persons involved or meant or referred to
understand	**be circumspect** - marked by caution and earnest attention to all significant circumstances and possible consequences of action (as actions to be undertaken) and usually by prudence and discretion
people	**flock** - all Christians in their relation to Christ
instruct	**understand** - grasp the meaning of: UNDERSTAND
many	**abundant** - occurring or existing in great quantity
they	**they** - those ones
fall	**falter** - to hesitate in purpose or action: WAVER, FLINCH: to lose drive, effectiveness, or momentum in some way
sword	**sword** - an instrument of destruction: a military force: coercive power or jurisdiction
flame	**flash** - SHOW, DISPLAY; especially: a vulgar ostentatious display: a showy ostentatious person: something or someone that attracts notice (as by gaudiness or excellence)
captivity	**exile** - forced removal from one's native country: voluntary absence from one's country
spoil	**booty** - PLUNDER, SPOILS: loot taken in war: REWARD, PRIZE, GAIN
days	**day** - the period of existence or prominence of a person or thing

DANIEL 11:34

*Now when **they** shall **fall, they** shall **be holpen with** a **little help:** but **many** shall **cleave** to them **with flatteries.***

■ Matthew 24:10-13 And then many will be offended, will betray one another, and will hate one another. Then many false prophets will rise up and deceive many. And because lawlessness will abound, the love of many will grow cold. But he who endures to the end shall be saved.

■ 2 Peter 2:1-3, 13b, 17-19 But there were also false prophets among the people, even as there will be false teachers among you, who will secretly bring in destructive heresies, even denying the Lord who bought them, and bring on themselves swift destruction. And many shall follow their pernicious ways; by reason of whom the way of truth shall be evil spoken of. And through covetousness shall they with feigned words make merchandise of you: whose judgment now of a long time lingereth not, and their damnation slumbereth not.

■ Spots they are and blemishes, sporting themselves with their own deceivings while they feast with you;

Michelle Lynn

■ These are wells without water, clouds that are carried with a tempest; to whom the mist of darkness is reserved for ever. For when they speak great swelling words of vanity, they allure through the lusts of the flesh, through much wantonness, those that were clean escaped from them who live in error.

■ While they promise them liberty, they themselves are the servants of corruption: for of whom a man is overcome, of the same is he brought in bondage.

■ Jude 4 For there are certain men crept in unawares, who were before of old ordained to this condemnation, ungodly men, turning the grace of our God into lasciviousness, and denying the only Lord God, and our Lord Jesus Christ.

■ Jude 11 Woe unto them! For they have gone in the way of Cain and ran greedily after the error of Balaam for reward, and perished in the gainsaying of Core.

■ Jude 12 These are spots in your feasts of charity, when they feast with you, feeding themselves without fear: clouds they are without water, carried about of winds; trees whose fruit withereth, without fruit, twice dead, plucked up by the roots;

■ Jude 16 These are murmurers, complainers, walking after their own lusts; and their mouth speaketh great swelling words, having men's persons in admiration because of advantage.

■ Jude 17 But, beloved, remember ye the words which were spoken before of the apostles of our Lord Jesus Christ;

■ Jude 18 How that they told you there should be mockers in the last time, who should walk after their own ungodly lusts.

■ James 1:26-27 If any man among you seem to be religious, and bridleth not his tongue, but deceiveth his own heart, this man's religion is vain. Pure religion and undefiled before God and the Father is this, To visit the fatherless and widows in their affliction, and to keep himself unspotted from the world.

they	**they** - those ones
fall	**stumble** - to fall into sin, error, or waywardness
they	**they** - those ones
be	**be** - to exist under conditions specified
holpen	**aid** - HELP
with	**with** - by means of
little	**little** - something not very extensive (as in amount or quantity): practically nothing
help	**aid** - HELP
many	**abundant** - occurring or existing in great quantity
cleave	**remain** - to stay in the same place or with the same person or group: RESIDE, DWELL
with	**with** - used as a function word to indicate a related or supplementary fact or circumstance
flatteries	**blandishment** - speech, action, or device that flatters and tends to coax or cajole
	treacherous - marked by ready disposition to betray confidence or faith pledged: DISLOYAL, FALSE, PERFIDOUS, TRAITOROUS: UNRELIABLE, UNTRUSTWORTHY: characterized by usually hidden dangers, hazards, or perils

DANIEL 11:35

*And some of them of **understanding** shall **fall,** to **try** them, and to **purge,** and to make them **white,** even to the **time** of the **end:** because it **is yet for** a time **appointed.***

■ Jeremiah 9:7-8 Therefore thus saith the Lord of hosts, Behold, I will melt them, and try them; for how shall I do for the daughter of my people? Their tongue is as an arrow shot out; it speaketh deceit; one speaketh peaceably to his neighbor with his mouth, but in heart he layeth his wait . . .

■ Zechariah 13 I will bring the one-third through the fire, will refine them as silver is refined, and test them as gold is tested.

■ Malachi 3:3 He will sit as a refiner and a purifier of silver; He will purify the sons of Levi, and purge them as gold and silver, that they may offer to the Lord an offering in righteousness.

■ Isaiah 48:10 Behold, I have refined you, but not as silver; I have tested you in the furnace of affliction.

■ James 1:2-4, 12 My brethren, count it all joy when ye fall into divers temptations; Knowing this, that the trying of your faith worketh patience. But let patience have her perfect work, that ye may be perfect and entire, wanting nothing . . . Blessed is the man that endureth temptation: for when he is tried, he shall receive the crown of life, which the Lord hath promised to them that love him.

DANIEL 11 : 35

understanding *intelligent* - marked by quick, active perception and understanding: showing or having some special knowledge, skill, or aptitude

fall *stumble* - to fall into sin, error, or waywardness: ERR: to falter through lack of knowledge or experience: BLUNDER

try *refine* - to free (as the mind or soul) from moral imperfection, grossness, dullness, earthiness: SPIRITUALIZE

purge *clarify* - to make clear and bright by lightening the darkness and obscurity of

brighten - to cause to shine

white *be white* - free from spot or blemish

time *time* - a point or period when something occurs

end *extremity* - HEIGHT, APEX, CLIMAX: the fullest possible extent

yet *still* - FARTHER: to a greater extent

for *causal* - expressing or indicating cause

appointed *a fixed time* - the moment of an event, process, or condition: OCCASION

Michelle Lynn

DANIEL 11:36

And the **king** shall **do** according to his **will;** and **he** shall **exalt** himself, and **magnify** himself **above every god,** and shall **speak marvelous** things **against** the **God** of **gods,** and shall **prosper till** the **indignation be accomplished: for that that is determined** shall **be done.**

For more than a thousand years after the fall of Rome, Europe was held together by a concept of order based on a largely feudal society united by the bonds of religion.[156] Now, instead, rulers all over Europe tried to concentrate all power in their own hands—a concept which became known as absolutism . . . The most brilliant example of the absolute monarch was Louis XIV of France (1643-1715), the 'Grand Monarque' who became a model for imitation in other countries. His object was unfettered power at home, expansion abroad . . . Louis believed that he was God's Lieutenant, called to rule, and he spent at least a nine-hour day at affairs of state. All other institutions—the Church, the nobility, the courts—became obviously subordinate . . . A remark attributed to Louis typifies his attitude: 'L'Etat c'est moi (I am the state)'.[157] He provoked universal imitation. Every king and princelet in Europe was building his own Versailles as much beyond his means as his subjects and credits would permit.[158]

Architecture was designed to glorify the monarch who became known as the 'Sun King'. His palace of Versailles took 47 years to complete, a Vatican for the secular pope.[159]

This new way of life, 'absolute monarchy', presses forward and continues until the blood bath of the French Revolution.[160]

LOUIS XIV

Louis XIV of France ranks as one of the most remarkable monarchs in history. He reigned for 72 years, 54 of them he personally controlled French government. The 17th century is labeled as the age of Louis XIV. Since then his rule has been hailed as the supreme example of a type of government—absolutism. He epitomized the ideal of kingship. During his reign France stabilized and became one of the strongest powers in Europe.

During his reign France became the ideal culture since he put great care into its enhancement so he could boast it to the world. The country changed drastically from savage mediaeval ways to a more refined, exquisite living—evident from his palace in Versailles. Within 54 years he did what several kings worked on for centuries. French culture became one of the most appealing in the world, and the name Louis XIV has been associated with greatness and glory.

Louis XIV was a great monarch, and he was capable of maintaining strong kingdom because he never, in his entire life, doubted his right to be king.

His autocracy was indeed amazing, and truly an example of the kind. He lived and ruled as a king should have. Louis XIV became the ideal king, and many have tried unsuccessfully to live up to his glory.[161]

The Age of Absolutism

It's difficult to determine precisely when the Enlightenment begins. Since the Enlightenment is primarily about changes in the world view of European culture, the process cannot really be said to have a beginning, for when a world view changes it essentially draws on previous shifts in world view. The Enlightenment is commonly dated to the middle of the eighteenth century and the activity of the *philosophes*, the French rationalist philosophers who fully articulated the values and consequences of Enlightenment thought.

However, the Enlightenment is more convincingly dated to the new natural science of Isaac Newton, the social and political theories of thinkers such as Hobbes, the empirical psychology of John Locke, and the epistemological revolutions of Blaise Pascal and René Descartes. All of these thinkers and innovations have clear antecedents: Newtonian thought derives from the thought and science of Francis Bacon, Galileo, Kepler, Copernicus, and ultimately, Roger Bacon in the thirteenth century. The social and political theories of Hobbes can be traced back to the Northern Renaissance, and the empirical psychology of Locke has antecedents in the fifteenth and sixteenth centuries.

Finally, the epistemological crises of Pascal and Descartes are in a long line of epistemological crises dating back to the fourteenth century and clearly articulated in the philosphical skepticism of Michel de Montaigne in the middle of the sixteenth century. For our purposes then, we'll use the term "Pre-Enlightenment," since it's a standard historical category, but we'll use it in the sense of "the transition to the full Enlightenment," or simply, "the transitional period."

European history throughout the seventeenth and eighteenth centuries took a variety of contradictory turns. England saw the complete overthrow of the monarchy in the middle of the seventeenth century and its replacement first by a republic and thenby a weakened monarchy later in the century; finally, at the end of the seventeenth century England would see the revolutionary erosion of the monarch's powers in England's "Glorious Revolution." For all this drama, however, the rest of Europe saw an astonishing growth in the power of monarchs over their states. The two centuries that bracket the Enlightenment saw the development of **absolute** monarchies and more tightly-centralized national governments; the growth of the absolute monarchy is regarded by many historians as the origin of the modern state. Europe consequently saw the gradual erosion of local power and autonomy and the rise of national legislation and civil bureaucracies. Because of this growth in absolute and centralized power of the national government and the monarchy, this age in European history is generally called the **Age of Absolutism** (1660-1789). It begins in the reign of Louis XIV and ends with the French Revolution.

Absolutism was by and large motivated by the crises and tragedies of the sixteenth and seventeenth centuries. The Reformation had led to a series of violent and cruel wars of religions; states erupted into civil war and thousands of innocents met their deaths in the name of national religions. Absolute monarchies were originally proposed as a solution to these violent disorders, and Europeans were more than willing to have local autonomy taken away in exchange for peace and safety.

In order to achieve this stability, absolutists asserted that in practical affairs several key elements of the national government should be solely in the hands of the monarch: the military, tax collection, and the judicial system. These were powers normally enjoyed by the aristocracy and local gentry; the national administration of these functions required the formation of a national civil bureaucracy whose officials were answerable only to the king. This bureaucracy had to stand against the most powerful institutional forces opposed to the king: the nobility, the church, representative legislative bodies, and autonomous regions. So the absolutists faced a problem very similar to that faced by the Japanese after the Meiji Restoration; in order to centralize the administration of the state, the government had to somehow take political authority out of the hands of the nobility and others who were not especially interested in giving that authority up.

In Europe absolute monarchs could not completely break the power of the nobility, so they incorporated them into their new bureaucratic institutions. The church, however, was a different matter. Most absolutist monarchs tried to get around the church by nationalizing it, that is, by imitating the actions of England's Henry VIII in the early sixteenth century. While Henry had himself named head of the church of England, the absolute monarchs in Europe only managed to gain some administrative and judicial control over the clergy. The most difficult battles, however, would be with representative legislative bodies; it was such a battle that precipitated the French Revolution.

Medieval political theory justified kingship by arguing that the king ruled by the will of God. Jacques-Benigne Bossuet (1627-1704) adapted the medieval concept of kingship in his theory of the Divine Right of Kings, which argued that the king ruled absolutely by will of God, andthat to oppose the king in effect constituted rebellion against God. Although the people should be excluded from power, God's purpose in instituting absolute monarchy was to protect and guide society.

Bossuet spelled out his arguments in the treatise *Politics Drawn from the Very Words of Scripture* in 1709; most of these theories he developed for Louis XIV in France. In this work, Bossuet argues that God institutes monarchy for the welfare of the people; for that reason, absolute rule is not arbitrary rule. The monarch cannot do as he pleases, but must rather consistently act in the best interests of society. As a political theorist attached to Louis XIV, he helped Louis establish the first and fullest absolute monarchy in Europe.

Louis XIV

This monarch who fully embodied absolutist principles—Louis XIV, the Sun King—ruled France from 1643 to 1715. In many ways, Louis was the embodiment of the modern age for the whole of Europe. Many countries and monarchs turned to him as a model for the new, modern government, while some countries, such as England, reacted against this model. Historians like to consider the reign of Louis XIV as the beginning of the modern state. Most of the practices of the modern state were more or less instituted in the France of Louis XIV: centralized government, a centralized civil bureaucracy, national legislation, a national judiciary that controlled most judicial activity, a large, standing military under the direct, rather than indirect, control of national authorities, and a national tax collection mechanism in which taxes went straight to the national government rather than passing through the hands of regional nobility.

Historians also credit Louis with inventing the **"theater" of national government.** This claim, though compelling in some ways, is not entirely true. Earlier monarchs had, since the beginning of the sixteenth century, largely thought of the monarchy as theater, as show, and as display. The purpose of this theater was to demonstrate both the power and the benevolence of the individual monarch;

such a display was integral to the legitimation of the monarch's authority and the dedication of the monarch's subject to the state itself. Louis, however, elevated the "theater of power" to unprecedented heights and clearly thought that every public aspect of the monarch should contribute to this theater of power.

Fundamental to Louis's theater of power was the display of monarchical wealth, power, and largesse. To this end, he moved the monarchical residence out of the center of Paris to a suburb in Versailles. There he built the single most opulent palace ever built for a king of Europe: the palace of Versailles. It was an awe-inspiring structure and was built as a stage on which to perform the public rituals and to display monarchical power. The building itself was a little over a third of a mile long; the outside was surrounded by magnificent gardens and over 1400 fountains employing the newest hydraulic technologies. The inside was an altar to French military might, room after room decorated with paintings, tapestries, and statues celebrating French military victories, heroes, and, especially, French kings.

Louis required every noble to spend some time at the palace at Versailles. There he would stage elaborate performances and rituals designed to show the nobility both his power and his benevolence.

In these displays of monarchical power he assumed the role of "Sun King." Neoplatonic philosophers of the Renaissance and seventeenth century argued that the sun, as the source of light, was the proper symbol for god and wisdom. Louis adopted the Neoplatonic symbol for God to symbolize his own role as God's monarchical representative.

The power and the benevolence that Louis put on display was to some measure real power and real benevolence. In order to secure his power, Louis had to centralize the military, take control of national taxes, reign in independent territories such as Brittany and Languedoc, break up the legislative assemblies, and impose a religious unity on the country

Until Louis XIV, the military in France had been largely a private affair. Individual regions raised and paid for their own armies; when the king required military help, the army came from these semi-private sources. Louis began to build a state army of professional soldiers and began to bleed the military power from these individual regions. This new centralized military would owe allegiance only to the king; the danger of factionalism and rebellion subsequently declined.

In order to pay for his new military as well as his expensive theater of power, Louis seized control of national taxes. Until Louis's time, taxes throughout Europe were collected largely by individual nobility on a region by region basis.

Nobles had been required to submit a certain amount of taxes to the crown, but they were free to collect whatever they pleased and keep the excess. In all the states in Europe, this was a massively inefficient affair, at least from a monarch's perspective. When Louis assumedpower, only 30 percent or so of the taxes due to the monarch actually got paid.

Louis effectively cut out the middlemen. Rather than charging nobility to collect taxes, Louis set up a bureaucracy to collect taxes directly from the peasantry (the tax burden did not fall on the nobility at all). By the end of his reign, Louis was collecting over eighty percent of the taxes due to the monarchy. But Louis did not spend this money only on himself: he and his finance minister, Jean Baptiste Colbert (1619-1683), used much of this money to expand and improve roads and to invest in national industry. In fact, historians usually credit Colbert as creating the first modern state in terms of financial management: collecting taxes and then reinvesting those taxes in the infrastructure and industries of the country.

Louis broke regional independence by dividing the country into thirty-six *generalités* ; each *generalité* was administered by an intendant, who was generally appointed from the upper middle classes rather than the nobility. No intendant was ever appointed to a region that he lived in; in this way, corruption would be kept to a minimum. These intendants were appointed by the king and answerable only to the king. For the most part, this bureaucracy functioned to collect taxes. In the most autonomous regions, such as Languedoc and Brittany, Louis ruthlessly imposed obedience to the crown.

In the matter of legislative assemblies, Louis had no patience whatsoever. The *parlements* of France were largely regional in nature rather than national. Not only did these *parlements* represent a diffusion of power from the king to the populace, they also represented a diffusion of power from the king to separate regions. Louis solved the problem of the *parlements* directly and simply: if any *parlement* vetoed monarchical legislation, all the members of that *parlement* would be exiled from France. Simple as that. The national legislative assembly, called the **Estates General,** was never called into session by Louis; in fact, it would not be called until 1789 at the heart of the crisis that precipitated the French Revolution.

Finally, decades of bloodshed over religion made it obvious that political unity would only be a dream unless religious unity were achieved first. To that end, Louis, a Roman Catholic, actively worked to get rid of heterodox religious groups: the Protestant Huguenots, the Quietists (mystical Christians), and the Jansenists, whose beliefs were a combination of Calvinism and Catholicism. The greatest threat to religious unity, as Louis saw it, were the Protestant Huguenots. He destroyed their churches and burned their schools and forced Protestants, under pain of imprisonment or death, to convert to Catholicism. Finally, he overturned the Edict of Nantes and declared Protestantism to be a crime against the state. All Protestant clergy were exiled from France. Most French Protestants chose to leave France rather than convert; the latter half of the seventeenth century saw the expansion of French culture throughout Europe as middle-class French Huguenots brought their culture, language, and artisanal skills to countries all over Europe.

In all the documents that we can find, it seems that Louis conceived his role as absolute monarch in terms of benevolence. His reign, he argued, was primarily about benefitting the people of France materially, spiritually, and militarily. He saw the political and religious unification of France as a means of protecting his French subjects from the ravages of political unrest and religious civil war. The collecting of taxes made this possible, and the reinvesting of taxes in infrastructure and industry were seen as means of increasing the general national wealth of the country.

Prussia

All throughout continental Europe, rulers began to adopt the principles and practices of Louis's absolute monarchy and centralized government. They met with varying degrees of success, and the process of converting European governments into centralized states went on for over a hundred years. The surprising twist in history, though, is that the most successful centralized and

Michelle Lynn

absolutist states were not to be created until the twentieth century—and they all started as democracies (such as fascist Germany) or they are democracies still (such as the United States).

In the eighteenth century, the first European power to fully adopt absolutist principles was a tiny, more or less powerless kingdom called **Brandenburg-Prussia** in what is now modern day Germany; as a result of this centralization, it would become one of the most powerful states in Europe. Throughout the sixteenth century, this area was part of the Holy Roman Empire, a disparate collection of semi-autonomous states from northern Germany to eastern Europe to the Mediterranean. These states were never fully unified politically or culturally. The rise of the Reformation severely frayed the political bonds between these separate states, and the Thirty Years' War severed them completely. What was once a significant empire fragmented into an array of tiny, inconsequential kingdoms.

After the disintegration of the empire, Prussia was transformed through the efforts of **Frederick William**, or **Frederick the Great**, the Elector (head of state) of Brandenburg-Prussia from 1640-1688. He adopted all the strategies that Louis had innovated in France. His state consisted of two semi-autonomous and semi-hostile territories—Brandenburg in the north and Prussia in the southeast. In order to effect political unity, he built a large standing army (which would eventually become the largest army in the European world), and he built a centralized and ruthless taxation system. In order to manage this army, he put it under the control of a military commission which not only ran the military but managed the industries which manufactured military goods. This model—later named the "military-industrial complex" by U.S. president Dwight Eisenhower—would become a standard feature of the modern, centralized state. As in France, taxes were levied only on the peasants and the middle class; the landlord nobility, called **Junkers**, were exempt. But although the Junkers thought that they had gotten away with something, in reality Frederick William's centralization of the military and the taxation system drained regional power from the Junkers and placed it in the hands of Frederick William.

Austria

Austria was an empire throughout the sixteenth and seventeenth centuries which was, like the Holy Roman Empire, only a loosely-unified state. It included three culturally different regions: 1) the German-speaking regions in what is modern day Austria and the German-speaking region of Silesia, 2) the Czech-speaking regions of what is now southeastern Germany and Czechoslovakia, and 3) the Magyar-speaking regions in what is now modern-day Hungary. The Austrians, or more precisely the Hungarians, were also the European front line against Ottoman Turk invasions of Europe. Whenever the Ottomans got a notion to invade Europe, they always started with the Austrian Empire. From 1583 onwards, the history of Austria is one long series of wars with Turkey over control of Hungarian territory. In 1683, the Ottomans made it all the way to Vienna and besieged the capital city itself.

This loose and volatile political territory was ruled by the **Hapsburg** emperors. They had, you might say, one of the worst jobs in Europe. This job wasn't made any easier when the Hapsburgs decided to adopt absolutist principles and impose them on this diverse set of territories and cultures. Beginning with Frederick I (ruled 1637-1657) and Leopold I (ruled 1658-1705), the Hapsburgs tried to centralize the government of Austria and break the power of the noble landlords. They managed this by making deals with the landed nobility; in the

Czech-speaking territories, for instance, the Hapsburgs passed national legislation that required peasants to work three days every week for their landlords in order to produce agricultural exports. In exchange for this inhumane increased demand for peasant labor, the landlords gave away the powers of their regional assemblies to the Hapsburgs.

Hungary, however, was a different matter. Not only were the regions controlled by an autonomous aristocracy, the Hungarians had their own king and jealously guarded their right to appoint their own king. Leopold I managed to talk them out of that right in 1687, but he didn't get rid of the Hungarian monarchy. However, from this point onward the Hapsburg Emperors would appoint kings that they knew they could trust: themselves. That's as far as Hapsburg dreams of unity got in Hungary. They tried many strategies to break the power of the Hungarian aristocracy: granting large tracts of land to German-speaking landlords, imposing religious unity by exiling large numbers of non-Catholics (mainly Eastern Orthodox but a few Protestants as well), and trying to set up a military administration of the country. The Hungarian nobility resisted and would, for the rest of the history of the Austrian empire, function as a more or less autonomous state with a Hapsburg as the titular monarch.

Peter the Great

The seventeenth century marks a political and cultural transformation of Russia that is epic in its scale. Russia, for the most part, can be culturally and politically considered as a separate people, even a separate continent. The Russians were a mixture of peoples; in western Russia, they were mainly Indo-Europeans who had settled the area in waves beginning with the original Indo-European migrations and ending with the Germanic migrations of the sixth, seventh, and eighth centuries AD. These Indo-Europeans were Eastern Orthodox in their religion. In the east, Russians were largely derived from peoples living north of China. The Mongol invasions of Russian territory had infused a strong Mongol character into the Russian world view in the same way the Mongol invasions had greatly changed Persian and Turkish culture.

The Russians, then, were a mixture of cultures and world views and saw themselves as neither continuous with Europeans to the west, Muslims to the south, or Asians to the east. It is probably fair to say that Russians saw themselves as having more in common with Asians than with Europeans. Be that as it may, Russians in the late Middle Ages and the early modern period primarily saw themselves as a separate people with their own traditions and their own culture. The Russian state was, by European standards, economically, politically, and technologically "backward." This was not, by and large, a fair assessment of the situation of medieval and early modern Russia; however, it was an assessment that Peter I, or Peter the Great, accepted completely.

Peter I became Tsar (or Czar—both words come from "Caesar") of Russia in 1682 and ruled until 1725. He was a member of the Romanov family which had established its dynasty in 1613. The Russian Empire was a truly fragmented affair. The various peoples under the control of the Russian Empire were highly diverse and often hostile to one another: Ukranians, Russians, and a large number of nomadic peoples were constantly at one another's throats. Not only that, they didn't like being ruled by an emperor. So volatile was the situation that the Russian Empire nearly fell beneath the sword of a Cossack rebel named Stenka Razin who led a huge popular revolt against the Romanovs.

Peter felt that the Empire could only be preserved by adopting Western European culture, industries, and political management. His first task was to bring Western European industry to Russia; in 1689, he went to Holland and England and brought back skilled workers. He also demanded that the nobility adopt Western cultural habits, such as going beardless or wearing only short beards, eating with utensils, wearing European clothes, and engaging in the habits of "polite" speech.

More than anything else, however, Peter was determined to bring new European political practices in Russia, in particular, the practice and theater of absolute monarchy. Unlike the European kings, however, Peter had inherited a Russian tradition that the monarch was entirely above the law. Peter's power, therefore, was far greater than any of his European contemporaries, and he wielded it with an arbitrary cruelty that would have sent any European monarch to their execution. He did, however, wield it with a purpose: his singular goal was to convert Russia into a Western European culture.

Peter imitated European armies by creating a standing army that was only answerable to him; he created this army by drafting five percent of the male population of Russia to serve in the army **for life**. This army was supplied by state-run factories; the factories were staffed by peasants who had been drafted to work in these factories. He centralized the tax system—you can probably guess how—by taxing the peasants of Russia directly rather than indirectly through landed nobles. As in other European states, the nobility were exempt from this tax. He created a bureaucracy and staffed it with both nobility and civil servants.

In pursuit of his aims, Peter did use a level of severity that almost boggles the mind. The peasants who served in his army and factories were, for all practical purposes, slaves.

He suppressed any dissent with swift and harsh capital punishment; he directed this harshness even towards his son, Alexis, who opposed him in his innovations. So Peter ordered him to be tortured to death.

Peter was determined to orient Russia towards the West; in order to do this, he needed a port that would allow him to enter the Baltic Sea at all times of the year. Most of his foreign wars were directed at this goal until he finally beat Sweden and acquired coastal territory. He instantly moved his capital to this new territory and built a city dedicated to himself: St. Petersburg. There he built a palace that was meant to imitate and even rival Louis XIV's palace at Versailles; this palace became the staging ground for the theater of power that would demonstrate his power and benevolence to his nobility, peasants, and the world.

When Peter died, he was followed by a series of Tsars and Empresses that never were able to rule as strongly, single-mindedly, or effectively as Peter. Russia would not see a strong absolutist government again until Catherine II, the Great, became Empress in 1762.

While Europe steadily developed strong, absolutist, and centralized governments, there was one exception. During this period, the tiny kingdom of England would undergo some of the most radical changes in the early modern state: from republic to a limited monarchy, the English were setting out in different directions in the long struggle to forge a new, modern state.[162]

DANIEL 11:36

king	**king** - one that holds supreme or preeminent position in a particular sphere or class
do	**do** - carry out
will	**delight** - to have or take great satisfaction or pleasure
he	**self** - MYSELF, HIMSELF, HERSELF
exalt	**raise** - to advance in rank, position, or esteem
magnify	**be large** - involving few restrictions: permitting considerable liberty (as of action or consequence)
above	**over** - used as a function word to indicate the possession or enjoyment of authority, power, or jurisdiction in regard to some thing or person
every	**all** - that is the whole amount or quantity of
God	**deity** - one that holds or wields supreme power or influence in some field
speak	**speak** - give expression to thoughts, opinions, or feelings
marvellous	**be great** - considerable or remarkable in magnitude, power, intensity, degree, or effectiveness
against	**against** - with respect to: relating to
God	**Almighty** - having absolute power over all
gods	**God** - the supreme or ultimate reality
prosper	to **push** forward - advance persistently or courageously
till	**until** - up to the time that
indignation	**fury** - violent anger: extreme wrath
be	**become** - to come to exist or occur

accomplished	**prepare** - to make ready beforehand for some purpose
for	**causal** - expressing or indicating cause
that	**that** - being the person, thing, or idea pointed to, mentioned, or or understood from the situation
that	**that** - being the person, thing, or idea pointed to, mentioned, or or understood from the situation
is	**become** - to emerge as an entity: grow to manifest a certain essence, nature, development, or significance
determined	**decide** - to make evident or give evidence of: serve as a means of revealing
be	**become** - come to exist or occur
done	**do** - to take place: HAPPEN

DANIEL 11:37

Neither shall he regard the God of his fathers, nor the desire of women, nor regard any god: for he shall magnify himself above all.

While the absolute rule of Louis XIV prevented any criticism of established authority in France, the new science and philosophy of Newton and Locke flourished in England, where two kings—Charles I and James II—were overthrown during the 17th century.

From England, the new theories, and a new questioning of all authority, spread across Europe, and became known as the Enlightenment. It drew together scholars who opposed the established Church and who were hostile to despotic government. The German philosopher Immanuel Kant was to summarize the movement when he urged men: 'Dare to know! Have the courage to use your own intelligence!' The early *philosophes* were largely people who believed that God was a master planner, 'the Eternal Geometer', who had created an intricate mechanism and left it to run itself.[163]

The next reign of Louis XV, was the age of that supreme mocker Voltaire (1694-1778), an age in which everybody in French society conformed to the Roman Catholic Church and hardly anyone believed in it.[164] Voltaire was a savage critic of the Church, because of the intolerance of the clergy . . . The Papacy—that 'infamous thing', as he called it—and the Church, were favorite targets.[165] His brilliant wit and cynicism dominated the intellectual life of Europe for over a quarter of a century and played a large part in undermining its existing social order. Voltaire proclaimed himself as a non-Christian.[166]

To Voltaire official Christianity was *"l'infame"*; something that limited people's lives, interfered with their thoughts, and persecuted harmless dissentients.[167]

17th Century Enlightenment Thought

As a historical category, the term "Enlightenment" refers to a series of changes in European thought and letters. It is one of the few historical categories that was coined by the people who lived through the era (most historical categories, such as "Renaissance," "early modern," "Reformation," "Tokugawa Enlightenment," etc., are made up by historians after the fact). When the writers, philosophers and scientists of the eighteenth century referred to their activities as the "Enlightenment," they meant that they were breaking from the past and replacing the obscurity, darkness, and ignorance of European thought with the "light" of truth.

Although the Enlightenment is one of the few self-named historical categories, determining the beginning of the Enlightenment is a difficult affair, as we noted earlier in this module. Not only can we not easily find a beginning to the Enlightenment, we can't really identify an end point either. For we still more or less live in an Enlightenment world; while philosophers and cultural historians have dubbed the late nineteenth and all of the twentieth century as "post-Enlightenment," we still walk around with a world view largely based on Enlightenment thought.

So in the spirit of not dating the Enlightenment, we will simply refer to the changes in European thought in the seventeenth century as "Seventeenth Century Enlightenment Thought," with the understanding that our use of the term may invite criticism.

The main components of Enlightenment thought are as follows:

The universe is fundamentally rational, that is, it can be understood through the use of reason alone;

Truth can be arrived at through empirical observation, the use of reason, and systematic doubt;

Human experience is the foundation of human understanding of truth; authority is not to be preferred over experience;

All human life, both social and individual, can be understood in the same way the natural world can be understood; once understood, human life, both social and individual, can be manipulated or engineered in the same way the natural world can be manipulated or engineered;

Human history is largely a history of progress;

Human beings can be improved through education and the development of their rational facilities;

Religious doctrines have no place in the understanding of the physical and human worlds;

There are two distinct developments in Enlightenment thought: the scientific revolution which resulted in new systems of understanding the physical world (this is covered in a later chapter), and the redeployment of the human sciences that apply scientific thinking to what were normally interpretive sciences. In the first, the two great innovations were the development of empirical thought and the mechanistic world view. Empiricism is based on the notion that human observation is a reliable indicator of the nature of phenomena; repeated human observation can produce reasonable expectations about future natural events. In the second, the universe is regarded as a machine. It functions by natural and predictable rules; although God created the universe, he does not interfere in its day to day runnings. Once the world is understood as a machine, then it can be manipulated and engineered for the benefit of humanity in the same way as machines are.

These ideas were steadily exported to the human sciences as well. In theories of personality, human development, and social mechanics, seventeenth century thinkers moved away from religious and moral explanations of human behavior and interactions and towards an empirical analysis and mechanistic explanation of the laws of human behavior and interaction.

Thomas Hobbes

The first major thinker of the seventeenth century to apply new methods to the human sciences was Thomas Hobbes (1588-1679) whose book *Leviathan* is one of the most revolutionary and influential works on political theory in European history. Hobbes was greatly interested in the new sciences; he spent some time in Italy with Galileo and eagerly read the work of William Harvey, who was applying the new physical science methods to human physiology. After the English Civil War, Hobbes determined that political philosophy had to be seriously revised. The old political philosophy, which relied on religion, ethics, and interpretation, had produced what he felt was a singular disaster in English history. He proposed that political philosophy should be based on the same methods of exposition and explanation as were being applied to the physical sciences.

When he applied these explanatory principles to politics and states, he arrived at two radical and far-reaching conclusions:

All human law derives from natural law; when human law departed from natural law, disaster followed;

All monarchs ruled not by the consent of heaven, but by the consent of the people.

These were radical ideas. In the first, Hobbes believed that human beings were material, physical objects that were ruled by material, physical laws. Everything that human beings feel, think, and judge, are simply physical reactions to external stimuli. Sensation produces feeling, and feeling produces decision, and decision produces action. We are all, then, machines. The fundamental motivation that spurs human beings on is **selfishness**: all human beings wish to maximize their pleasure and minimize their pain. As long as political philosophy is built on some other principle, such as morality, the human inclination to selfishness will always result in tragedy.

Since all human beings are selfish, this means that no person is really safe from the predations of his or her fellow beings. In its natural state, humanity is at war with itself. Individuals battle other individuals in a perpetual struggle for advantage, power, and gain. Hobbes argued that the society was a group of selfish individuals that united into a single body in order to maximize their safety—to protect themselves from one another. The primary purpose of society is to maximize the happiness of its individuals. At some early point, individuals gathered into a society and agreed to a "social contract" that stipulated the laws and rules they would all live by.

Michelle Lynn

Human beings, however, could not be trusted simply to live by their agreements. For this reason, authority was created in order to enforce the terms of the social contract. The creation of authority, by which Hobbes meant a monarch, transformed society into a *state*. For Hobbes, humanity is better off living under the circumscribed freedoms of a monarchy rather than the violent anarchy of a completely equal and free life.

Using this reasoning, Hobbes argued for unquestioning obedience of authority. In a twist of fate, however, both his methods of inquiry and his basic assumptions would form the basis of arguments against absolute authority.

Baruch Spinoza

Baruch Spinoza (1632-1677) was a Jewish philosopher living in the Netherlands who applied the new sciences to questions of ethics and philosophy. His most famous work, the *Ethics*, attempts to use a system of demonstration first outlined by Francis Bacon and fully theorized by René Descartes that begins with certain definitions and draws from these consequent axioms and corollaries. His basic definition of good ("The highest good of the mind is knowledge of God and the highest virtue of the mind is to know God") formed the foundation of all of his ethical statements, including some highly controversial statements ("Pity is not a virtue"). The work was extraordinarily controversial, for from his base definitions he derived the notion that God and nature were essentially identical. He argued the same thing that the Greek philosopher Parmenides did almost two thousand years earlier: there is one and only one thing in the universe and that one thing is God. Everything else is simply a part of God. Anyproposition concerning the physical is, then, a proposition about the nature of God. For Spinoza the new physical sciences were, by and large, coterminous with theology. This position would be reiterated by Isaac Newton and the deists, who argued that understanding the rational workings of the universe would also mean understanding the rational workings of its creator, God.

Like Hobbes, Spinoza believed that human action was fundamentally mechanistic. Human actions resulted from two things: the external environment and internal passions. The relationship between the environment, passions, and human action was a mechanistic relationship; all human actions, then, could be explained in terms of laws. The fundamental drive that animates all human beings is the effort to preserve themselves and their own autonomy in relation to external things. However, the one area of human activity that is free from the influence of the external environment and human passions is rational thought; the more that thought is disengaged from the external world and human passsion, that is, the more abstract that thought is, the more free the individual. Human freedom, for Spinoza, existed only in abstract thinking.

In political theory, Spinoza argued that human beings fundamentally act in accordance with natural law. Like Hobbes, Spinoza believed that human beings pursue their own self-preseveration. In a natural state, the only "wrong" that a human being can commit is an action that results in his or her destruction or downfall. Since human beings cannot preserve themselves in isolation, they form societies by which individual "right" is subsumed under "common right," a notion very similar to Hobbes' social contract. The means by which a society enforces its common right on the individual is "dominion" (in Latin, "imperium"). Dominion takes three forms: dominion by the multitude (democracy), by a select few (aristocracy), or by a single individual (monarchy). The concepts of right and wrong,

Michelle Lynn

justice and injustice are only established when the common right is articulated through dominion; that is, when a ruler asserts something as right or wrong, it is then right or wrong (in nature there is no right or wrong, justice or injustice). The relationship between the right (power) of the individual and the right of the dominion is an inverse relationship: the more power that accrues to individuals, the less is available to the dominion; the more power that accrues to authorities, the less is available to individuals. Surprisingly, Spinoza implies that democracy is the best way to balance individual and common right since it more closely guarantees that the beliefs of the multitude will correspond with the beliefs and actions of the dominion.

John Locke

The last important philosopher, besides Pascal and Descartes, of human sciences in the seventeenth century was John Locke (1632-1704). Locke was steeped in the new physical sciences; he was an avid reader of Francis Bacon and Isaac Newton, and he was a close friend of Robert Boyle, one of the founders of modern chemistry. He also read Pascal and Descartes avidly. He wrote two far-reaching and massively influential works on human sciences, *An Essay Concerning Human Understanding* (1690) and *Two Treatises on Government* (1690).

The *Essay* takes as its subject human psychology and cognition; it is, undoubtedly, the first European work on human cognition. Locke applied the new science to explaining the human mind itself and all its operations; he started with a radical definition of the human mind. For Locke, the human mind enters the world with no pre-formed ideas whatsoever. The human mind at birth is a blank, a *tabula rasa* (erased board). Human sensation:taste, touch, smell, hearing, and especially vision filled the empty mind with objects of sensation. From these sensations, humans eventually derive a sense of order and rationality. All human thought, then, and all human passion is ultimately derived from sensation and sensation alone. In Locke's view, the human mind is completely **empirical**. Not only is he arguing that the best knowledge is empirical knowledge, he was arguing that the only knowledge is empirical knowledge; there is no other kind.

One of the consequences of this empirical view of humans means that every human being enters the world with all the same capacities. No one is by virtue of birth more moral or knowledgeable than anyone else. Since all moral behavior arises from one's empirical experiences, that means that immoral behavior is primarily a product of the environment rather than the individual. If you accept that line of reasoning, that means that you can change moral and intellectual outcomes in human development by changing the environment. Locke proposed that education above everything else was responsible for forging the moral and intellectual character of individuals; he proposed in part an extension of education to every member of society. This view of education still dominates Western culture to this day.

In the *Two Treatises*, Locke argued that government and authority was based on natural law. Unlike Hobbes, Locke believed that natural law dictated that all human beings were fundamentally equal; he derived this argument from his theories of human development. Since every human being walked into the world with the same capacities as every other human being, that meant that inequality was an unnatural result of the environments that individuals are forced to live in, a belief that still underlies the Western notion of human development. Human beings have a natural inclination to preserve their equality and independence, since these are natural aspects of humanness. For Locke, humans enter into social contracts only to help adjudicate disputes between individuals or groups. Absolute power, then, is an unnatural development in human history.

For Locke, the purpose of authority is to protect human equality and freedom; this is why social groups agree to a "social contract" that places an authority over them. When that authority ceases to care for the welfare, independence, and equality of individual humans, the social contract is broken and it is the duty of the members of society to overthrow that ruler. This work was published shortly after the Glorious Revolution and clearly reflects the political fallout from that event. It would also serve as one of the central influences in the formation of the American government. *Richard Hooker*[168]

Philosophes

The European Enlightenment developed in part due to an energetic group of French thinkers who thrived in the middle of the eighteenth century: the **philosophes.** This group was a heterogenous mix of people who pursued a variety of intellectual interests: scientific, mechanical, literary, philosophical, and sociological. They were united by a few common themes: an unwavering doubt in the perfectibility of human beings, a fierce desire to dispel erroneous systems of thought (such as religion) and a dedication to systematizing the various intellectual disciplines.

The rallying cry for the *philosophes* was the concept of **progress.** By mastering both natural sciences and human sciences, humanity could harness the natural world for its own benefit and learn to live peacefully with one another. This was the ultimate goal, for the *philosophes*, of rational and intentional progress.

The central ideas of the *philosophe* movement were:

Progress: Human history is largely a history of the improvement of humanity in three respects: a) developing a knowledge of the natural world and the ability to manipulate the world through technology; b) overcoming ignorance bred of superstitions and religions; c) overcoming human cruelty and violence through social improvements and government structures.

Deism: Deism is a term coined in the *philosophe* movement and applies to two related ideas: a) religion should be reasonable and should result in the highest moral behavior of its adherents; b) the knowledge of the natural world and the human world has nothing to do whatsoever with religion and should be approached completely free from religious ideas or convictions.

Tolerance: The greatest human crimes, as far as the *philosophes* were concerned, have been perpetrated in the name of religion and the name of God. A fair, just, and productive society absolutely depends on religious tolerance. This means not merely tolerance of varying Christian sects, but tolerance of non-Christian religions as well (for some *philosophes*).

The miracle years for the *philosophes* occurred between 1748 and 1751: all the outstanding works of the *philosophes* first saw the light of day during these intellectually exciting years: Montesquieu's *Spirit of the Laws* (1748), Rousseau's *Discourse on the Moral Effects of the Arts and Sciences* (1750), and, finally, the great capstone of the French *philosophes* movement, the first edition of Denis Diderot's *Encyclopédie* in 1751.

None of the *philosophes* engaged in speculative philosophy or abstract thinking (very much; they were primarily concerned with the betterment of society and human beings so their focus was overwhelmingly practical. This concern was focused on reforming individual human beings and on outdated human institutions and belief systems.

Voltaire

Besides Jean-Jacques Rousseau, the most influential of the French *philosophes* was François Marie Arouet or, as he signed his books, **Voltaire**. Voltaire concentrated on two specific philosophical projects. First, he untiringly worked to introduce empiricism, as it was practiced by the English, into French intellectual life. Second, he persisted in proselytizing for religious tolerance; in fact, most of his works that we still read today had as their theme religious tolerance.

Empiricism: Empirical philosophy, which was first systematized by Aristotle in the fourth century BC, was reintroduced into Western culture with a vengeance by English scientists in the seventeenth century. Like Descartes, English philosophers such as Isaac Newton began by doubting everything. Unlike Descartes, who developed a non-empirical philosophy to answer that doubt, Newton and his crew based all human certainty on empirical verification through the senses. Voltaire spat all over the French rationalist tradition and worked tirelessly to develop a French philosophy based on empiricism. Although the French solidly remained rooted in rationalism, much of French empirical science owes its origins to the works of Voltaire.

*A **Treatise on Tolerance*** : Voltaire had written most of his life on religious tolerance and had gained a large audience. In 1762, however, he was fired into action by the execution of an innocent Protestant in Toulouse. This man, Jean Calas, was accused of murdering his son before that son could convert to Catholicism. Like the OJ Simpson case, this murder created a sensation all throughout largely Catholic France. Calas was inhumanly tortured and eventually strangled, but he never confessed to the crime. When Voltaire heard about this gross miscarriage of justice, he made Jean Calas's case his cause and in 1763 he published *A Treatise on Tolerance* that focused entirely on the Calas case.

Voltaire's argument was very simple: the most inhuman crimes perpetrated by humanity throughout its enitre history have been perpetrated in the name of religion. Mass extermination, torture, infanticide, regicide: behind just about every abominable human crime lay some religious zealotry or passionate religious commitment. The most vicious crimes, though, are those perpetrated by Christians against other Christians who belong to a different sect or church. Since religion does not admit of certainty, and since so many sects and religions have so many things in common, the *Treatise* argues that people should be allowed to practice whatever religion they see fit, particularly if it's a Christian religion. Individual governments should not impose religious systems on an entire state. The ultimate argument of the book is that secular values should take precedence over religious values; until that happens, human history will be marked by viciousness and inhumanity.

Candide : Voltaire's most famous book, however, is *Candide*, a novel which he published in 1759. Although Voltaire is the most representative *philosophe* of his time, *Candide* is a strange book in that it attacks many of the assumptions of the *philosophe* movement.

In particular, the novel makes fun of those who think that human beings can endlessly improve themselves and their environment. The main character of the novel, Candide, is set adrift in a hostile world and futilely tries to hold on to his optimistic belief that this "is the best of all possible worlds" as his tutor, Dr. Pangloss, keeps insisting. He travels throughout Europe, South America, and the Middle East, and on the way he encounters terrible natural disasters and even more terrible disasters perpetrated by human beings on their fellow human beings. He learns in the end that the only solution is productive work that benefits those around you.

Denis Diderot and Jean le Rond d'Alembert

The great manifesto of the *philosophe* movement was no small document; by the late 1740's, everyone understood that the sum total and the entire spirit of the movement was contained in the **Encyclopédie** of Denis Diderot and Jean le Rond d'Alembert, known simply as Diderot's *Encyclopedia*.

The *Encyclopedia* was in fact the collective effort of over one hundred French thinkers. The central purpose of the work was to secularize learning and, above all other things, to refute what the authors felt were dangerous carry-overs from the Middle Ages. For the Encyclopedists, human improvement was not a religious issue, but simply a matter of mastering the natural world through science andtechnology and mastering human passions through an understanding of how individuals and societies work.

Diderot was a prolific writer who wrote on just about every topic and in just about every format. He wrote on philosophy, science, music, and art, and wrote novels, essays, and dramatic pieces. D'Alembert was a mathematician and scientist; he was responsible for the

Encyclopedia 's "Preface." This preface is a vitally important document in explaining the *philosophe* attitude towards knowledge. In it, d'Alembert explains that the *Encyclopedia* has been organized around the categories of human knowledge. This, ultimately, is an Aristotelean principle, and it became the standard working principle of the *Encyclopedia*. This division of knowledge in the *Encyclopdia* was ultimately responsible for the division of human sciences we see today: the division between human and natural sciences, as well as the division between natural and mechanical sciences all owe their origin to the *Encyclopedia* and d'Alembert's theoretical preface.

Montesquieu

The baron de Montesquieu concerned himself entirely with political theory. His *Spirit of the Laws* (1748) sought to explain how different groups of people end up with different and varying forms of government. He argued that climate, terrain, and agricultural conditions largely predetermined both human behavior and various forms of authority. However, Montesquieu also believed that there was a single, best form of government and that humans could overcome any and all geographical and climatic conditions. For Montesquieu, the best form of human government was embodied in the English constitution after the Glorious Revolution. In particular, the English constitution divided state powers into three independent branches of government: the executive, the legislative, and the judicial. Since no one person or group was in charge, the maximum amount of political and economic freedom was made available to the general population. He called this equal distribution of power "checks and balances," and his theories of government would be the single most powerful influence upon the formation of American government at the end of the century.

English Philosophes

The *philosophes* movement was not confined to France, but soon spilled over into other European countries. In England, the movement was championed by David Hume, Adam Smith, and Edward Gibbon. It was natural that the English would take to the new ideas, since the French *philosophes* were so heavily influenced by English thought: Voltaire by English empiricism and Montesquieu by English government.

David Hume (1711-1776) is perhaps the most important English philosopher of the eighteenth century. He was a radical skeptic and his most influential work, *An Inquiry Concerning Human Understanding*, argued that human beings can know nothing whatsoever with certainty. Even more influential were his ideas on ethics; he argued for a moral relativism. Since no one can know anything for certain, that means that no individual is in a position to pass judgement on alternative moral systems.

Adam Smith (1723-1790) is one of the most important theorists of the eighteenth century period. His book, *An Inquiry into the Nature and Causes of the Wealth of Nations* (1776), was the first book to systematically theorize capitalism and stands as the book that pretty much invented economics in the Western world.

Smith has one and only one concern in the book: to explain how nations as a collective grow wealthier. While other eighteenth century thinkers were concerned about improvements in knowledge and society, Smith believed that human progress largely consisted in the steady improvement of human life through the increasing wealth of a nation as a whole. The *Wealth of Nations* is a systematic attempt to explain the processes whereby the collective wealth of a nation grows.

Smith identifies several characteristics of growing economies. The first and foremost is **division of labor.** The revolution in labor in the seventeenth and eighteenth centuries, in which productive tasks were divided among a number of workers each doing a single task, produced a revolution in production in which output was increased a hundredfold. Smith's foundational argument is that all meaning and value in human life is to be found in productive labor; the exponential increase of production, then, not only resulted in more wealth for the nation, but greater meaning and value for human life.

Second, all monopolies and regulations stifle productive labor. Human beings work for their own profit; regulations and monopolies do away with the profit incentive and so discourage human productivity. In place of these regulations, Smith proposed a natural system of **economic liberty,** in which each individual in a society is free to choose how to expend their productive labor and their capital. This economic liberty was called *laissez faire* (let them do as they please); if individuals were allowed to pursue their own selfish aims, then the wealth of the nation as a whole would increase. This selfishness, though, would not result in social injustice; behind this natural economic liberty lay an "invisible hand" which guided people into right action.

Third, the material world was an infinite store of resources that could be exploited for the benefit of humankind. It was incumbent on humans to approach material resources, not as scarce, but as infinitely abundant. The idea that the world is an infinite storehouse of resources open to human exploitation is such a common aspect of our lives that it's hard to realize that it's a modern idea that can be dated back to Smith's book.

Edward Gibbon (1737-1794) wrote a monumental history of Rome, *The Decline and Fall of the Roman Empire*, which was published between 1776 and 1788. You can still find people dutifully reading this book as a classic of history. However, the book is important for articulating political and social ideas of the *philosophe* movement in relationship to history. Gibbon argued that Rome fell for two reasons. First, Rome was overwhelmed by barbarians. Second, Rome declined when it adopted Christianity, which he called "servile and pusillanimous" and a religion which "debased" the Roman mind and soul. The Romans replaced scientific rationalism with a "vile" religion; this, above all, made Rome vulnerable to internal degradation and external predation.

Italian Philosophes

In Italy, the most influential adherent of the *philosophe* movement was Cesare Beccaria (1738-1794), whose book, *On Crimes and Punishments* (1764) radically changed the European outlook on justice and the penal system. Beccaria argued that judicial punishment should not be used *for punishment*, but rather should be used to protect society. Incarceration of the criminal prevented the criminal from committing other crimes, and closely watching and training incarcerated criminals taught them moral and social values that would prevent them from committing crimes once they were released.

All other forms of punishment, including corporal and capital punishment, were excessive; understand that Beccaria wrote this at a time when most serious crimes were capital crimes and that executions were a common public sight. Beccaria's book completely changed the face of European society: forty years after it was written, most European countries had abolished torture and maiming as well as severely trimmed the number of crimes punishable by death. In addition, prisons changed to reflect the new mentality towards prisoners. Prison became a place where prisoners interiorized proper social behavior. Rather than being thrown into a hole, prisoners were held in large and open places that allowed for them to be constantly watched to assure that their behavior conformed to proper norms.

German Philosophes

In Germany, the most prominent thinker influenced by the *philosophe* movement was Gotthold Lessing (1729-1781). The movement never gained much ground in Germany and the Papal States, for censorship was very tight and religious authorities, particularly in Protestant states, were extremely intolerant of new ideas. Lessing primarily argued for religious tolerance; his most famous work is *Nathan the Wise*, written in 1779. In it, he argued for religious tolerance of the Jews and, even further, that human excellence was in no way related to religious affiliation. He carried this argument even further in his work, *On the Education of the Human Race* in 1780. This is the classic work of the history of human progress; Lessing argues that all world religions, including Christianity, are steps in the intellectual, social, and spiritual progress of humanity. The ultimate goal of this progress is the point at which humanity abandons religion entirely in favor of pure reason.

Social Agitation

Since the *philosophes* of all countries believed that human beings and human society was perfectible, the *philosophes* were energetic activists and agitators, sometimes incurring great personal risk for their beliefs and actions. They believed that human society could be perfected a bit at a time. Some of these efforts were useless, while others, such as agitation for judicial reform following the principles outlined in Beccaria's book, led to significant improvement. It should not be overlooked, however, that the most effective agitators using the ideas of the *philosophe* movement were the American revolutionaries in the latter quarter of the century. The foundation and formation of the American Republic was, by and large, the product of putting *philosophe* ideas into practice at great personal risk.

However, the center of gravity for social reform in the eighteenth century was a single writer: Jean-Jacques Rousseau. *Richard Hooker*[169]

DANIEL 11: 37

neither	**not** - in no manner or degree
he	**he, she, it** - the person or thing spoken of
regard	**distinguish** - make eminent: give prestige to
God	**God** - the holy, infinite, and eternal spiritual reality presented in the Bible as the creator, sustainer, judge, righteous sovereign, and redeemer of the universe who acts with power in history in carrying out his purpose
fathers	**father** - FOREFATHER, ANCESTOR
desire	**delight** - lively pleasure: JOY: extreme satisfaction
women	**woman** - one possessing in high degree the qualities considered distinctive of womanhood
nor	**not** - in no manner or degree
regard	**distinguish** - make eminent: give prestige to
any	**any** - one, some, or all indiscriminately of whatever quantity
god	**deity** - one that holds or wields supreme power or influence in some field
for	**causal** - expressing or indicating cause
he	**self** - MYSELF
magnify	**be large** - having more than usual power, capacity, range, or scope: involving few restrictions: permitting considerable liberty (as of action or conscience)
above	**above** - higher or superior in rank, position, or power
all	**all** - that is the whole amount or quantity of

Michelle Lynn

DANIEL 11:38

*But in his **estate** shall **he honour** the **God** of **forces**: and a god whom his **fathers knew not** shall **he honour with gold,** and **silver,** and **with precious stones** and **pleasant** things.*

Revolution . . . On another continent, the ideas of the Enlightenment were influencing another group of intellectuals who were not content merely to talk about change. The thinkers of America were about to put their ideas into practice, and to make America the scene of the first revolution fought for the sake of the new ideals.[170] Americans were forced to pay taxes without representation. They raised an outcry 'No taxation without representation' and all taxes were taken away except for the tea tax.

In France, the tax money which was paid by the poor French peasants and workers was wasted for luxuries of the gorgeous court. The poor people, of course, were never invited to see the royal display or to eat the fine food served in the handsome hall. They lived in huts, with piles of straw for beds, and were lucky to have enough black bread to eat. The peasants were having a hard time in France. The king made many bad laws and repealed many good ones. For example, Louis gave a certain company the right to sell salt in France. Then he ruled that every person over seven years old must buy seven pounds of salt each year, whether he needed it or not. This was called the salt tax . . . Matters grew worse and worse until many of the people were actually starving. News from other countries helped to rouse the French. They learned how the English people had taken away some of the power from their king and forced him to treat them fairly. They saw how the American colonies had freed themselves from the English king when he tried to tax them without giving them a part in the government. These events in America and England roused the French people. Men wrote circulars about liberty and passed them out for the common people to read. "If the English people can free themselves, why can't we?" they asked. "If the Americans fought for liberty, why can't we?"[171]

Jean Jacques Rousseau

Perhaps the single most important Enlightenment writer was the philosopher-novelist-composer-music theorist-language theorist-etc. Jean-Jacques Rousseau (1712-1778), who is important not merely for his ideas (which generally recycled older Enlightenment ideas) but for his passionate rhetoric, which enflamed a generation and beyond. The central problem he confronted most of his life he sums up in the first sentence of his most famous work, *The Social Contract* :

"Man is born free but everywhere is in chains."

The central concept in Rousseau's thought is "liberty," and most of his works deal with the mechanisms through which humans are forced to give up their liberty. At the foundation of his thought on government and authority is the idea of the "social contract," in which government and authority are a mutual contract between the authorities and the governed; this contract implies that the governed agree to be ruled only so that their rights, property and happiness be protected by their rulers. Once rulers cease to protect the ruled, the social contract is *broken* and the governed are free to choose another set of governors or magistrates. This idea would become the primary animating force in the *Declaration of Independence,* which is more or less a legal document outlining a breach of contract suit. In fact, all modern liberation discourse at some level or another owes its origin to *The Social Contract* and Rousseau's earlier treatise, *The Discourse on Inequality.*

Written for an essay contest sponsored by the city of Geneva, Switzerland, in 1754 (Rousseau won the contest), *The Discourse on*

Inequality outlines all the key ideas that were to greatly influence modern culture: a) the idea of the noble savage, that is, the happiest state of humankind is a middle state between completely wild and completely civilized; b) the idea of social contract; c) the nature of human distinctions; d) the criticism of property; and e) the nature of human freedom. As you read this essay, you should get a good handle on each of these topics. In particular, you should compare these ideas to their earlier incarnations (such as Luther's idea of "freedom") and keep them in mind as we explore later ideas in modern human cultures.

Rousseau first argued that civilization had corrupted human beings in his essay, *Discourse on the Moral Effects of the Arts and Sciences* in 1750. This corruption was largely a moral corruption; everything that civilized people have regarded as progress—urbanization, technology, science, and so on—has resulted in the moral degradation of humanity. For Rousseau, the natural moral state of human beings is to be compassionate; civilization has made us cruel, selfish, and bloodthirsty. In the *Discourse on Inequality*, Rousseau also argued that civilization has robbed us of our natural freedom. While semi-civilized humanity looked to itself for its values and happiness, civilized human beings live outside themselves in the opinions and authority of others. The price of civilization is human freedom and human individuality:

In reality, the difference is, that the savage lives within himself while social man lives outside himself and can only live in the opinion of others, so that he seems to receive the feeling of his own existence only from the judgement of others concerning him. It is not to my present purpose to insist on the indifference to good and evil which arises from this disposition, in spite of our many fine works on morality, or to show how, everything being reduced to appearances,

Michelle Lynn

there is but art and mummery in even honour, friendship, virtue, and often vice itself, of which we at length learn the secret of boasting; to show, in short, how abject we are, and never daring to ask ourselves in the midst of so much philosophy, benevolence, politeness, and of such sublime codes of morality, we have nothing to show for ourselves but a frivolous and deceitful appearance, honour without virtue, reason without wisdom, and pleasure without happiness.

In 1762, Rousseau published *The Social Contract*, which, though it was largely unread when it first came out, became one of the most influential works of abstract political thought in the Western tradition. In the *Discourse on Inequality*, Rousseau had tried to explain the human invention of government as a kind of contract between the governed and the authorities that governed them. The only reason human beings were willing to give up individual freedom and be ruled by others was that they saw that their rights, happiness, and property would be better protected under a formal government rather than an anarchic, every-person-for-themselves type of society. He argued, though, that this original contract was deeply flawed. The wealthiest and most powerful members of society "tricked" the general population, and so installed inequality as a permanent feature of human society. Rousseau argued, in *The Social Contract*, that this contract between rulers and the ruled should be rethought. Rather than have a government which largely protects the wealth and the rights of the powerful few, government should be fundamentally based on the rights and equality of *everyone*. If any form of government does not properly see to the rights, liberty, and equality of everyone, that government has **broken** the social contract that lies at the heart of political authority. These ideas were essential for both the French and American revolutions; in fact, it is no exaggeration to say that the French and American revolutions are the direct result of Rousseau's abstract theories on the social contract.

It would be incorrect, though, to think of Rousseau as a thorough-going individualist. In fact, Rousseau believed that the social contract, if it were followed on all sides, bound every member of society to obedience to political authority. It was only when political authority *broke* the basic premises of the social contract and individual liberty was replaced by inequality that Rousseau believed that government should be torn down. Rousseau was trying to figure out a way to maximize individual liberty while preserving order, obedience, and harmony in society. He was really the first Enlightenment thinker to articulate the **contractual** basis of rights. Rights, or principles of individual autonomy or liberty, are not magical entitlements that come from heaven into this world the moment you pop out of the womb nor are they inscribed in our DNA. Rights and liberties are social contracts. You have rights and individual liberties *because the rest of* society *agrees that you have those rights and liberties.* If you don't have a right or liberty, then you must convince everyone to give you that right or liberty. For Rousseau, natural human beings are born completely self-sufficient and self-governing; social human beings are dependent and restricted. The rights and liberties that social human beings get are derived ultimately from a general social agreement. This is one reason, by the way, that the American and French revolutions resulted in "contracts" outlining the rights and liberties of the governed.

Rousseau also wrote a novel, *Emile*, which outlined the best way to educate human beings. His goal was to produce an education that maximized human potential rather than restricted it. Both European and American educational ideas were greatly influenced by this work; the American public school system, established in the first part of the nineteenth century, drew heavily from Rousseau's educational ideas.*Richard Hooker* [172]

IN CONGRESS, JULY 4, 1776
The unanimous Declaration of the thirteen united States of America

When in the Course of human events it becomes necessary for one people to dissolve the political bands which have connected them with another and to assume among the powers of the earth, the separate and equal station to which the Laws of Nature and of Nature's God entitle them, a decent respect to the opinions of mankind requires that they should declare the causes which impel them to the separation.

We hold these truths to be self-evident, that all men are created equal, that they are endowed by their Creator with certain unalienable Rights, that among these are Life, Liberty and the pursuit of Happiness.—That to secure these rights, Governments are instituted among Men, deriving their just powers from the consent of the governed,—That whenever any Form of Government becomes destructive of these ends, it is the Right of the People to alter or to abolish it, and to institute new Government, laying its foundation on such principles and organizing its powers in such form, as to them shall seem most likely to effect their Safety and Happiness. Prudence, indeed, will dictate that Governments long established should not be changed for light and transient causes; and accordingly all experience hath shewn that mankind are more disposed to suffer, while evils are sufferable than to right themselves by abolishing the forms to which they are accustomed. But when a long train of abuses and usurpations, pursuing invariably the same Object evinces a design to reduce them under absolute Despotism, it is their right, it is their duty, to throw off such Government, and to provide new Guards for their future security.

—Such has been the patient sufferance of these Colonies; and such is now the necessity which constrains them to alter their former Systems of Government. The history of the present King of Great Britain is a history of repeated injuries and usurpations, all having in direct object the establishment of an absolute Tyranny over these States. To prove this, let Facts be submitted to a candid world.

He has refuted his Assent to Laws, the most wholesome and necessary for the public good.

He has forbidden his Governors to pass Laws of immediate and pressing importance, unless suspended in their operation till his Assent should be obtained; and when so suspended, he has utterly neglected to attend to them.

He has refused to pass other Laws for the accommodation of large districts of people, unless those people would relinquish the right of Representation in the Legislature, a right inestimable to them and formidable to tyrants only.

He has called together legislative bodies at places unusual, uncomfortable, and distant from the depository of their PublicRecords, for the sole purpose of fatiguing them into compliance with his measures.

He has dissolved Representative Houses repeatedly, for opposing with manly firmness his invasions on the rights of the people.

Michelle Lynn

He has refused for a long time, after such dissolutions, to cause others to be elected, whereby the Legislative Powers, incapable of Annihilation, have returned to the People at large for their exercise; the State remaining in the mean time exposed to all the dangers of invasion from without, and convulsions within.

He has endeavoured to prevent the population of these States; for that purpose obstructing the Laws for Naturalization of Foreigners; refusing to pass others to encourage their migrations hither, and raising the conditions of new Appropriations of Lands.

He has obstructed the Administration of Justice by refusing his Assent to Laws for establishing Judiciary Powers.

He has made Judges dependent on his Will alone for the tenure of their offices, and the amount and payment of their salaries.

He has erected a multitude of New Offices, and sent hither swarms of Officers to harass our people and eat out their substance.

He has kept among us, in times of peace, Standing Armies without the Consent of our legislatures.

He has affected to render the Military independent of and superior to the Civil Power.

He has combined with others to subject us to a jurisdiction foreign to our constitution, and unacknowledged by our laws; giving his Assent to their Acts of pretended Legislation:

For quartering large bodies of armed troops among us:

For protecting them, by a mock Trial from punishment for any Murders which they should commit on the Inhabitants of these States:

For cutting off our Trade with all parts of the world:

For imposing Taxes on us without our Consent:

For depriving us in many cases, of the benefit of Trial by Jury:

For transporting us beyond Seas to be tried for pretended offences:

For abolishing the free System of English Laws in a neighbouring Province, establishing therein an Arbitrary government, and enlarging its Boundaries so as to render it at once an example and fit instrument for introducing the same absolute rule into these Colonies

For taking away our Charters, abolishing our most valuable Laws and altering fundamentally the Forms of our Governments:

For suspending our own Legislatures, and declaring themselves invested with power to legislate for us in all cases whatsoever.

He has abdicated Government here, by declaring us out of his Protection and waging War against us.

He has plundered our seas, ravaged our Coasts burnt our towns, and destroyed the lives of our people.

He is at this time transporting large Armies of foreign Mercenaries to compleat the works of death, desolation, and tyranny, already begun with circumstances of Cruelty & Perfidy scarcely paralleled in the most barbarous ages, and totally unworthy the Head of a civilized nation.

He has constrained our fellow Citizens taken Captive on the high Seas to bear Arms against their Country, to become the executioners of their friends and Brethren, or to fall themselves by their Hands.

He has excited domestic insurrections amongst us, and has endeavoured to bring on the inhabitants of our frontiers, the merciless Indian Savages whose known rule of warfare, is an undistinguished destruction of all ages, sexes and conditions.

In every stage of these Oppressions We have Petitioned for Redress in the most humble terms: Our repeated Petitions have been answered only by repeated injury. A Prince, whose character is thus marked by every act which may define a Tyrant, is unfit to be the ruler of a free people.

Nor have We been wanting in attentions to our British brethren. We have warned them from time to time of attempts by their legislature to extend an unwarrantable jurisdiction over us. We have reminded them of the circumstances of our emigration and settlement here. We have appealed to their native justice and magnanimity, and we have conjured them by the ties of our common kindred. to disavow these usurpations, which would inevitably interrupt our connections and correspondence. They too have been deaf to the voice of justice and of consanguinity. We must, therefore, acquiesce in the necessity, which denounces our Separation, and hold them, as we hold the rest of mankind, Enemies in War, in Peace Friends.

We, therefore, the Representatives of the United States of America, in General Congress, Assembled, appealing to the Supreme Judge of the world for the rectitude of our intentions, do, in the Name, and by Authority of the good People of these Colonies, solemnly publish and declare, That these United Colonies are, and of Right ought to be Free and Independent States, that they are Absolved from all Allegiance to the British Crown, and that all political connection between them and the State of Great Britain, is and ought to be totally dissolved; and that as Free and Independent States, they have full Power to levy War, conclude Peace contract Alliances, establish Commerce, and to do all other Acts and Things which Independent States may of right do.—And for the support of this Declaration, with a firm reliance on the protection of Divine Providence, we mutually pledge to each other our Lives, our Fortunes and our sacred Honor.

—John Hancock

New Hampshire:
Josiah Bartlett, William Whipple, Matthew Thornton

Massachusetts:
John Hancock, Samuel Adams, John Adams, Robert Treat Paine, Elbridge Gerry

Rhode Island:

Stephen Hopkins, William Ellery

Michelle Lynn

Connecticut:
Roger Sherman, Samuel Huntington, William Williams, Oliver Wolcott

New York:
William Floyd, Philip Livingston, Francis Lewis, Lewis Morris

New Jersey:
Richard Stockton, John Witherspoon, Francis Hopkinson, John Hart, Abraham Clark

Pennsylvania:
Robert Morris, Benjamin Rush, Benjamin Franklin, John Morton, George Clymer, James Smith, George Taylor, James Wilson, George Ross

Delaware:
Caesar Rodney, George Read, Thomas McKean

Maryland:
Samuel Chase, William Paca, Thomas Stone, Charles Carroll of Carrollton

Virginia:
George Wythe, Richard Henry Lee, Thomas Jefferson, Benjamin Harrison, Thomas Nelson, Jr., Francis Lightfoot Lee, Carter Braxton

North Carolina:
William Hooper, Joseph Hewes, John Penn

South Carolina:

Edward Rutledge, Thomas Heyward, Jr., Thomas Lynch, Jr., Arthur Middleton

Georgia:

Button Gwinnett, Lyman Hall, George Walton[173]

Declaration of the Rights of Man

The representatives of the French people, constituted as a National Assembly, and considering that ignorance, neglect, or contempt of the rights of man are the sole causes of public misfortunes and governmental corruption, have resolved to set forth in a solemn declaration the natural, inalienable and sacred rights of man: so that by being constantly present to all the members of the social body this declaration may always remind them of their rights and duties; so that by being liable at every moment to comparison with the aim of any and all political institutions the acts of the legislative and executive powers may be the more fully respected; and so that by being founded henceforward on simple and incontestable principles the demands of the citizens may always tend toward maintaining the constitution and the general welfare.

In consequence, the National Assembly recognizes and declares, in the presence and under the auspices of the Supreme Being, the following rights of man and the citizen:

1. Men are born and remain free and equal in rights. Social distinctions may be based only on common utility.

2. The purpose of all political association is the preservation of the natural and imprescriptible rights of man. These rights are liberty, property, security, and resistance to oppression.

3. The principle of all sovereignty rests essentially in the nation. No body and no individual may exercise authority which does not emanate expressly from the nation.

4. Liberty consists in the ability to do whatever does not harm another; hence the exercise of the natural rights of each man has no other limits than those which assure to other members of society the enjoyment of the same rights. These limits can only be determined by the law.

5. The law only has the right to prohibit those actions which are injurious to society. No hindrance should be put in the way of anything not prohibited by the law, nor may any one be forced to do what the law does not require.

6. The law is the expression of the general will. All citizens have the right to take part, in person or by their representatives, in its formation. It must be the same for everyone whether it protects or penalizes. All citizens being equal in its eyes are equally admissible to all public dignities, offices, and employments, according to their ability, and with no other distinction than that of their virtues and talents.

7. No man may be indicted, arrested, or detained except in cases determined by the law and according to the forms which it has prescribed. Those who seek, expedite, execute, or cause to be executed arbitrary orders should be punished; but citizens

summoned or seized by virtue of the law should obey instantly, and render themselves guilty by resistance.

8. Only strictly and obviously necessary punishments may be established by the law, and no one may be punished except by virtue of a law established and promulgated before the time of the offense, and legally applied.

9. Every man being presumed innocent until judged guilty, if it is deemed indispensable to arrest him, all rigor unnecessary to securing his person should be severely repressed by the law.

10. No one should be disturbed for his opinions, even in religion, provided that their manifestation does not trouble public order as established by law.

11. The free communication of thoughts and opinions is one of the most precious of the rights of man. Every citizen may therefore speak, write, and print freely, if he accepts his own responsibility for any abuse of this liberty in the cases set by the law.

12. The safeguard of the rights of man and the citizen requires public powers. These powers are therefore instituted for the advantage of all, and not for the private benefit of those to whom they are entrusted.

13. For maintenance of public authority and for expenses of administration, common taxation is indispensable. It should be apportioned equally among all the citizens according to their capacity to pay.

14. All citizens have the right, by themselves or through their representatives, to have demonstrated to them the necessity of public taxes, to consent to them freely, to follow the use made of the proceeds, and to determine the means of apportionment, assessment, and collection, and the duration of them.

15. Society has the right to hold accountable every public agent of the administration.

16. Any society in which the guarantee of rights is not assured or the separation of powers not settled has no constitution.

17. Property being an inviolable and sacred right, no one may be deprived of it except when public necessity, certified by law, obviously requires it, and on the condition of a just compensation in advance.[174]

Daniel 11:38

estate	*stand* - a place or port where one stands: STATION, POSITION
he	*that* - with which: by which: in which
honor	*make weighty* - having much importance or consequence: MOMENTOUS
God	*deity* - a person or thing that is exalted or revered as supremely good or great
forces	*defense* - an argument prepared or advanced to defend an action, policy or thesis :
god	*deity* - one that holds or wields supreme power or influence in some field
whom	*which* - the one who
fathers	*father* - ANCESTOR, FOREFATHER
knew	*know (properly to ascertain by seeing)* - to have perception, cognition, or understanding of especially to an extensive or complete extent
not	*not* - in no way
he	*he, she, it* - the person or thing spoken of
honor	*make weighty* - having much importance or consequence: MOMENTOUS
with	*with* - in consequence of: because of
gold	*gold* - MONEY, RICHES
silver	*silver* - silver money
with	*with* - in consequence of: because of
precious	*valuable* - characterized by usefulness, worth, or serviceableness usually for a specified purpose

Michelle Lynn

stones   **stone** - a concretion of earthy or mineral matter of igneous, sedimentary, or metamorphic origin: a building block

pleasant   to **delight** in - to have or take great satisfaction or pleasure

Daniel 11:39

*Thus shall **he do** in the **most strong holds with** a **strange god, whom** he shall **acknowledge** and **increase with glory:** and **he** shall cause them to **rule** over **many,** and shall **divide** the **land for gain.***

Another revolution was taking place which was to have equally far-reaching effects as the French Revolution. The Industrial Revolution.

New machines, using first water power then steam power, ushered in the modern industrial age. The first of these machines were almost all British. Britain was the pioneering industrial society, blessed at the outset by rich supplies of coal and iron ore . . . One result of the Industrial Revolution was to bring the factory system into being. It made for the concentration of people in towns, since factories, other than textile mills, no longer had to be near streams . . . Towns all over Europe soon became industrial centers for textiles, metal working, coal and steel. Behind all these developments lay money, especially in London, Paris, and Amsterdam. The effect of new inventions was most dramatic in Germany, where a web-like spread of railway lines enabled rich supplies of coal and iron to be exploited, and factories boomed through the use of steam engines. The story of Alfred Krupp of Essen was typical of one aspect of German—and European—industrial growth. What in 1826 was a near-bankrupt household business had become by 1870 a vast private, paternalist empire of steel and bronze and guns, with pension schemes, hotels and stores. In the 60 years between 1850 and 1910 iron production rose 26-fold in Germany—and only trebled in Britain. Germany was now the dominant industrial force in Europe.[175]

The Industrial Revolution

The most far-reaching, influential transformation of human culture since the advent of agriculture eight or ten thousand years ago, was the industrial revolution of eighteenth century Europe. The consequences of this revolution would change irrevocably human labor, consumption, family structure, social structure, and even the very soul and thoughts of the individual. This revolution involved more than technology; to be sure, there had been industrial "revolutions" throughout European history and non-European history. In Europe, for instance, the twelfth and thirteenth centuries saw an explosion of technological knowledge and a consequent change in production and labor. However, the industrial revolution was more than technology—impressive as this technology was. What drove the industrial revolution were profound social changes, as Europe moved from a primarily agricultural and rural economy to a capitalist and urban economy, from a household, family-based economy to an industry-based economy. This required rethinking social obligations and the structure of the family; the abandonment of the family economy, for instance, was the most dramatic change to the structure of the family that Europe had ever undergone—and we're still struggling with these changes.

In 1750, the European economy was overwhelmingly an agricultural economy. The land was owned largely by wealthy and frequently aristocratic landowners; they leased the land to tenant farmers who paid for the land in real goods that they grew or produced. Most non-agricultural goods were produced by individual families that specialized in one set of skills: wagon-wheel manufacture, for instance. Most capitalist activity focused on mercantile activity rather than production; there was, however, a growing manufacturing industry growing up around the logic of mercantilism.

The European economy, though, had become a global economy. In our efforts to try to explain why the Industrial Revolution took place, the globalization of the European economy is a compelling explanation. European trade and manufacture stretched to every continent except Antarctica; this vast increase in the market for European goods in part drove the conversion to an industrial, manufacturing economy. Why other nations didn't initially join this revolution is in part explained by the monopolistic control that the Europeans exerted over the global economy. World trade was about making *Europeans* wealthy, not about enriching the colonies or non-Western countries.

Another reason given for the Industrial Revolution is the substantial increase in the population of Europe; this is such an old chestnut of historians that we don't question it. Population growth, however, is a mysterious affair to explain; it most often occurs when standards of production rise. So whether the Industrial Revolution was started off by a rise in population, or whether the Industrial Revolution started a rise in population is hard to guess.

It's clear, though, that the transition to an industrial, manufacturing economy required more people to labor at this manufacture. While the logic of a national economy founded centrally on the family economy and family production is more or less a subsistence economy—most production is oriented around keeping the family alive, the logic of a manufacturing economy is a surplus economy. In a manufacturing economy, a person's productive labor needs to produce more than they need to keep life going. This surplus production is what produces profits for the owners of the manufacture. This surplus economy not only makes population growth possible, it makes it desirable.

England

While it's hard to pinpoint a beginning to the Industrial Revolution, historians generally agree that it basically originated in England, both in a series of technological and social innovations. Historians propose a number of reasons. Among the most compelling is the exponential increase in food production following the enclosure laws of the eighteenth century; Parliament passed a series of laws that permitted lands that had been held in common by tenant farmers to be enclosed into large, private farms worked by a much smaller labor force. While this drove peasants off the land, it also increased agricultural production *and* increased the urban population of England, since the only place displaced peasants had to go were the cities. The English Parliament, unlike the monarchies of Europe, was firmly under the control of the merchant and capitalist classes, so the eighteenth century saw a veritable army of legislation that favored mercantile and capitalist interests.

Because of the strong role of Parliament in English government and the incredible influence of capitalists and mercantilists, social values had also been steadily shifting in England. In continental Europe, the aristocracy represented the fullest embodiment of social values. They believed that they were born with higher virtues than the common people, who, because of their birth would never attain these virtues to the same level. They also believed that the pursuit of money was a characteristic of common people; the mercantile and capitalist revolutions throughout Europe, in England, was achieved by the non-aristocratic classes—it was a middle-class or **bourgeois** revolution.

The diminished role of the aristocracy in English government and society, however, allowed for a steady shift in values; the values of the mercantile and capitalist classes slowly became the norm—the most important of these values was the pursuit of wealth. Adam Smith's *The Wealth of Nations* proposed that the only legitimate goal of national government and human activity is the steady increase in the overall wealth of the nation. This is not an idea that would have flown two hundred years earlier.

Mercantilism had thrived in England in ways that it hadn't on the continent. In particular, the English had no internal tariffs or duties on commerce, which wasn't true of any of the continental European states. Moving goods around in continental Europe was an expensive affair as you had to pay taxes and duties every hundred miles or so; moving goods around in England was cheap, and profits soared. In addition, England had come to monopolize overseas trade. Every time England fought a war in the eighteenth century it always acquired new overseas territory. It completely monopolized trade with the North American colonies—in fact, one-half of all British exports went to America in the 1780's—but it also began to control the South American and, most importantly, the Indian trade. All this trade produced the largest merchant marine in the world as well as a navy to protect this merchant marine fleet. Like Periclean Athens, England shot to the forefront of the new capitalist economy primarily through its navy.

The technological innovations followed these social and economic changes. The first major technological innovation was the cotton gin. Cotton is a plant grown in America and India; it was a small industrythrough much of the seventeenth century but exploded in the middle of the eighteenth. Most cotton was produced in British colonies; because it was a labor-intensive

Michelle Lynn

agriculture, it fueled the traffic in African slaves to the colonies—the cotton shroud that fell over the history of Africa. The first innovation in cotton manufacture was the fly-shuttle, which greatly speeded up the process of weaving cotton threads into cloth. That wasn't enough, though, for cotton had to be stretched out or spun into threads to begin with; this process was done slowly, one thread at a time, by a machine called a spinning wheel. This slow process was mechanized by James Hargreaves, a carpenter, in what is usually pointed to as one of the typological major technological innovations of the Industrial Age: the "spinning jenny." Patented in 1767, the spinning jenny was a series of simple machines rather than a single machine, and it spun sixteen threads of cotton simultaneously. These two qualities: multiple machines in a single machine as well as a machine that was designed not just to speed up work, but to do the work of several laborers simultaneously, was the hallmark of all subsequent technological innovations. In 1793, the American, Eli Whitney, invented the cotton gin which mechanized the separating of seeds from cotton fibers. These innovations made cotton incredibly cheap and infinitely expandable; since cotton clothing was tougher than wool, the manufacture of cotton clothing shot through the roof. By the end of the eighteenth century, the manufacture of thread and cloth was slowly moving out of the family economy and into large factory mills, though this transition would not be fully realized until the middle of the nineteenth century.

While the spinning jenny is frequently pointed to as the first, major technological innovation of the industrial revolution, the invention that really drove the revolution in the eighteenth century was invented several decades earlier: the steam engine. Along with the growth in the cotton industry, the steel industry began to grow by leaps and bounds.

This was largely due to a quirk in English geography: England sits on vast quantities of coal, a carbon based mineral derived from ancient life forms. Coal burns better and more efficiently than wood and, if you have lots of coal, is infinitely cheaper. The English figured out that they could substitute coal for wood in the melting of metals, including iron, and blissfully went about tearing coal from the ground while manufacturers in Europe looked on jealously.

Mining coal, however, was not an easy task. As you drew more and more coal out of the ground, you had to mine deeper and deeper. The deeper the mine, the more it fills with water. In 1712, Thomas Newcomen built a simple steam engine that pumped water from the mines. It was a single piston engine, and so it used vast amounts of energy. Because of its inefficiency, nobody could think of any use for it besides pumping water.

Until a Scotsman named James Watt added a separate cooling chamber to the machine in 1763; this cooling chamber condensed the steam so the cylinder itself didn't have to be cooled. Patented in 1769, Watt's steam engine had the efficiency to be applied to all kinds of industries. He was not, however, good at doing busines and it was only when he had teamed up with the businessman, Matthew Boulton, that the steam engine began to change the face of English manufacture. By 1800, Watt and Boulton sold 289 of these new engines; by the middle of the next century, the steam engine replaced water as the major source of motive power in England and Europe. The changes that the steam engine wrought, however, is a story for another day.

And it is here, with 289 steam engines pumping and steaming around England that we'll leave the story of the Industrial Revolution— half-completed, you might say. The nineteenth century saw the exporting of the Industrial Revolution to Europe in the decades after 1830, and the explosion of factory-based, technology driven manufacture. The Age of Absolutism and the waning years of the Enlightenment saw Europe just beginning a new phase in its history, one that would irreperably severe it from the traditions and certainties of the past. *Richard Hooker ©1996,*[176]

DANIEL 11:39

he	**he, she, it** - the person or thing spoken of
do	**make** - cause to exist, appear, or occur
most	**a fortified** (*past of* **fortify**) *place* - to add material to for the strong purpose of studying or improving
holds	**fortification** - increase in the content of an ingredient by addition: ENRICHMENT
with	**with** - by means of
strange	**foreign** - not native or domestic
god	**deity** - one that holds or wields supreme power or influence in some field
whom	**who** - what one or ones out of a group
he	**he, she, it** - the person or thing spoken of
acknowledge	**acknowledge** - recognize, honor, or respect especially publicly: to take notice of: indicate recognition and acceptance of
increase	**increase** - to become great in some respect (as in size, quantity, number, degree, value, intensity, power, authority, reputation, wealth): GROW, ADVANCE, WAX
with	**with** - used as a function word to indicate accompaniment or companionship
glory	**weight** - the relatively great importance or authority accorded something: measurable influence in determining the acts of others
he	**same** - something that has previously been defined or described

Michelle Lynn

rule	*rule* - to control, direct, or influence the mind, character, or actions of: to exercise authority or power over
many	*abundant* - occurring or existing in great quantity
divide	*apportion* - to divide and share out according to a plan; *especially*: to make a proportionate division or distribution of
land	*soil* - firm land: EARTH, COUNTRY, LAND
for	*causal* - expressing or indicating cause: marked by cause and effect
gain	*wages* - RECOMPENSE, REQUITAL, REWARD

DANIEL 11:40

*And at the **time** of the **end** shall the **king** of the **south push***
*at him: and the **king** of the **north** shall **come against** him*
*like a **whirlwind, with chariots,** and **with horsemen,** and*
***with many ships;** and **he** shall **enter** into the **countries,** and*
*shall **overflow** and **pass** over.*

World War I. The continued growth of nationalism early in the 20th century led to the most devastating war ever fought up to that point. Stimulated by the rise of nationalism, pan-Slavism grew with the awakening of the Slavs within the Austrian and Ottoman Empires. Slavs wanted to for a single unified Slavic nation, Yugoslavia. That desire would set off the war.[177] A Bosnian-Serb, Gavrillo Princip, assassinated Archduke Francis Ferdinand on June 28,1914. This sets off the war. Austria-Hungary, backed by Germany, declared war on Serbia.

The fading Ottoman Empire allied with Germany, Austria-Hungary, and Bulgaria, which became known as the Central Powers, so fighting spread to the Middle East. France, Britain, Russia, Serbia, Belgium, and later Japan became the Allied Powers.[178]

Mechanized warfare, employment of modern mobile attack and defense tactics that depend upon vehicles powered by gasoline and diesel engines. Automobiles were of great use in WWI.[179] The tank together with the airplane, opened up modern warfare, which had been immobilized and stalemated by the use of rifled guns.[180]

This was a new kind of war, one so destructive and widespread that it was known as the Great War and "the war to end all wars." Later it became known as the World War I because of the many countries it involved and the wide area over which it raged.[181]

Michelle Lynn

World War I

(1914-18)

International conflict between the Central Powers—Germany, Austria-Hungary, and Turkey—and the Allied Powers—mainly France, Britain, Russia, Italy, Japan, and (from 1917) the U.S. or *First World War* After a Serbian nationalist assassinated Archduke Francis Ferdinand of Austria in June 1914, a chain of threats and mobilizations resulted in a general war between the antagonists by mid-August. Prepared to fight a war on two fronts, based on the Schlieffen Plan, Germany first swept through neutral Belgium and invaded France. After the First Battle of the Marne (1914), the Allied defensive lines were stabilized in France, and a war of attrition began. Fought from lines of trenches and supported by modern artillery and machine guns, infantry assaults gained little ground and were enormously costly in human life, especially at the Battles of Verdun and the Somme (1916). On the Eastern Front, Russian forces initially drove deep into East Prussia and German Poland (1914) but were stopped by German and Austrian forces at the Battle of Tannenberg and forced back into Russia (1915). After several offensives, the Russian army failed to break through the German defensive lines. Russia's poor performance and enormous losses caused widespread domestic discontent that led to the Russian Revolution of 1917. Other fronts in the war included the Dardanelles Campaign, in which British and Dominion forces were unsuccessful against Turkey; the Caucasus and Iran (Persia), where Russia fought Turkey; Mesopotamia and Egypt, where British forces fought the Turks; and northern Italy, where Italian and Austrian troops fought the costly Battles of the Isonzo. At sea, the German and British fleets fought the inconclusive Battle of Jutland, and Germany's use of the submarine against neutral shipping eventually brought the U.S. into the war in 1917. Though Russia's armistice with Germany in December 1917 released German troops to fight on the Western Front, the Allies were reinforced by U.S. troops in early 1918. Germany's unsuccessful offensive in the Second Battle of the Marne was countered by the Allies' steady advance, which recovered most of France and Belgium by October 1918 and led to the November Armistice. Total casualties were estimated at 10 million dead, 21 million wounded, and 7.7 million missing or imprisoned. [182]

DANIEL 11:40

time	*time* - a point or period when something occurs
end	*extremity* - a culminating point (as of emotion or pain): HEIGHT, APEX, CLIMAX
king	*king* - one that holds a supreme or preeminent position in a particular sphere or class
south	*south* - regions or countries lying to the south of a specified or implied point of orientation
push	*war* - a state of usually open and declared armed hostile conflict between political units (as states or nations)
king	*king* - one that holds a supreme or preeminent position in a particular sphere or class
north	*north* - regions or countries lying to the north of a specified or implied point of orientation
come	*storm* - to blow with violence
against	*over* - indicating a relation of superiority, advantage, or preference to another
whirlwind	*shiver* - to undergo trembling (as from cold, fear, or the application of physical force)
with	*with* - by means of
chariots	*vehicle* - a means of carrying or transporting something: CONVEYANCE
with	*with* - used as a function word to indicate accompaniment or companionship
horsemen	*driver* - one that drives something: as: a person in actual physical control of a vehicle (as an automobile)
with	*with* - by means of
many	*abundant* - AMPLE, PLENTIOUS, COPIOUS

ships   *ship* - any large vessel

he   *he, she, it* - the person or thing spoken of

enter   *go* - to move on a course

countries *land* - REALM, DOMAIN

overflow   *gush* - to give free reign to a sudden copious flow or
                   issuing forth

pass   *cover* - spread over: ENVELOP, FILM, COAT

DANIEL 11:41

He shall **enter** *also into the* **glorious land,** *and* **many** *countries shall* **be overthrown:** *but* **these** *shall* **escape out** *of his* **hand,** *even* **Edom,** *and* **Moab,** *and the* **chief** *of the* **children** *of* **Ammon.**

The collapse of Russia, which withdrew (from the war) after the Bolshevik Revolution, put extra pressure on the Allied Powers. They were aided in 1917 when the United States came into the war, irritated by the loss of American lives in the sinking of passenger ships by Germany and alarmed at news of a secret agreement between Germany and Mexico. Over the next two years the injection of U.S. troops and war material helped turn the tide in Europe. In the Middle East the British and Arabs defeated the Turks. Austria-Hungary and Turkey surrendered . . . and on November 11, 1918, Germany signed an armistice.[183]

As a result of WWI many countries were adversely affected. Austria was reduced in size, Hungary lost territories, and the Ottoman Empire came to an end, thus starting modern Turkey's history.

To calculate the total losses caused by the war is impossible. About 10 million dead (two million of those being German) and 20 million wounded is a conservative estimate. Starvation and epidemics raised the total in the immediate postwar years.[184]

In biblical times, the area that Jordan covers today contained the Semitic kingdoms of Moab, Edom, Ammon, and Gilead. Jordan was dominated by the Ottoman Turks for four centuries (1516-1918).[185]

In 1922, Britain mandated the land east of the Jordan to the peoples east of the Jordan. This land became the independent Emirate of Transjordan ("beyond the Jordan"), under the rule of Emir Abdullah ibn Hussein. Hussein was a member of the Hashemite family, which claims descent from Muhammad.[186]

Jordan

Country, Middle East, lying east of the Jordan River. *officially Hashemite Kingdom of Jordan* It is bordered by Syria, Iraq, Saudi Arabia, Israel, and the West Bank territory. Jordan has 12 miles (19 km) of coastline on the Gulf of Aqaba. Area: 34,495 sq mi (89,342 sq km). Population (2002 est.): 5,260,000. Capital: Amman. The vast majority of the population are Arabs, about two-thirds of whom are Palestinian Arabs who fled to Jordan from Israel and the West Bank as a result of the Arab-Israeli wars. Language: Arabic (official). Religion: Islam (official), with more than nine-tenths of the population Sunnite. Currency: Jordan dinar. Four-fifths of Jordan is occupied by desert, and less than one-tenth of the land is arable. The highest point of elevation, Mount Ramm (5,755 ft [1,754 m]), rises in the uplands region on the east bank of the Jordan River. The Jordan Valley region contains the Dead Sea. Jordan's economy is based largely on manufacturing and services (including tourism); exports include phosphate, potash, pharmaceuticals, fruits and vegetables, and fertilizers. Jordan is a constitutional monarchy with two legislative houses; the head of state and government is the king, assisted by the prime minister. Jordan shares much of its history with Israel, since both occupy parts of the area known historically as Palestine. Much of present-day Jordan was once part of the kingdom of Israel under David and Solomon (*c.* 1000 BC). It fell to the Seleucids in 330 BC and to Muslim Arabs in the 7th century AD. The Crusaders extended the kingdom of Jerusalem east of the Jordan River in 1099. The region became part of the Ottoman Empire during the 16th century. In 1920 the area comprising Jordan (then known as Transjordan) was established within the British mandate of Palestine. Transjordan became an independent state in 1927, although the British mandate did not end until 1948. After hostilities with the new State of Israel ceased in 1949, Jordan annexed the West Bank and east Jerusalem, administering the territory until Israel gained control of them in the Six-Day War of 1967. In 1970-71 Jordan was wracked by fighting between the government and guerrillas of the Palestine Liberation Organization (PLO), a struggle that ended in the expulsion of the PLO from Jordan. In 1988 King Hussein renounced all Jordanian claims to the West Bank in favour of the PLO. In 1994 Jordan and Israel signed a full peace agreement.[187]

Michelle Lynn

he   *he, she, it* - the person or thing spoken of

enter   *go* - to reach a certain point: ATTAIN, EXTEND

               come - to arrive at a particular place, end, result, or conclusion

glorious   *splendor* - MAGNIFICENCE, POMP, GLORY, BEAUTY, EXCELLENCE, VALUE, WORTH

               conspicuous - obvious to the eye or mind: plainly visible: MANIFEST: attracting or tending to attract attention by reason of size, brilliance, contrast, station: STRIKING, EMINENT

land   *land* - REALM, DOMAIN

many   *abundant* - occurring or existing in great quantity

countries   *land* - REALM, DOMAIN

be   *be* - to exist under conditions specified

overthrown   *falter* - WEAKEN, DECLINE, FAIL

these   *these* - these

escape   *release* - to loosen or remove the force or effect of: ALLEVIATE: set free from restraint, confinement or servitude

out   *out of* - used as a function word to indicate movement or direction away from the center

hand   *hand* - personal possession

Edom   *Edom {Edomite}* - a member of an ancient people who were descended from Esau and who lived southeast of the Dead Sea

Moab   *Moab {Moabite}* - a member of a people living in Old Testament times east of the Dead

Sea, north of the Edomites, and at one period, south of the Ammonites

chief   *first* - CHIEF

children   *nation* - a community of people composed of one or more nationalities and possessing a more or less defined territory and government

Ammon   *Ammon* - a member of a people who in Old Testament times lived east of the Jordan between the Jabbok and the Arnon

Michelle Lynn

DANIEL 11:42

He shall *stretch* forth his *hand* also *upon* the *countries:*
and the *land* of *Egypt* shall *not escape.*

With its vast economic resources intact (after the war), the
United States was able to aid Europe's recovery. Huge loans from
the financiers of Wall Street emphasized Europe's dependence
on the New World. One thought united the Western world in the
immediate post-war period—that the war of 1914—18 had been the
'war to end all wars'. International institutions based on good will,
such as the League of Nations, would ensure that no generation
would ever have to fight again.[188]

The 'West' set mandates (*mandate—an order or commission
granted by the League of Nations to a member nation for the
establishment of a responsible government over a former German
colony or other conquered territory*) and wielded its power over less
powerful states in order to promote peace.

Egypt, which had been under British control, was declared
independent in 1922, as a result of increasing nationalist demands. A
Western-type constitution was proclaimed, with a parliament, and
the country became a kingdom under Faud I. But British troops still
occupied the country (and controlled most of the economic life and
the canal), and Britain refused to consider Egyptian claims to the
Anglo-Egyptian Sudan.[189]

British Occupation Period

The British occupation had no physical changes on Cairo since the British had been ruling Egypt indirectly for years. Tawfik remained the khedive, the consular courts dealt justice, the administration was foreign and the British occupied the Citadel. They did need foreigners to help rule Cairo simply because they did not want the commerce in Cairo to be controlled by the Egyptians. However, it was very important that the city be organized by dependable people that were not Egyptian.

Lord Cromer was the man responsible for the consolidation of the absolute rule in Cairo. He became the British Agent in Egypt in 1883 and ruled Egypt for 24 years. Before this, he had been in control of the Public Debt in Cairo as British Commissioner. He was responsible for the manipulation that helped the British occupation of Egypt. He was also responsible for keeping the French, Belgians and Italians away from the Nile. Under Cromer, Cairo was a very political and social city.

Cromer left Cairo in 1907 and left control of the city to Sir Eldon Gorst. Cairo began to change its appearance after the English arrived. By the year 1900 there were four tramways in Cairo and a fifth was being built to run from Giza to the pyramids. Trains had been built that ran from Helwan and Tura. English department stores and shopping districts had been set up.

After Gorst, Lord Kitchener became resident minister of Egypt and set up a legislative assembly in Cairo. This was the beginning of the parliamentary life of Egypt, which was an imitation of England. The British resident minister was similar to the prime minister in

England. Each minister was always afraid that somehow the Egyptian people might discover that there might be another way to rule itself other than the English parliament way. During World War I the people did finally recognize this from the political events that resulted from the war.

The war brought many Australian, British, New Zealand and colonial troops to Cairo. In Arabia, the Arabs revolted against the Turks in a fight for national liberation. This soon became a policy that all Egyptians could agree on. European Cairo was a madhouse because of the British and their self-indulgences. However, Egyptian Cairo became a place of politics, preparation and whispers. The prices began to rise steeply in Cairo while the British soldiers were enjoying things that they had never had before. The people in the countryside began to suffer greatly from poverty and malnutrition. It was so bad that during the year 1918 more people died than were born.

In the city itself, some things were more prosperous. The Australians that came in 1914 spent a great deal of money each day in Cairo. Eventually the soldiers began to have too much fun and were thinking more of fun than of the job they had been sent to do. The citizens of Cairo watched the soldiers and began to want more and more an independent country.

In 1916 martial law was introduced in Cairo. Military courts judged civilians and had them punished. England began to treat Egypt more like a country that was the enemy instead of a friend. In 1917, the British began to encourage the kidnapping of peasants to serve in their labor groups in Palestine. Thousands of fellahin were sent to Syria, Mesopotamia and to France.

After the war, U.S. President Wilson's Fourteen Points gave Egypt a hope of independence. Saad Zaghlul went to the British Residency and demanded the Egypt be given the right to self-determination. He was allowed to speak and leave, but was arrested a month later and sent to Malta. Egypt revolted on the news of this. Overnight Cairo became a revolutionary city as every town and city was seized by Egyptians. Everything stopped. Trains and trams stopped, no one went to work and strikes began. Eight British soldiers were killed on March 18, 1919 while on their way to Cairo. Trenches were dug and the city was barricaded. Many people were killed either in the fighting or executed for killing British officers.

The resident minister was replaced by General Allenby and he immediately had Zaghlul released from Malta. Allenby was criticized for years for this as being too compromising, but this probably saved Egypt for Britain more than anything else. He declared martial law and stopped the strikes one by one. Zaghlul had been released from Malta, but was not allowed to come to Egypt yet. He went to Paris where he tried to get someone to help him get Egypt's independence. On April 20, 1919 the United States recognized the British protection of Egypt. This all but ended the hope the Egyptians had of being free.

After the war, cotton returned to the world market. Food crops were replaced by cotton and fortunes were made. However, no food was grown and people were starving. The politics between the British and the Egyptians were getting worse. In 1922 Egypt was allowed sovereignty and Fuad became king. In the next 18 months, seventeen British officials were killed and twenty more were attacked in broad daylight. In 1936 the Anglo-Egyptian treaty was signed which gave Egypt a little bit of independence although superficially. In 1937, the Tribunaux Mixtes, which were the foreign courts, were done away with. The Egyptians still were not satisfied. The British were still in occupation, controlled most of the economic life and still controlled the canal. The reason that the British would not give up its hold completely was the cotton, the land and the link to India.

The British did very little to improve the way of life for the Egyptian people. They never drilled an artesian well that could pump pure water to a village or set up medical services for Egyptians. They didn't even try to educate or improve the conditions of the majority of the population. They weren't brutal occupiers, but they failed miserably at making the conditions livable to the citizens of Egypt. The Europeans that were born in Cairo were not directly to blame for the situation, but they did contribute to it. They lived, ate and slept well and they thought this was all that was expected of them. [190]

DANIEL 11:42

he	**he, she, it** - the person or thing spoken of
stretch	**to send** out - ISSUE: **issue** - to go out or come out or flow out
hand	**power** - a position of ascendancy: ability to compel obedience
upon	**above** - higher or superior in rank, position, or power
countries	**land** - REALM, DOMAIN
land	**land** - REALM, DOMAIN
Egypt	**Mitsrajim** - Egypt
not	**not** - in no way
escape	**deliverance** - the act of freeing or state of being freed (as from restraint, captivity, peril): RESCUE, LIBERATION, RELEASE

Michelle Lynn

DANIEL 11:43

But *he* shall have **power** over the **treasures** of **gold** and of **silver,** and over **all** the **precious** things of **Egypt:** and the **Libyans** and the **Ethiopians** shall **be** at his **steps.**

An agreement in 1936 (the Anglo-Egyptian treaty) ended the military occupation but gave Britain the right to garrison the canal zone (Suez Canal). In 1875 Britain had gained a controlling interest in its stock. Britain considered the canal vital to the maintenance of maritime power and colonial interests. This is why Britain didn't want to relinquish control of the canal. Even today, the Suez Canal is an important trade route, and trade means commerce, and commerce means money.

Libya also had to endure Western occupation. In 1931 the Italians were able to occupy the whole of Libya.[191]

Some 3000 years ago, Egypt established outposts in Sudan, from which grew the kingdom of Kush. In AD 350, the Ethiopian kingdom of Axum overthrew Kush.[192] This leaves us with the nation of Sudan as the actual descendent of the Kushite kingdom. Britain and Egypt governed the Sudan jointly both before and after the Second World War.[193]

The modern Suez Canal

At the end of the 18th century, <u>Napoleon Bonaparte</u>, while in Egypt, contemplated the construction of a canal to join the Mediterranean and Red Seas. His project was abandoned, however, after a French survey erroneously concluded that the waters of the Red Sea were higher than those of the Mediterranean, making a lockless canal impossible.

In 1854 and 1856 <u>Ferdinand de Lesseps</u> obtained concessions from <u>Said Pasha</u>, the viceroy of Egypt, whom de Lesseps had as a French diplomat come to know in the 1830s. Said Pasha authorized the creation of a company for the purpose of constructing a maritime canal open to ships of all nations according to plans created by <u>Austrian</u> engineer <u>Alois Negrelli</u>. By way of a lease of the relevant land, the company was to operate the canal for 99 years from its opening to navigation. The Suez Canal Company (<u>*Compagnie Universelle du Canal Maritime de Suez*</u>) came into being on <u>December 15, 1858</u>.

The excavation operations took nearly eleven years to accomplish, mostly through the forced labor of poor Egyptians. Involuntary labor ceased on the project, however, after the Viceroy conceded to strong anti-slavery sentiment and condemnation by the British government that reached a climax during the <u>American Civil War</u>. (It should be noted that the British had an ulterior motive, as the canal was an important trade route.) Although numerous technical, political, and financial problems were overcome, the final cost was more than double the original estimate. The canal opened to traffic on <u>November 17, 1869</u>.

Michelle Lynn

The canal had an immediate and dramatic effect on world trade. Combined with the completion of the American Transcontinental Railroad six months earlier, the entire world could be circled in record time. It played an important role in increasing European penetration and colonization of Africa. External debts forced Said Pasha's successor, Isma'il Pasha, to sell his country's share in the canal to the United Kingdom in 1875. The Convention of Constantinople in 1888 declared the canal a neutral zone under the protection of the British, after British troops had moved in to protect it while they newly settled on civil war torn Egypt in 1882. Under the Anglo-Egyptian Treaty of 1936, the United Kingdom insisted on retaining control over the canal.[194]

Libya
North Africa

officially Socialist People's Libyan Arab Jamāhīriyyah Area: 678,400 sq mi (1,757,000 sq km). Population (2002 est.): 5,368,000. Capital: Tripoli. Berbers, once the major ethnic group, have been largely assimilated into the Arab culture. Italians, Greeks, Jews, and sub-Saharan Africans are among the other ethnic groups. Languages: Arabic (official), Hamitic (Berber). Religions: Islam (official), small percentage Christianity. Currency: dinar. All but two tiny fractions of Libya are covered by the Sahara: Tripolitania in the northwest and Cyrenaica in the northeast. Tripolitania is Libya's most important agricultural region and its most populated area. The production and export of petroleum are the basis of Libya's economy; other resources include natural gas, manganese, and gypsum. Livestock raising, including sheep and goats, is important in the north. Libya is a socialist state with one policy-making body; the head of governmentis the prime minister, but Muammar al-Qaddafi has been the de facto head of state and real power in Libya since 1970. The early history is that of Fezzan, Cyrenaica, and Tripolitania, which the Ottoman Empire combined under one regency in Tripoli in the 16th century. In 1911 Italy claimed control of Libya, and by the outbreak of World War II (1939-45) 150,000 Italians had immigrated there. The scene of much fighting in the war, it became an independent state in 1951 and a member of the Arab League in 1953. The discovery of oil in 1959 brought wealth to Libya. A decade later a group of army officers led by al-Qaddafi deposed the king and made the country an Islamic republic. Under al-Qaddafi, Libya supported the Palestinian Liberation Organization (PLO) and allegedly provided aid for international terrorist groups. Intermittent warfare with Chad that began in the 1970s ended with Libya's defeat in 1987. International relations in the 1990s were dominated by the consequences of a U.S. trade embargo (endorsed by the UN) that was imposed on Libya for its purported connection to terrorism.[195]

The Sudan

officially Republic of the Sudan Area: 966,757 sq mi (2,503,890 sq km). Population (2002 est.): 37,090,000. Capital: Khartoum. Muslim Arab ethnic groups live in the northern and central two-thirds of the country, while Dinka, Nuer, and Zande peoples live in the south. Languages: Arabic (official), Beja, Zande, Dinka. Religions: Islam (official), traditional religions, Christianity. Currency: Sudanese dinar. The largest country in Africa, The Sudan encompasses an immense plain with the Sahara Desert in the north, sand dunes in the west, semiarid shrub lands in the south-central belt, and enormous swamps and tropical rainforests in the south. The Nile River flows the entire length of the country. Wildlife includes lions, leopards, elephants, giraffes, and zebras.

Michelle Lynn

It has a developing mixed economy based largely on agriculture. One of the largest irrigation projects in the world provides water to farms between the White and the Blue Nile. Chief cash crops are cotton, peanuts, and sesame; livestock is also important. Major industries include food processing and cotton ginning. The country is ruled by an Islamic military regime. Evidence of inhabitation dates back tens of thousands of years. From the end of the 4th millennium BC, Nubia (now northern Sudan) periodically came under Egyptian rule, and it was part of the kingdom of Cush from the 11th century BC to the 4th century AD. Christian missionaries converted the Sudan's three principal kingdoms during the 6th century AD; these black Christian kingdoms coexisted with their Muslim Arab neighbours in Egypt for centuries, until the influx of Arab immigrants brought about their collapse in the 13th-15th centuries. Egypt had conquered all of the Sudan by 1874 and encouraged British interference in the region; this aroused Muslim opposition and led to the revolt of al-Mahdī, who captured Khartoum in 1885 and established a Muslim theocracy in the Sudan that lasted until 1898, when his forces were defeated by the British. The British ruled, generally in partnership with Egypt, until the region achieved independence as The Sudan in 1956. Since then the country has fluctuated between ineffective parliamentary government and unstable military rule. The non-Muslim population of the south has engaged in ongoing rebellion against the Muslim-controlled government of the north, leading to famines and the displacement of some four million people.[196]

Daniel 11:43

he	*he, she, it* - the person or thing spoken of
power	*rule* - to exercise authority or power over: GOVERN
treasures	*treasure* - wealth of any kind or in any form: RICHES
gold	properly something *carved* out - to cut or hew out
silver	*money* - a measure of value or a means of payment
all	*all* - that is the whole amount or quantity of
precious	to *delight* in - to have or take great satisfaction or pleasure
Egypt	*Mitsrajim*—Egypt
Libyans	*Libyans* - a member of any of the peoples indigenous in historical ancient times to the regions immediately west of Egypt
Ethiopians	*Cushite* - a native or inhabitant of ancient Cush {Cush, an ancient country in the Nile valley adjoining Egypt}
be	*be* - exist under conditions specified
steps	*step* - pace with or as if with another

Michelle Lynn

DANIEL 11:44

*But **tidings out** of the **east** and **out** of the **north** shall **trouble***
*him: therefore **he** shall **go forth with great fury to destroy,***
*and utterly to make **away many.***

The Treaty of Versailles, which concluded World War I, demanded that Germany accept blame for the war and pay huge reparations to the Allies for the damage it had caused. The German economy collapsed, and its people were angry and dispirited, looking for a savior. Then the racist, anti-Semitic orator, Adolf Hitler, promised a way out of economic decline. He built a powerful military force, all the time assuring countries such as Britain and the United States that he meant them no harm. In Italy Benito Mussolini was building a dictatorial regime that also reveled in military power. Japan, now highly industrialized and dominated by military adventurists, sought more territory for the raw materials it needed. Eventually Germany, Italy, and Japan united as the Axis Powers.[197]

By mid-1940 Hitler had occupied France, Denmark, Norway, Belgium, the Netherlands, and Luxembourg and had driven Britain's troops off the European mainland. The next year, Yugoslavia and Greece would fall as well . . . The Japanese attacked the U.S. fleet at Pearl Harbor in Honolulu, Hawaii. The U.S entered the war, allied with Britain and the USSR[198]

Ever since a British scientist, Ernest Rutherford, had split the atom in 1919, many European scientists had been looking into the structure of atoms and speculating on their potential for creating energy . . . It took five years for scientists to realize that the neutrons were actually splitting a uranium-235 nucleus in two, releasing four times as much radioactive energy as had existed in the single nucleus. As the nucleus split, it released more neutrons, which split more atoms, releasing more neutrons, and on and on in a chain reaction known as fission . . . In December 1942, with WWII well under way, teams of scientists working with Enrico Fermi in Chicago successfully began a nuclear reaction that created heat before they stopped it. The next step was to allow it to continue, creating an atomic explosion. The atomic bomb itself was produced amid high secrecy at Los Alamos, New Mexico . . . the bomb was dropped on Hiroshima. So powerful was it that it created a huge fireball 250 yards in diameter. At least 100,000 people were killed either outright by the blast or by the firestorm that followed it.[199] Broadly speaking, it destroyed the whole city and all living things therein. A similar result followed from the dropping of a second, differently designed atom bomb on Nagasaki three days later.[200]

World War II

... also known as the Second World War, was a large scale military conflict that took place between 1939 and 1945. It engulfed much of the globe and is accepted as the largest and deadliest war in human history. The war was initially fought between Germany and the Allies, at first consisting of the United Kingdom (with the British Empire), France (with the French Empire) and Poland. Germany was later joined by Italy, jointly known as the Axis Powers, and Japan. Some of the nations that Germany conquered also sent military forces, particularly to the Eastern front, while others joined the Allies. The Soviet Union had signed a non-aggression treaty with Germany, but 22 June 1941 Germany invaded the Soviet Union, pulling that country into the war as well. In the same year, 7 December 1941 the United States of America entered the war on the Allies' side after first Japan and then Germany attacked and declared war on the US. China, which had been engaged in war with Japan since the mid-1930s, also entered the Allies camp. The war ended in 1945 with the unconditional surrenders of both Germany and Japan.

Approximately 62 million people died as a result of the war, almost half of which were Russians (at the decisive Eastern Front). This figure includes acts of genocide such as the Holocaust and General Ishii Shiro's Unit 731 experiments in Pingfan, incredibly bloody battles in Europe, North Africa and the Pacific Ocean, and massive bombings of cities, including the atomic bombings of Hiroshima and Nagasaki in Japan, the firebombing of Dresden and Pforzheim in Germany and the blitz on British cities such as Coventry and London. Few areas of the world were unaffected; the war involved the "home front" and bombing of civilians to a greater degree than any previous conflict. Atomic weapons, jet aircraft, rockets and radar, the *blitzkrieg* (or *"lightning war"*), the massive use of tanks, submarines, torpedo bombers and destroyer/tanker formations, are only a few of many wartime inventions and new tactics that changed the face of conflict. It was the first time that a number of newly developed technologies, including nuclear weapons, were used against either military or civilian targets. It is estimated to have cost about 1 trillion US dollars in 1945 (adjusted for inflation; roughly 10.5 trillion in 2005), not including subsequent reconstruction. The vast outcomes of the war, including new technology and changes to the world's geopolitical, cultural and economic arrangement, were unprecedented in human history.[201]

DANIEL 11:44

tidings	*heard* - to be informed of or gain knowledge of by hearing
out	*from* - used as a function word to indicate the source or original or moving force of something
east	*sunrise* - the apparent rising of the sun above the horizon *east* - the general direction of sunrise
north	*north* - regions or countries lying to the north of a specified or implied point of orientation
trouble	*make alarmed* {*alarm*} - a call to arms (as on the approach of an enemy)
he	*he, she, it* - the person or thing spoken of
go	*go out* - ATTAIN, EXTEND
with	*with* - by means of: by the use or agency of
great	*great* - considerable or remarkable in magnitude, power, intensity, degree, or effectiveness
fury	*heat* - the energy associated with the random motions of the molecules, atoms, or smaller structural units of which matter is composed
destroy	*desolate* - DEPOPULATE: to lay waste: RAVAGE: to leave in a ruinous or barren state
away	*seclude* - to exclude or debar from a privilege, rank, or dignity: expel or bat from a membership or office
many	*abundant* - occurring or existing in great quantity

Daniel 11:45

> And **he** shall **plant** the **tabernacles** of his **palace between**
> the **seas** in the **glorious holy mountain;** yet **he** shall **come**
> to his **end, and none** shall **help** him.

The United States emerged from the Second World War as the unquestioned leader of the Western world.[202] She has grown during the present (last) century into the world's richest and most powerful nation. America's wealth is a magnet to the world, much of which remains poor and backward. Emergent countries wish to learn the secret of Americas 'know-how'.[203]

America is located between the Atlantic Ocean and the Pacific Ocean, and is possessed of several mountain ranges. The Puritans believed devoutly that this country, and they in particular, were the beneficiaries of God's special favor. Novelist Herman Melville believed that "we Americans are the peculiar chosen people, the Israel of our time; we bear the ark of liberties of the world".[204] From earliest times religion has offered strength and solace to Americans of many faiths. It has also been a factor in shaping the Nation's history.[205]

Closely read the definitions for **come, extremity, non-entity, surround.** New material expectations were developed by the spread of affluence and the impact of American-style advertising. More and more people came to regard as necessities of life objects, which before the war had been thought of as luxuries.

To the motorcar, refrigerator, vacuum-cleaner and washing-machine were added the products of a new technology-such as tape recorders and transistor radios. By the mid-50s, television was no longer a novelty.[206] (This reference was written in the

1970s—our technology has far surpassed tape recorders and transistor radios).

Man has set foot on the moon. We are fast reaching the furthest extent of our capabilities and at the same time we are surrounded by things that are not necessary for life or significant in the final end of things—in fact these "things" are now an integral part of our world.

America The Beautiful

Here is a note from Katharine Lee Bates:

"One day some of the other teachers and I decided to go on a trip to 14,000-foot Pikes Peak. We hired a prairie wagon. Near the top we had to leave the wagon and go the rest of the way on mules. I was very tired. But when I saw the view, I felt great joy. All the wonder of America seemed displayed there, with the sea-like expanse."

America the Beautiful—1913

O beautiful for spacious skies,
For amber waves of grain,
For purple mountain majesties
Above the fruited plain!
America! America!
God shed his grace on thee
And crown thy good with brotherhood
From sea to shining sea!

O beautiful for pilgrim feet
Whose stern, impassioned stress
A thoroughfare for freedom beat
Across the wilderness!
America! America!
God mend thine every flaw,
Confirm thy soul in self-control,
Thy liberty in law!

O beautiful for heroes proved In liberating strife.
Who more than self the country loved
And mercy more than life!
America! America!
May God thy gold refine
Till all success be nobleness
And every gain divine!

O beautiful for patriot dream
That sees beyond the years
Thine alabaster cities gleam
Undimmed by human tears!
America! America!
God shed his grace on thee
And crown thy good with brotherhood
From sea to shining sea!

O beautiful for halcyon skies,
For amber waves of grain,
For purple mountain majesties
Above the enameled plain!
America! America!
God shed his grace on thee
Till souls wax fair as earth and air
And music-hearted sea!

O beautiful for pilgrims feet,
Whose stern impassioned stress
A thoroughfare for freedom beat
Across the wilderness!

America ! America !
God shed his grace on thee
Till paths be wrought through
wilds of thought
By pilgrim foot and knee!

O beautiful for glory-tale
Of liberating strife
When once and twice,
for man's avail
Men lavished precious life !
America! America!
God shed his grace on thee
Till selfish gain no longer stain
The banner of the free!

O beautiful for patriot dream
That sees beyond the years
Thine alabaster cities gleam
Undimmed by human tears!
America! America!
God shed his grace on thee
Till nobler men keep once again
Thy whiter jubilee!

Michelle Lynn

Twentieth Century Archive Clipreels

How We Lived 1900-1969

1900-1909

00:04 American Farm Scenes

00:30 Western Frontier Scenes

00:51 Logging Camps / Pacific Northwest

01:11 American West—Cattle Ranches, Rodeos

01:34 Buffalo Bill

01:44 "Wish Books" (Mail Order Catalogue From Sears, Montgomery Ward)

02:34 Rural "Free Delivery" Trucks

02:48 Mailmen

02:59 New York City

03:11 New York Society People

03:34 Henry Flagler's Hotels

03:52 Mrs. John McLean / Hope Diamond

04:02 Black Americans In Cities

04:28 Black American Children

04:36 Booker T. Washington

04:45 George Washington Carver

04:49 Education Of Black Americans

04:56 Hampton Institute (Vocational For Blacks)

05:08 Tuskegee Institute

05:22 Booker T Washington

05:33 Ellis Island—Immigrants

06:09 Immigrants in Manhattan

07:05 Crowded New York Streets

07:08 Baltimore Fire Of 1902

07:16 San Francisco Earthquake And Fire

07:46 Army Relief Troops, San Francisco

1910-1919

08:17 Henry Ford—Peace Mission To Europe

08:29 Henry Ford

08:31 Thomas Edison And Luther Burbank

08:35 Helen Keller

08:38 Theodore Roosevelt

08:53 Charles Evans Hughes

09:04 Woodrow Wilson

09:09 Woodrow Wilson Re-election

09:24 Woodrow Wilson Inauguration

09:42 Wilson Announces US Involvement In World War I (Americans prepare for war, US soldiers leave for France) April 6, 1917

12:28 American Soldiers And Supplies In France WWI

12:50 American Women Take Over "Mens Jobs" During WWI

13:14 American Women Build Planes And Guns WWI

13:38 Red Cross Nurse, WWI

13:46 Red Cross Nurse, WWI

14:01 US Soldiers Fighting In France

1920-1929

16:12 US Census Taken

16:21 Cities Of America, 1920

16:48 Mechanization Of Farming Communities

17:51 Automobile Industry

18:11 Oil Industry

18:21 Mass Production—Machinery

18:43 Men's Fashion—"Business Suit"

19:03 Businessmen In Service Clubs

19:24 Women Vote, 1920

19:43 Women Run For Office—1st Woman Governor Elected, 1924

19:50 Women Police Officers

20:00 Women Working, Blue Collar Jobs

20:10 Women Telephone Operators, stenographers and clerks

20:25 First Piggly Wiggly Grocery

20:43 1920's Grocery Prducts

21:15 Product Advertising

21:56 Magazine Industry

22:26 Middle Class America

22:29 Telephones And Radios

22:42 Family Cars

23:17 Gas Stations

23:20 Streets Filled With Cars

1930-1939

24:01 The Great Depression

24:15 "Hoovervilles"

24:28 Corpses; Deaths Blamed On The Great Depression

24:57 US Communists March And Riot Against Hunger

25:31 The Poor Of The Depression

25:37 President Franklin Roosevelt Speaks

26:17 Middle Class Housewife Speaks Supporting FDR

26:35 Father Coughlin (Radio Priest Who Was Opposed To FDR)

27:01 FDR Appealing To Youth

27:23 Youth Of America

27:28 Civilian Conservation Corps

28:00 Depressed Farmers—Dust Bowl

28:34 Farmers Migrating West

28:59 1936 Huge US Floods

Daniel XI

29:25 Depressed Blacks—Some Blacks Emerging As Middle Class

29:59 Discrimination—Black Man Lynched

30:23 Women Waterskiing

30:31 Violence, Strikes

30:54 John L. Lewis, UMW

31:02 Autoworkers—Sit-Down Strike

31:09 Union Movements, Strikes, Demonstrations

31:29 Union Leader

1940-1949

32:20 Boy Scouts Collect Scrap During World War II

32:29 Collecting Scrap Metal And Rubber

32:42 FDR Appeals To Conserve Rubber

33:36 Petrol Rationing During WWII

33:52 Conserving Petrol—Carpooling, Riding The Bus, Storing Cars

34:02 Women Give Up Silk And Nylon Stockings For War Effort

34:15 Cigarette Shortage—US Women Turn To Pipes, Rolling Their Own

34:44 Food Rationing—Ration Stamps

34:54 Food Rationing—Instructions

35:26 Americans Grow Their Own Food

35:40 Americans Plant Victory Gardens

36:04 "How To Grow Bigger Tomatoes" Jimmy Durante, Gary Moore

36:36 WWII Housing

37:07 Japanese American Citizens, After Pearl Harbour Bombing

37:46 Japanese Americans Interned In Detention Camps During WWII

38:35 Americans Shop For houses After WWII Ends

38:56 Post-War Apartment Buildings

39:06 *Post-War Spending Spree*

39:18 Post-War—New Cars

39:26 Post-War—New Motels, New Fast Food Restaurants

39:33 New Post-War Appliances, Washers, First Telvision Sets

1950-1959

40:03 Americans Enlist—Korean War

40:24 Women Enlist—Korean War

40:34 WWII Veterans Support Korean War

40:58 Soviet Spies And US Reds Deported

41:15 President Truman Speaks On Atomic War

41:51 US Builds Home Bomb Shelters

42:09 Booming Economy In The 1950s

42:22 Exploding Use Of Automobiles And Gas Stations

43:31 Growing Suburbia

43:38 Homebuilding, Architecture

44:17 New Shopping Centres

44:47 Suburban Housewives

45:17 Corporate Wives

45:28 Businessman's Dress Code

45:59 Advertisements For Luxury Goods

46:44 Dining Out

47:09 Convenience Foods At Home

47:22 Teens—Drive-In Restaurants and Theatres

47:37 Suburban School Kids

47:41 School Sports, Clubs, Social Organisations

1960-1964

48:21 John And Jacqueline Kennedy

49:35 Peace Corps Program\

50:31 Civil Rights Movement

50:40 Civil Rights Protests

51:03 Black American Registering To Vote

51:12 JFK Sends Federal Troops To University Of Miss. After Governor Refuses Admission To Black Students

51:44 Governor Wallace Attempts To Prevent Registration Of Black Students At University Of Alabama

52:36 Kennedy Speaks On Civil Rights

53:13 Largest Civil Rights Demonstration In Washington, D.C

53:37 Martin Luther King's "I Have A Dream Speech"

55:56 Green Berets

56:27 American Soldiers In Vietnam (Buddhist Monks Protest, Saigon)

57:05 Madame Nu (First Lady Of Vietnam)

1965-1969

57:39 Television In American Homes

57:43 TV Cameras In Vietnam

58:08 TV Commercial For "Anacin"

58:22 TV War Scene (Helicopter)

58:30 American Soldiers In Vietnam

58:49 US Soldiers Grow Disenchanted

59:21 Americans Protesting Vietnam

59:49 Black Americans Fighting To Improve Conditions At Home

60:27 Vietnam War, 1967

61:08 Eugene McCarthy Anti-War Speech

61:51 Students Burn Draft Cards

62:07 Students Strike At Columbia University

62:23 Leftist Students Protest, France

62:37 Clashes Between Students And Riot Police

62:44 Violence At Democratic Convention, Chicage 1968

63:19 Vice President Humphrey Speech On Violence

DANIEL 11:45

he	**he, she, it** - the person or thing spoken of
plant	**plant** - to establish or institute in a particular place or region
tabernacles	**tent** - ABODE, DWELLING, HABITATION
palace	**pavilion** - a large often sumptuous tent
between	**between** - from one to the other of
seas	**sea** - the great body of salty water that covers much of the earth's surface
glorious	**conspicuous** - obvious to the eye or mind: plainly visible: MANIFEST: attracting or tending to attract attention by reason of size, brilliance, contrast, station: STRIKING, EMINENT
holy	*a* **sacred** *place or thing* - religious in nature, association, or use: not secular or profane **profane** - not devoted to the sacred and the holy
mountain	**range** *of hills* - mountainous country
he	**he, she, it** - the person or thing spoken of
come	**come** - to arrive at a particular place, end, result or conclusion
end	**extremity** - the fullest possible extent: utmost limit: utmost degree
none	**non-entity** - something of no consequence or significance: something totally lacking in distinction
help	**surround** - to constitute part of the determining environment or accustomed condition of: ENVIRON

Michelle Lynn

STUDY ON ANTICHRIST

> ◆ 2 Thessalonians 2:3 Let no man deceive you by any means: for that day shall not come, except there come a falling away first, and that man of sin be revealed, the son of perdition.

2 Thessalonians 2:3

no	a primary particle of qualified _negation_; adverbial) _not_, (conjunction) _lest_; also (as an interrogative implying a _negative_ answer, _whether_
man	_some_ or _any_ person or object
deceive	to _seduce wholly_
you	_you_ (as the object of a verb or preposition)
any	_not even one_ (man, woman, thing)
means	a _turn_, i.e. (by implication) _mode_ or _style_ (especially with preposition or relative prefix as adverb _like_); figuratively _deportment_ or _character_
for	a primary article; properly assigning a _reason_ (used in argument, explanation or intensification; often with other particles)
that	_that_ one (or [neuter] thing)
	or
	demonstrative _that_ (sometimes redundant); causative _because_
not	_no_ or _not_
come	to _come_ or _go_
except	_if not_, i.e. _unless_
come	to _come_ or _go_
falling	_defection_ from truth (properly the state) ["apostasy"]

away	_defection_ from truth (properly the state) ["apostasy"]
first	_firstly_ (in place, time, order, or importance)
and	a primary particle having a _copulative_ and sometimes also a _cumulative_ force; _and_, _also_, _even_, _so_, _then_, _too_, etc.; often used in connection (or composition) with other particles or small words
that	_that_ one (or [neuter] thing)
	or
	demonstrative _that_ (sometimes redundant); causative _because_
man	_man-faced_, i.e. a _human_ being
sin	_sin_

(Falling away is the sin spoken of.)

be	I _exist_ (used only when emphatic)
revealed	to take _off the cover_, i.e. _disclose_

(Revealed, indicating that it has been here all along only now will be manifest. Reference 1 John 2:18-19)

the	the definite article; _the_ (sometimes to be supplied, at others, omitted, in English idiom)
son	a _"son"_ (sometimes of animals), used very widely of immediate, remote or figurative kinship
perdition	_ruin_ or _loss_ (physical, spiritual, or eternal)

(This falling away is the result of spiritual ruin.)

Michelle Lynn

2 Thessalonians 2:4

who	the definite article; *the* (sometimes to be supplied, at others omitted, in English idioms)
opposeth	to *lie opposite*, i.e. *be adverse* (figuratively) *repugnant* to
and	a primary particle having a *copulative* and sometimes also a *cumulative* force; *and, also, even, so, then, too*, etc. often used in connection (or composition) with other particles or small words
exalteth	to *raise* oneself *over*, i.e. (figuratively) to *become haughty*
himself	*him*—(*her-, it-, them-*, also [in conjunction with the personal pronoun of the other persons] *my-, thy-, our-, your-*) *self* (*selves*), etc.

The exaltation of self has always been here, but at the time of the Renaissance it becomes dominant.

above	properly meaning *superimposition* (of time, place, order, etc.) as a relation of *distribution* [with the genitive], i.e. *over, upon*, etc.; of *rest* (with the dative), *at, on*, etc.; of *direction* (with the accusative) *toward, upon*, etc.
all	a primary word; *all, any, every*, the *whole*
that	*that* one (or [neuter] thing)

or

	demonstrative *that* (sometimes redundant); causative *because*
is	*he* (*she* or *it*) is; also (with neuter plural) they *are*
called	a primary verb; properly to "lay" forth, i.e. (figuratively) relate (in words [usually of systematic or set discourse]); by implication to mean
God	a *deity*, especially the supreme *Divinity*; figuratively a *magistrate*; by Hebrew *very*
or	a primary particle of distinction between two connected terms; disjunctive, *or*, comparative, *than*
that	*that* one (or [neuter] thing) or demonstrative *that* (sometimes redundant); causative *because*
is	*he* (*she* or *it*) *is*; also (with neuter plural) they *are*
worshipped	something *adored*, i.e. an *object of worship* (god, altar, etc.)
so	*so too*, i.e. *thus therefore* (in various relation of *consecution*)
that	*that* one (or [neuter] thing)
	or
	demonstrative *that* (sometimes redundant); causative *because*
he	the reflexive pronoun *self*, used of the third person, and (with the proper personal pronoun) of the other persons
as	*which how*, i.e. *in that manner* (very variously used)
God	a *deity*, especially the supreme *Divinity*; figuratively a *magistrate*; by Hebrew *very*
sitteth	to *seat down*, i.e. *set* (figuratively *appoint*); intransitively to *sit* (down); figuratively to *settle* (*hover*, *dwell*)
in	a primary preposition denoting (fixed) *position* (in place, time, or state), and (by implication)

Michelle Lynn

	instrumentality (medially or constructively), i.e. a relation of rest; *"in"*, *at*, (up-), *on, by*, etc.
the	the definite article; *the* (sometimes to be supplied, at others omitted, in English idioms
temple	a *fane, shrine, temple*
God	a *deity*, especially the supreme *Divinity*; figuratively a *magistrate*; by Hebrew *very*

```
■  1 Corinthians 3:16-18 Know ye not that ye are
the temple of God, and that the Spirit of God
dwelleth in you? If any man defile the temple
of god, him shall God destroy; for the temple
of God is holy, which temple ye are. Let no man
deceive himself. If any man among you seemeth
to be wise in this world, let him become a fool
that he may be wise.
```

shewing	to *show off*, i.e. *exhibit*; figuratively to *demonstrate*, i.e. *accredit*
himself	*him—(her-, it-, them-*, also [in conjunction with the personal pronoun of the other persons] *my-, thy-, our-, your-) self (selves)*, etc.
that	*that* one (or [neuter] thing) or demonstrative *that* (sometimes redundant); causative *because*
he	the reflexive pronoun *self*, used of the third person, and (with the proper personal pronoun) of the other persons
is	*he (she* or *it) is*; also (with neuter plural) they *are*

god   a _deity_, especially the supreme _Divinity_; figuratively a _magistrate_; by Hebrew _very_

◉ Luke 9:23-25 And he said to them all, If any man will come after me, let him deny himself, and take up his cross daily, and follow me. For whosoever will save his life will lose it: but whosoever will lose his life for my sake, the same shall save it. For what is a man advantaged, if he gain the whole world, and lose himself, or be cast away?

◆ 2 Thessalonians 2:5-6 Remember ye not, that, when I was yet with you, I told you these things? And now ye know what withholdeth that he might revealed in his time.

2 Thessalonians 2:6

and   a primary particle having a _copulative_ and sometimes also a _cumulative_ force; _and, also, even, so, then, too,_ etc.; often used in connection (or composition) with other particles or small words

now   a primary particle of present time; "now" (as adverb of date, a transition or emphasis); also as noun or adjective present or immediate

ye   _you_ (as subject of verb)

know	properly to _see_ (literally or figuratively); by implication (in the perfect only) to _know_
what	the definite article; _the_ (sometimes to be supplied, at others omitted, in English idioms
withholdeth	to _hold down_ (_fast_), in various applications (literal or figurative)
that	_that_ one (or [neuter] thing)
	or
	demonstrative _that_ (sometimes redundant); causative _because_
he	the reflexive pronoun _self_, used of the third person and (with other proper personal pronoun) of the other persons
be	I _exist_ (used only when emphatic)
revealed	to take _off the cover_, i.e. _disclose_
in	a primary preposition denoting (fixed) _position_ (in place, time, or state), and (by implication) _instrumentality_ (medially or constructively), i.e. a relation of _rest_; _"in"_, _at_, (up-), _on_, _by_, etc.
his	_self_ (in some oblique case or reflexive relation)
time	an _occasion_, i.e. a _set_ or _proper_ time

Time is all they were waiting for.

◆ 2 Thessalonians 2:7 For the mystery of iniquity doth already work: only he who now letteth will let until he be taken out of the way,

---

for	a primary particle; properly assigning a <u>reason</u> (used in argument, explanation, or Intensification; often with other particles
the	the definite article; <u>the</u> (sometimes to be supplied, at others, omitted, in English idiom
mystery	a <u>secret</u> or <u>"mystery"</u> (through the idea of <u>silence</u> imposed by initiation into religious rites)
iniquity	<u>illegality</u>, i.e. <u>violation of law</u> or (generally) <u>Wickedness</u>
already	<u>even now</u>
work	to <u>be active</u>, <u>efficient</u>
only	<u>merely</u>
he	the reflexive pronoun <u>self</u>, used of the third person, and (with the proper personal pronoun) of the other persons
letteth	to <u>hold down</u> (<u>fast</u>), in various applications (literal or figurative)
let	to <u>hold down</u> (<u>fast</u>), in various applications (literal or figurative)
until	<u>until</u> (of time and place)
he	the reflexive pronoun <u>self</u>, used of the third person, and (with the proper personal pronoun) of the other persons
be	I <u>exist</u> (used only when emphatic)
taken	**to <u>cause to be</u> ("gen-" <u>erate</u>), i.e. (reflexively) to <u>become</u> (<u>come into being</u>), used with great latitude (literal, figurative, intensively, etc.)**

Nothing is taken, but something comes into being.

Michelle Lynn

out	a primary preposition denoting _origin_ (the point _whence_ motion or action proceeds), _from_, _out_ (of place, time, or cause; literal or figurative; remote or direct)
the	the definite article; _the_ (sometimes to be supplied, at others, omitted, in English idiom
way	_middle_ **(as an adjective or [neuter] noun)**

> ■ Daniel 9:27 And he shall confirm the covenant with many for one week: and in the **midst** of the week he shall cause the sacrifice and oblation to cease, and for the overspreading of abominations he shall make it desolate, even until the consummation, and that determined shall be poured upon the desolate.

For a Study on Abomination of Desolation see page 353.

> ◆ 2 Thessalonians 2:8 And then shall that Wicked be revealed, whom the Lord shall consume with the spirit of his mouth, and shall destroy with the brightness of his coming.

2 Thessalonians 2:8

and	a primary particle having a _copulative_ and sometimes also a _cumulative_ force; _and, also, even, so, then, too,_

	etc.; often used in connection (or composition) with other particles or small words
then	_the when_, i.e. _at the time_ that (of the past or future, also in consecution)
that	_that_ one (or [neuter] thing)

or

demonstrative _that_ (sometimes redundant)

causative (_because_)

wicked	_lawless_, i.e. (negatively) _not subject to_ (the Jewish) _law_; (by implication a _Gentile_), or (positively) _wicked_
revealed	to take _off the cover_, i.e. _disclose_

◆ 2 Thessalonians 2:9-10 Even him, whose coming is after the working of Satan with all power and signs and lying wonders, And with all deceivableness of unrighteousness in them that perish; because they received not the love of the truth, that they might be saved.

◉ "In all fields the men of the Renaissance challenged accepted ideas. It is this that marks them out as modern men, no longer content to accept ideas handed down by authority, even when those ideas seemed to be the plainest truth."

◱ 2 Thessalonians 2:11-14 And for this cause God shall send them strong delusion, that they should believe a lie: That they all might be damned who believed not the truth, but had pleasure in unrighteousness. But we are bound to give thanks always to God for you, brethren beloved of the lord, because God hath from the beginning chosen you to salvation through sanctification of the Spirit and belief of the truth: Whereunto he called you by our gospel, to the obtaining of the glory of our Lord Jesus Christ.

STUDY ON ABOMINATION OF DESOLATION

(Daniel 9:24-27)

■ Daniel 9:24-26 Seventy weeks are determined upon thy people and upon thy holy city, to finish the transgression, and to make an end of sins, and to make reconciliation for iniquity, and to bring in everlasting righteousness, and to seal up the vision and prophecy, and to anoint the most Holy.

■ Know therefore and understand, that from the going forth of the commandment to restore and to build Jerusalem unto the Messiah the Prince shall be seven weeks, and threescore and two weeks: the street shall be built again, and the wall, even in troublous times.

■ And after threescore and two weeks shall *Messiah be cut off*, but not for himself: and the people of the prince that shall come shall destroy the city and the sanctuary; and the end thereof shall be with a flood, and unto the end of the war desolations are determined.

Messiah will be cut off.

To **cut**—to *cut* (off, down or asunder); by implication to *destroy* or *consume*; specifically to *covenant* (i.e. make an alliance or bargain, originally by cutting flesh and passing between pieces)

> Daniel 9:27 And **he** shall **confirm** the _covenant_
> with **many** **for** **one** **week**: and in the **midst** of
> the **week** _he_ shall cause the **sacrifice** and
> **oblation** to **cease**, and **for** the **overspreading**
> of **abominations** _he_ shall make it **desolate**, even
> **until** the **consummation**, and **that** **determined**
> shall **be** **poured** **upon** the **desolate**.

Bold-type words are the only ones that should be there.

To **_covenant_**—(in the sense of _cutting_); a _compact_ (because made by passing between _pieces_ of flesh)

The only one mentioned making a covenant is Messiah. Salvation is the covenant that is confirmed for the final week.

The pronoun _**he**_ can mean—he (_she_ or _it_); only expressed when emphatic or without a verb; also (intensively) _self_, or especially with the article) the _same_; sometimes (as demonstrative) _this_ or _that_, occasionally (instead of copula) _as_ or _are_

Rome destroys the city and the sanctuary; Christ confirms the covenant with many for one week.

So, what is this abomination of desolation that occurs in the midst of the final week?

Read Matthew 23 paying particular attention to verse 38.

Michelle Lynn

Then:

> ■ Proverbs 6:16-19 These six things doth the Lord hate: yea, seven are an abomination unto him: A proud look, a lying tongue, and hands that shed innocent blood, An heart that deviseth wicked imaginations, feet that be swift in running to mischief, A false witness that speaketh lies, and he that soweth discord among the brethren.

> ■ Luke 11:17 But He, knowing their thoughts, said to them: "Every kingdom divided against itself is brought to desolation, and a house divided against a house falls.

Considering the schism that occurred about 1000 years after Christ's resurrection and the subsequent history . . . .

> ■ 1 Corinthians 3:16-18 Know ye not that ye are the temple of God, and that the Spirit of God dwelleth in you? If any man defile the temple of God, him shall God destroy; for the temple of God is holy, which temple ye are. Let no man deceive himself. If any man among you seemeth to be wise in this world, let him become a fool, that he may be wise.

. . . . I present that the abomination has taken its place in the temple already.

DANIEL XI
DEFINED

A

abomination

11:31

disgusting, i.e. filthy; especially idolatrous or (concretely); an idol

above

11:5,36,37

above, over, upon, against

accomplished

11:36

to end, whether intransitive (to cease, be finished, perish) or transitive (to complete, prepare, consume)

acknowledge

11:39

properly to scrutinize, i.e. look intently at; hence (with recognition implied) to acknowledge, be acquainted with, care for, respect, revere, or (with suspicion implied), to disregard, ignore, be strange toward, reject, resign, dissimulate (as if ignorant or disowning)

after

11:13

an extremity; adverbially (with prepositional prefix) after

against

11:14,24,25,28,30,36,40

above, over, upon, against

11:16

properly denoting motion towards, but occasionally used of a quiescent position, i.e. near, with, or among; often in general, to

agreement

11:6

evenness, i.e. (figuratively) prosperity or concord; also straitness, i.e. (figuratively) rectitude (only in plural with singular sense; often adverbial)

all

11:2,37,43

properly whole, hence all, any, or every

also

11:8, 22

from an unused root meaning to gather; properly assemblage; used only adverbially also, even, yea, though; often repeated as correlation both . . . and

Ammon

11:41

tribal, i.e. inbred; Ammon, a son of Lot; also his posterity and their country

anger

11:20

properly the nose or nostril; hence, the face, and occasionally a person; also (from the rapid breathing in passion) ire

any

11:37

properly the whole; hence, all, any or every

appointed

11:27,29,35

properly an appointment; i.e. a fixed time or season; specifically a festival; conventionally a year; by implication an assembly (as convened for a definite purpose); technically the congregation; by extension the place of meeting; also a signal (as appointed beforehand)

arm

11:6   the arm (as stretched out), or (of animals) the foreleg; figuratively force

arms

11:15,22,31   the arm (as stretched out), or (of animals) the foreleg; figuratively force

army

11:7,13,25,26   probably a force, whether of men, means, or other resources; an army, wealth, virtue, valor, strength

assemble

11:10   to gather for any purpose; hence to receive, take away, i.e. remove (destroy, leave behind, put up, restore, etc.)

at

11:27   above, over, upon, against

away

11:31   to turn off (literal or figurative)

11:44   to seclude; specifically (by a ban) to devote to religious uses (especially destruction); to be blunt as to the nose

B

battle

11:20,25

(in the sense of fighting); a battle (i.e. the engagement); generally war (i.e. warfare)

be

11:2,4,5,6,10,11,12,15,16, 17,19,20,22,25,27,28, 29,30,32,34,36,41 43

to exist, i.e. be or become, come to pass (always emphatic, and not a mere copula or auxiliary)

become

11:23

to bind fast, i.e. close (the eyes); intransitively to be (causatively make) powerful or numerous denominative to crunch the bones

before

11:16,22

the face (as the part that turns); used in a great variety of applications (literal and figurative); also (with prepositional prefix) as a preposition (before, etc.)

begat

11:6

to bear young; causatively to beget; medically, to act as midwife; specifically to show lineage

behold

11:2

lo!

beside

11:4

properly separation; by implication a part of the body, branch of a tree, bar for carrying; figuratively chief of a city; especially (with prepositional prefix) as adverb, apart, only, beside

Michelle Lynn

between

11:45   a <u>distinction</u>; but used only as a preposition
<u>between</u> (repeated before each noun, often with
other particles); also as a conjunction, <u>either</u> . . . or

both

11:27   <u>two</u>; also (as ordinal) <u>twofold</u>

branch

11:7   in the sense of <u>greenness</u> as a striking color; a
<u>shoot</u>; figuratively a <u>descendant</u>

broken

11:4,22   to <u>burst</u>

brought

11:6   to <u>go</u> or <u>come</u>

C

captives

11:8   exiled; captured; as noun, exile (abstract or concrete
                    and collective); by extension booty

captivity

11:33   exiled; captured; as noun, exile (abstract or concrete
                    and collective); by extension booty

carry

11:8   to go or come

cast

11:12   to fall, in a great variety of applications (intransitive
                    or causative, literal or figurative)

11:15   to spill forth (blood, a libation, liquid metal; or even
                    a solid, i.e. to mound up); also (figurative) to expend
                    (life, soul, complaint, money, etc.)

cease

11:18   to repose, i.e. desist from exertion

certain

11:13   time, especially (adverbially with preposition) now,
                    when, etc.

chariots

11:40   a vehicle; by implication a team; by extension cavalry;
                    by analogy a rider, i.e. the upper millstone

chief

11:41   the first, in place, time, order or rank (specifically a
                    firstfruit)

Michelle Lynn

children

11:41   a son (as a builder of the family name), in the widest sense (of literal and figurative relationship, including grandson, subject, nation, quality or condition, etc.

Chittim

11:30   a Kittite or Cypriote; hence, an islander in general, i.e. the Greeks or Romans on the shores opposite Palestine

choler

11:11   properly to trickle; to be (causative make) bitter (literal and figurative)

chosen

11:15   select, i.e. best

cities

11:15   a city (a place guarded by waking or a watch) in the widest sense (even of a mere encampment or post)

cleave

11:34   properly to twine, i.e. (by implication) to unite, to remain also to borrow (as a form of obligation) or (causative) to lend

come

11:6,7,9,10,13,   to go or come (in a wide variety of applications)
15,21,29,30,45

11:11   to go (causatively bring) out

come

11:23   to ascend; intransitive (be high) or actually (mount); used in a great variety of senses, primitive and secondary, literal and figurative

11:40   to storm; by implication to shiver, i.e. fear

cometh

11:16   to go or come

confirm

11:1   to fasten upon; hence to seize, be strong (figuratively courageous, causatively strengthen, cure, help, repair, fortify), obstinate; to bind, restrain, conquer

consumed

11:16   to end, whether intransitively, (to cease, be finished, perish) or transitively (to complete, prepare, consume)

continue

11:8   to stand, in various relations (literal and figurative, intransitive and transitive)

corrupt

11:32   to soil, especially in a moral sense

corrupting

11:17   to decay, i.e. (causatively) ruin (literal and figurative)

countries

11:40,42   from an unused root probably meaning to be firm; the earth (at large, or partitively a land)

courage

11:25   the heart (as the most interior organ)

covenant

11:22,28,30,32   (in the sense of cutting); a compact (because made by passing between pieces of flesh)

D

daily

11:31

properly <u>continuance</u> (as indefinite extension); but used only (attributively as an adjective) <u>constant</u> (or adverbially <u>constantly</u>); elliptically the <u>regular</u> (daily) sacrifice

Darius

11:1

<u>Darejavish</u>, a title (rather than name of several Persian kings)

daughter

11:6,17

a <u>daughter</u>, (used in the same wide sense as other terms of relationship, literal and figurative)

days

11:20,33

from an unused root meaning to <u>be hot</u>; a <u>day</u> (as the <u>warm</u> hours), whether literally (from sunrise to sunset, or from one sunset to the next), or figuratively (a space of time defined by an associated term)

deal

11:7

to <u>do</u> or <u>make</u> (in the broadest sense and widest application)

deceitfully

11:23

in the sense of <u>deceiving</u>, <u>fraud</u>

desire

11:37

<u>delight</u>

desolate

11:31   to stun (intransitively) grow numb i.e. devastate (figuratively) stupefy (both usually in a passive sense

destroy

11:26 11:44   to burst (literal and figurative) to desolate

destroyed

11:20   to burst (literal and figurative)

determined

11:36   properly to point sharply, i.e. (literally) to wound; figuratively to be alert, to decide

devices

11:24,25   a contrivance; i.e. (concretely) a texture, machine, or (abstractly) intention, plan, (whether bad, a plot; or good, advice)

divide

11:35   to be smooth (figuratively); by implication (as smooth stones were used for lots) to apportion or separate

divided

11:4   to cut or split in two; to halve

do

11:3,16,17,24,28   to do or make (in the broadest sense and
30,32,36,39   widest application)

dominion

11:3,5b   a ruler or (abstractly) rule

| 11:4 | (1) empire (2) parallel |
| 11:5a | to rule |

done

| 11:24,36 | to do or make |

down

| 11:12 | to fall, in a great variety of applications, (intransitive or causative, literal or figurative) |

E

east

11:44   sunrise (i.e. the east)

Edom

11:41   red, Edom, the elder twin brother of Jacob; hence,
                               the region (Idumaea) occupied by him

Egypt

11:8,42,43   Mitsrajim, i.e. Upper and Lower Egypt

end

11:6,27,35,40,45   an extremity; adverbially (with prepositional prefix) after

enter

11:7,17,24,40,41   to go or come (in a wide variety of applications)

escape

11:41   properly to be smooth, i.e. (by implication) to escape
                               (as if by slipperiness); causatively to release or
                               rescue; specifically to bring forth young, emit sparks

11:42   deliverance; concretely an escaped portion

establish

11:14   to stand, in various relations (literal and figurative,
                               intransitive and transitive)

estate

11:7,20,21,38   used as a noun; a stand, i.e. pedestal or station

Ethiopians

11:43   a Cushite, or descendant of Cush

every

11:36   properly the whole; hence all, any or every

exalt

11:14   to lift, in a great variety of applications, literal and figurative, absolute and relative

11:36   to be high; actually to rise or raise

F

face

11:17,18,19

the <u>face</u> (as the part that
turns) used in a great variety of
applications (literal and figurative);
also (with prepositional prefix) as a
preposition (<u>before</u>, etc.)

fall

11:19,26

to <u>fall</u>, in a great variety of
applications (intransitive or
causative, literal or figurative)

11:14,33,34,35

to <u>totter</u> or <u>waver</u> through
weakness of the legs, especially
the ankles); by implication to <u>falter</u>,
<u>stumble</u>, faint or fall

far

11:2

<u>great</u> (in any sense); hence, <u>older</u>;
also <u>insolent</u>

fathers

11:24,37,38

<u>father</u>

fathers'

11:24

<u>father</u>

fattest

11:24

<u>fat</u>, i.e. (literal and abstract) <u>fatness</u>;
but usually (figurative and concrete)
a <u>rich</u> dish, a <u>fertile</u> field, a <u>robust</u> man

feed

11:26

to <u>eat</u> (literal and figurative)

Michelle Lynn

fenced

11:15
a <u>fortification</u>, <u>castle</u>, or <u>fortified</u> city; figuratively a <u>defender</u>

few

11:20
properly <u>united</u>, i.e. <u>one</u>; or (as an ordinal) <u>first</u>

fight

11:11
to <u>feed</u> on ; figuratively to <u>consume</u> by implication to <u>battle</u> (as <u>destruction</u>)

first

11:1
properly <u>united</u>, i.e. <u>one</u>; or (as an ordinal) <u>first</u>

flame

11:33
from an unused root meaning to <u>gleam</u>; a <u>flash</u>; figuratively a sharply polished <u>blade</u> or <u>point</u> of a weapon

flatteries

11:21,34
properly something <u>very smooth</u>; i.e. a <u>treacherous</u> spot; figuratively <u>blandishment</u>

11:32
<u>flattery</u>

flood

11:22
a <u>deluge</u> (literal or figurative)

for

11:4,6,13,17,18,23,24, 25,27,30,35,36,37,39
indicating <u>causal</u> relations of all kinds

forces

11:10   properly a <u>force</u>, whether of men, means, or other resources; an <u>army</u>, <u>wealth</u>, <u>virtue</u>, <u>valor</u>, <u>strength</u>

11:38   a <u>fortified</u> place; figuratively a <u>defense</u>

forecast

11:24,25   to <u>plait</u> or interpenetrate, i.e. (literal) <u>to weave</u> or (general) to <u>fabricate</u>; figuratively to <u>plot</u> or contrive (usually in a malicious sense); hence (from the mental effort) to <u>think</u>, <u>regard</u>, <u>value</u>. <u>compute</u>

former

11:13,29   <u>first</u>, in place, time or rank (as an adjective or noun)

forsake

11:30   to <u>loosen</u>, i.e. <u>relinquish</u>, <u>permit</u>, etc.

fort

11:19   a <u>fortified</u> place; figuratively a <u>defense</u>

forth

11:11a,44   to go (causative <u>bring</u>) <u>out</u>

11:11b   to <u>stand</u>, in various relations (literal and figurative, intransitive and transitive)

fortress

11:7,10   a <u>fortified</u> place; figuratively a <u>defense</u>

Michelle Lynn

found

11:19   properly to come forth to, i.e. appear or exist; transitively to attain, i.e. find or acquire; figuratively to occur, meet or be present

four

11:4   four

fourth

11:2   fourth; also (fractionally) fourth

fury

11:44   heat; figuratively anger, poison (from its fever)

G

gain

11:39   from an unused root meaning to buy; price, payment, wages

give

11:17,21   to give, used with greatest latitude of application (put, make, etc.)

given

11:6,11   to give, used with greatest latitude of application (put, make, etc.)

glorious

11:16,41,45   in the sense of prominence; splendor (as conspicuous); also a gazelle (as beautiful)

glory

11:20   honor; used (figurative) for the capital city

11:39   properly weight, but only figurative in a good sense, splendor or copiousness

go

11:44   to go (causatively bring) out God

God

1. Creator and Ruler of the world, Israel, and the church.

11:32,37   gods in the ordinary sense; but specifically used (in the plural thus, especially with the article) of the supreme God; occasionally applied by way of deference to magistrates; and sometimes as a superlative

          Michelle Lynn

11:38	a deity or the Deity
11:36	strength; as adjective mighty; especially the Almighty (but used also of any deity)

2. Any deity other than God

11:36	strength; as adjective mighty; especially of the Almighty (but used also of any deity)
11:37,38,39	a deity or the Deity

gods

11:8,36	God

gold

11:8,38,43	properly something carved out, i.e. ore; hence, gold (pure as originally mined)

great

11:5,13,25,28,44	great (in any sense); hence, older; also insolent

greater

11:13,29	abundant (in quantity, size, age, number, rank, quality)

Grecia

11:2	effervescing (i.e. hot and active); Javan, the name of a son of Joktan, and of the race (Ionians i.e. Greeks) descended from him, with there territory; also of a place in Arabia

grieved

11:30	to despond; causatively to deject

H

hand

11:11,16,41,42

a hand (the open one [indicating power, means, direction, etc.]

he

11:2,4,5,6,8,10,11,12,17,18,19,
20,21,23,24,25,28,29,30,32, 36,
37,38,39,40,41,42,43,44,45

he, (she or it); only expressed emphatically or without a verb; also self, or (especially with the article) the same; sometimes (as demonstrative) this or that; occasionally (instead of copula) as or are

heart

11:12,28

the heart (as the most interior organ)

hearts

11:27

the heart (as the most interior organ)

heaven

11:4

from an unused root meaning to be lofty; the sky (as aloft; the dual perhaps alluding to the visible arch in which the clouds move, as well as to the higher ether where the celestial bodies revolve)

help

11:45

to surround, i.e. protect or aid

11:34

aid

holds

11:24,39

a fortification, castle, or fortified city; figuratively a defender

holpen

11:34   to surround, i.e. protect or aid

holy

11:28,30,45   a sacred place or thing; rarely abstract sanctity

honour

11:21   grandeur (i.e. an imposing form or appearance)

11:38   to be heavy, i.e. in a bad sense (burdensome, severe, dull) or in a good sense (numerous, rich, honorable); causatively to make weighty (in the same two senses)

horsemen

11:40   a steed (as stretched out to a vehicle, not single nor for mounting); also (by implication) a driver (in a chariot), i.e. (collectively) cavalry

I

I

11:4,6,12,15,17,19,21,
24,25,27,29,38,42

I

increase

11:39   to increase (in whatever respect)

indignation

11:30   properly to foam at the mouth, i.e. to be
                                         enraged

11:36   strictly froth at the mouth, i.e. (figuratively)
                                         fury (especially of God's displeasure with sin)

instruct

11:33   to separate mentally (or distinguish), i.e.
                                         (generally) understand

intelligence

11:30   to separate mentally (or distinguish), i.e.
                                         (generally) understand

into

11:9b   a primitive particle; properly denoting motion
                                         towards, but occasionally used of a quiescent
                                         position, i.e. near, with, or among; often in
                                         general, to

is

11:35,36   to exist, i.e. be or become, come to pass
                                         always emphatic, and not a mere copula or
                                         auxiliary)

isles

11:18   properly a habitable spot (as desirable); dry

J

join

11:6   to join (literal or figurative); specifically (by means of spells) to fascinate

K

king

11:3,5,6,7,8,9,11,13,   a king
14,15,25,36,40

kingdom

11:4,9,17,20,21   a rule; concretely a dominion

king's

11:6   a king

kings

11:2   a king

kings'

11:27   a king

knew

11:38   to know (properly to ascertain by seeing); used in a great variety of senses, figurative, literal, euphemistically and inferentially (including observation, care, recognition; and causatively instruction, designation, punishment, etc.

know

11:32   see **knew**

L

land

11:16,19,28,41,42   from an unused root probably meaning to be firm; the earth (at large, or partitively a land)

11:9,39   soil (from its general redness)

latter

11:29   hinder; generally late or last; specifically (as facing the east) western

league

11:23   to join (literal and figurative) specifically (by means of spells) to fascinate

Libyans

11:43   patrial from a name probably derived from an unused root meaning to thirst, i.e. a dry region; apparently a Libyan or inhabitant of interior Africa (only in plural)

lies

11:27   to lie (i.e. deceive), literal or figurative

lifted

11:12   to be high; actually to raise or rise (in various applications, literal or figurative)

little

11:34   a little or few (often adverbial and comparative)

M

magnify

11:36,37

properly to twist, i.e. to be (causative make) large (in various senses, as in body, mind, estate or honor, also in pride)

make

11:6

to do or make

many

11:14,18,26,33a,34, 39,40,41,44

abundant (in quantity, size, age, number, rank, quality)

marvelous

11:36

properly perhaps to separate, i.e. distinguish literal or figurative); by implication to be (causative make) great, difficult, wonderful

meat

11:26

a dainty

Mede

11:1

a Madian or native of Madai

mighty

11:3

powerful; by implication warrior, tyrant

11:25

powerful (specifically a paw); by implication numerous

mischief

11:27

used as (abstract) noun, wickedness

Michelle Lynn

Moab

11:41   from (her [the mother's]) father; Moab, an incestuous son of Lot also his territory and descendants

most

11:39   a fortified place; figuratively a defense

mount

11:15   a military mound, i.e. rampart of besiegers

mountain

11:45   a mountain or range of hills (sometimes used figuratively)

multitude

11:10,11,12,13   a noise, tumult, crowd; also disquietude, wealth

N

neither

11:6,17,20,37   lo; a primitive particle; not (the simple or abstract negation); by implication no; often used with other particles

11:15   as if from a primitive root meaning to be nothing or not exist; a non-entity; generally used as a negative particle

none

11:16,45   as if from a primitive root meaning to be nothing or not exist; a non-entity; generally used as a negative particle

nor

11:4,20,37b   not (the simple abstract negation); by implication no; often used with other particles

north

11:6,7,8,11,13,15,40,44   properly hidden, i.e. dark; used only of the north as a quarter (gloomy and unknown)

not

11:4,6,12,15,17,19,21, 24,25,27,29,38,42   lo; a primitive particle; not (the simple or abstract negation); by implication no; often used with other particles

now

11:2   at this time, whether adverbial, conjunctional, or expletive

Michelle Lynn

O

obtain

11:21   to fasten upon; hence to seize, be strong (figuratively courageous, causative strengthen, cure, help, repair, fortify), obstinate; to bind, restrain, conquer

one

11:27   properly united, i.e. one; or (as an ordinal) first

others

11:4   properly hinder; generally next, other, etc.

out

11:7,41,44   properly a part of; hence, (prepositional), from or out of in many senses

over

11:40   to cross over; used very widely of any transition (literal or figurative; transitive, intransitive, intensive, or causative); specifically to cover (in copulation)

overflow

11:10,26,40   to gush; by implication to inundate, cleanse; by analogy to gallop, conquer

overflown

11:22   see **overflow**

overthrown

11:41   to totter or waver (through weakness of the legs, especially the ankle); by implication to falter, stumble, faint or fall

own

11:16   delight

P

palace

11:45   a <u>pavilion</u> or palace-tent

part

11:31   properly <u>smoothness</u> (of the tongue); also an <u>allotment</u>

pass

11:10,40   to <u>cross</u> over; used very widely of any <u>transition</u> (literal
                  or figurative, transitive, intransitive, intensive, or
                  causative); specifically to <u>cover</u> (in copulation)

peaceably

11:21,24   <u>security</u> (genuine or false)

people

11:14,15,32,33   a <u>people</u> (as a congregated <u>unit</u>); specifically a <u>tribe</u>
                  (as those of Israel); hence, (collectively) <u>troops</u> or
                  <u>attendants</u>; figuratively a <u>flock</u>

11:23   (in the sense of <u>massing</u>); a foreign <u>nation</u>; hence, a
                  <u>Gentile</u>; also (figurative) a <u>troop</u> of animals or a <u>flight</u> of
                  locusts Persia

11:2   <u>Paras</u> (i.e. <u>Persia</u>), an Eastern country, including its
                  inhabitants

place

11:31   to <u>give</u>, used with greatest latitude of application (<u>put</u>,
                  <u>make</u>, etc.)

plant

11:45   properly to <u>strike</u> in, i.e. <u>fix</u>; specifically to <u>plant</u> (literal
                  and figurative)

pleasant

11:38   to <u>delight</u> in

plucked

11:4   to <u>tear</u> away

pollute

11:31   properly to <u>bore</u>, i.e.(by implication) to <u>wound</u>, to <u>dissolve</u>; figuratively to <u>profane</u> (a person, place, or thing), to <u>break</u> (ones word), to <u>begin</u> (as if by an "opening wedge"); denominatively to <u>play</u> (the flute)

portion

11:26   a <u>dainty</u>

posterity

11:4   the <u>last</u> or <u>end</u>, hence, the <u>future</u>; also <u>posterity</u>

power

11:6,25   from an unused root meaning to be <u>firm</u>; <u>vigor</u>, literally (<u>force</u>, in a good or bad sense) or figuratively (<u>capacity</u>, <u>means</u>, <u>produce</u>); also (from its hardiness) a large <u>lizard</u>

11:43   to <u>rule</u>

precious

11:8   <u>delight</u>

11:38   <u>valuable</u> (objective or subjective)

11:43   to <u>delight</u> in

prevail

11:7 to <u>fasten</u> upon; hence, to <u>seize, be strong</u> (figurative courageous, causative <u>strengthen</u>, <u>cure</u>, <u>help</u>, <u>repair</u>, <u>fortify</u>), <u>obstinate</u>; to <u>bind</u>, <u>restrain</u>, <u>conquer</u>

prey

11:24 <u>booty</u>

prince

11:18 in the sense of <u>determining</u>; a <u>magistrate</u> (as <u>deciding</u>) or other <u>leader</u>

11:22 a <u>commander</u> (as occupying the <u>front</u>), civil, military or religious; generally (abstract plural), <u>honorable</u> themes

princes

11:5 a <u>head</u> person (of any rank or class)

11:8 properly something <u>poured</u> out, i.e. a <u>libation</u>; also a molten <u>image</u>; by implication a <u>prince</u> (as <u>anointed</u>)

prosper

11:27,36 to <u>push</u> forward, in various senses (literal or figurative, transitive or intransitive)

province

11:24 properly a <u>judgeship</u>, i.e. <u>jurisdiction</u>; by implication a <u>district</u> (as ruled by a judge); generally a <u>region</u>

purge

11:35 to <u>clarify</u> (i.e. <u>brighten</u>), <u>examine</u>, <u>select</u>

push

11:40 to <u>but</u> with the horns; figuratively to <u>war</u> against

R

raiser

11:20
to cross over; used very widely of a transition; specifically to cover (in copulation)

realm

11:2
a rule; concretely a dominion

regard

11:37
to separate mentally (or distinguish), i.e. (generally) understand

reproach

11:18
contumely, disgrace, the pudenda

retain

11:6
to inclose; by analogy to hold back; also to maintain, rule, assemble

return

11:9,10,13,28,29,30
to turn back (hence, away), transitive or intransitive, literal or figurative, (not necessarily with the idea of return to the starting point; generally to retreat; often adverbially again

richer

11:2
properly to accumulate; chiefly (specifically) to grow (causative make) rich

riches

11:2
see **richer**

11:13,24,28
property (as gathered)

robbers

11:14
violent, i.e. a tyrant

roots

11:7   a <u>root</u> (literal or figurative)

rule

11:3,39   to <u>rule</u>

ruled

11:4   to <u>rule</u>

S

sanctuary

11:31
a consecrated thing or place, especially a palace, sanctuary (whether of Jehovah or of idols) or asylum

scatter

11:24
to disperse

seas

11:45
from an unused root meaning to roar; a sea (as breaking in noisy surf) or large body of water; specifically (with the article) the Mediterranean; sometimes a large river, or an artificial basin; locally the west, or (rarely) the south

set

11:11,13
to stand, in various relations, (literal and figurative, intransitive and transitive)

11:17
to put, (used in a great variety of applications, literal, figurative, inferential, and elliptical)

she

11:6,17
he (she or it); only when expressed emphatically or without a verb; also self, or (especially with the article) the same; sometimes (as demonstrative) this or that; occasionally (instead of copula) as or are

shew

11:2
to show

ships

11:30
a ship (as a fixture)

11:40
a ship

silver

11:8,38,43   silver (from its pale color); by implication money

slain

11:26   pierced (especially to death); figuratively polluted

small

11:23   a little or few (often adverbial or comparative)

sons

11:10   a son (as a builder of the family name), in the widest
                          sense of literal and figurative relationships (including
                          grandson, subject, nation, quality or condition, etc.

south

11:5,6,9,11,14,   from an unused root meaning to be parched; the
15,25,29,40   south (from its drought); specifically the Negeb or
                          southern district of Judah, occasionally, Egypt (as
                          south to Palestine)

speak

11:27,36   properly to arrange; but used figuratively (of words),
                          to speak; rarely (in a destructive sense) to subdue

spoil

11:24,33   booty

stand

11:2,3,4,6,7,14,16,17,   to stand (in various relations, literal and figurative,
20,21,25,31   intensive and causative)

steps

11:43   a step; figuratively companionship

stir

11:2,25   through the idea of opening the eyes; to wake (literal or figurative)

stirred

11:10,25   properly to grate, i.e. (figuratively) to anger

stones

11:38   through the meaning to build; a stone

stood

11:1   to stand, in various relations (literal or figurative, intransitive or transitive)

strange

11:39   foreign, or (concrete) a foreigner, or (abstract) heathendom

strength

11:2   vehemence (usually in a bad sense)

11:15   from an unused root meaning to be firm; vigor, literally (force, in a good or bad sense) or figuratively (capacity, means, produce) also (from its hardiness) a large lizard

11:17   might or (figurative) positiveness

11:31   a fortified place; figuratively a defense

strengthen

11:1   a fortified place; figuratively a defense

strengthened

11:6   to fasten upon; hence, to seize, be strong (figuratively courageous, causatively strengthen, cure, help, repair, fortify), obstinate; to bind, restrain, conquer

| 11:12 | to be stout (literal or figurative) |

stretch

| 11:42 | to send away, for, or out |

strong

11:5,32	to fasten upon; hence to seize, be strong (figurative courageous, causatively strengthen, cure, help, repair, fortify), obstinate; to bind, restrain, conquer
11:23	to bind fast, i.e. close (the eyes); intransitive to be (causative make) powerful or numerous; denominatively to crunch the bones
11:24	a fortification, castle, or fortified city; figurative a defender
11:39	a fortified place; figuratively a defense

stumble

| 11:19 | to totter or waver (through weakness of the legs, especially the ankle); by implication to falter, stumble, faint or fall |

sword

| 11:33 | drought; also a cutting instrument (from its destructive effect), as a knife, sword, or other sharp implement |

T

tabernacles

11:45   a <u>tent</u> (as <u>clearly</u> conspicuous from a distance)

table

11:27   a <u>table</u> (as <u>spread</u> out); by implication a <u>meal</u>

take

11:15,18   to <u>catch</u> (in a net, trap or pit); generally to <u>capture</u> or occupy; also to <u>choose</u> (by lot); figuratively to <u>cohere</u>

11:31   to <u>turn</u> off (literal or figurative)

taken

11:12   to <u>lift</u>, in a great variety of applications, literal and figurative, absolute and relative

taxes

11:20   to <u>drive</u> (an animal, a workman, a debtor, an army); by implication to <u>tax</u>, <u>harass</u>, <u>tyrannize</u>

ten

11:12   a <u>myriad</u>, i.e. indefinite <u>large</u> <u>number</u>

than

11:13   properly a <u>part</u> of; hence (prepositional), <u>from</u> or <u>out of</u> in many senses

that

11:3,6,16,24,26,30,   who, <u>which</u>, <u>what</u>, <u>that</u>; also (as adverb and
31,32,33,36   conjunction) <u>when</u>, <u>where</u>, <u>how</u>, <u>because</u>, <u>in order that</u>, etc. **or** <u>this</u> or <u>that</u> **or** indicating <u>causal</u> relations of all kinds

these

11:41   these or those

they

11:2,6,14,21,22,25,   they (only used when emphatic)
26,27,31,33,34

those

11:4   these or those

11:14   they (used only when emphatic)

thousands

11:12   a myriad, i.e. indefinitely a large number

tidings

11:44   something heard, i.e. an announcement

till

11:36   as far (or long, or much) as, whether of space
                    (even unto) or time (during, while, until) or degree
                    (equally with)

time

11:24,35a,40   time, especially (adverbial with preposition) now,
                    when, etc.

times

11:6,14   see **time**

treasures

11:43   in the sense of hiding; treasure (as hidden)

trouble

11:44   to tremble inwardly (or palpitate), i.e. (figurative)
be (causative make) (suddenly) alarmed or agitated;
by implication to hasten anxiously

truth

11:2   stability; figurative certainty, truth, trustworthiness

try

11:35   to fuse (metal), i.e. refine (literal or figurative)

turn

11:18,19   to turn back (hence, away), (not necessarily with
the idea of return to the starting point), generally to
retreat; often adverbial again

U

understand

11:33

to <u>be</u> (causative <u>make</u> or <u>act</u>) <u>circumspect</u> and hence, <u>intelligent</u>

understanding

11:35

see **understand**

up

11:2,3,4,6,7,10,12,
14,15,20,21,23,25

properly the <u>upper</u> part, used only adverbially with prefix <u>upward</u>, <u>above</u>, <u>overhead</u>, <u>from the top</u>, etc.

upon

11:18,24,42

<u>above</u>, <u>over</u>, <u>upon</u>, or <u>against</u>

upright

11:17

<u>straight</u> (literal or figurative)

V

vessels

11:8   something <u>prepared</u>, i.e. any <u>apparatus</u> (as an implement, utensil, dress, vessel or weapon)

vile

11:21   to <u>disesteem</u>

vision

11:14   a <u>sight</u> (mentally), i.e. a <u>dream</u>, <u>revelation</u>, or <u>oracle</u>

W

which

11:4,24   who, which, what, that; also (as adverb and conjunction) when, where, how, because, in order that, etc.

whirlwind

11:40   to storm; by implication to shiver, i.e. fear

white

11:35   to be (or become) white; also to make bricks

whole

11:17   properly the whole; hence all, any or every

whom

11:21   above, over, upon, or against

11:38,39   who, which, what, that; also (as adverb and conjunction) when, where, how, because, in order that, etc.

wickedly

11:32   to be (causative do or declare) wrong; by implication to disturb, violate

will

11:3,16,36   delight

winds

11:4   wind; by resemblance breath, i.e. a sensible (or even violent) exhalation; figuratively life, anger, insubstantiality; by extension a region of the sky; by resemblance spirit, but only of a rational being (including its expression and functions)

Michelle Lynn

with

11:3,7,8,11,13,17,22, 23,25,28,30,34,38, 40,44

with (i.e. in conjunction with), in various applications; specifically equally with

without

11:18

properly a failure of, i.e. (used only as a negative particle, usually with prepositional prefix) not, except, without, unless, besides, because not, until, etc.

withstand

11:15

to stand, in various relations (literal and figurative, intransitive and transitive)

women

11:17,37

a woman

work

11:23

to do or make, in the broadest sense and widest application

Y

yea

11:22

from an unused root meaning to gather; properly assemblage; used only adverbially also, even, yea, though; often repeated as correlation both . . . and

year

11:1

a year (as a revolution of time)

years

11:6,8,13

a year (as a revolution of time)

yet

11:2,27,35

properly iteration or continuance; used only adverbially (with or without preposition) again, repeatedly, still, more

DICTIONARY
DEFINITIONS

A

above *prep*: superior to or surpassing in any respect: higher than (as in rank, position, quality, or degree): out of reach of: not likely to be affected by: not exposed to: in preference to: over against

above *adv*: higher or superior in rank, position, or power

abundant *adj*: possessing (as resources) in great quantity: having great plenty: RICH: amply supplied: ABOUNDING: more than sufficient: occurring or existing in great quantity: AMPLE, PLENTIFUL, COPIOUS

accumulate *vb*: to heap up in a mass: pile up: AMASS: COLLECT, GATHER: to grow or increase in quantity or number

acknowledge *vb*: to show by word or act that one has knowledge of and respect for the rights, claims, authority, or status of: recognize, honor, or respect especially publicly: to take notice of: indicate recognition and acceptance of

acquainted *adj*: being known to and having knowledge of

acquire *vb*: to come into possession, control, or power of disposal of often by some uncertain or unspecified means

act *n*: a thing done or being done: DEED, PERFORMANCE

advice *n*: the way in which one regards something: VIEW, OPINION: careful thought: CONSIDERATION, DELIBERATION: recommendation regarding a decision or course of conduct: COUNSEL

after *adv*: following in time or place: AFTERWARD, BEHIND

again *adv*: BACK: in the opposite direction: in return or in response: BACK: as a result or consequence: another time: once more: ANEW

against *prep*: in opposition or hostility to: not in conformity with: contrary to: in spite of: NOTWITHSTANDING: in competition with: with respect to: relating to :TOWARD

agitated *adj*: moving to and fro: QUIVERING, SHAKING: troubled in mind: DISTURBED, EXCITED

aid *vb*: to give help or support to: FURTHER, FACILITATE, ASSIST: contribute to: to give assistance: be of use to: HELP

alarm *n*: a call to arms (as on the approach of an enemy)

alert *adj*: marked by careful zealous watchfulness and promptness to counter threats and dangers and to cope with emergencies: marked by ready activity, brisk liveliness, or quick reactions

all *adj*: that is the whole amount or quantity of: that is the whole extent or duration of: as much as possible: the greatest possible

allotment *n*: something that is allotted: a part or portion distributed or assigned: as: something that is assigned by or as if by lot or by destiny

almighty *adj*: having absolute power over all—used especially of God: relatively unlimited in power

aloft *adv*: upward from an inferior position or from a depressing mood

also *adv*: in the same manner as something else: LIKEWISE: in addition: as well: BESIDES, TOO

Ammon *(see map in 11:41)*

among *prep*: surrounded by: in the midst of: intermingled with: through the midst of: DURING: in the course of: in or to the locality of: in company with: in association with: WITH

and *conj*: along with or together with: added to or linked to: as well as: again and again: also at the same time: THEN: in addition to being: but not less truly: YET

anger *n*: a strong feeling of displeasure and usually of antagonism: a cause or manifestation of anger: something resembling the state, appearance, or behavior of an angry person

Michelle Lynn

announce *vb*: to give notice of the arrival, presence, or readiness of: to point to or indicate in advance: declare beforehand: FORETELL

anoint *vb*: to choose by or as if by divine election: designate as if through the rite of anointment: CONSECRATE

any *adj*: one, some, or all indiscriminately of whatever quantity: one or more not none—used as a function word to indicate a positive but undetermined number or amount

apart *adj*: to or at one side: at a little distance: separately in space or time: away from one another: as a separate or distinct object of thought: INDEPENDENTLY, INDIVIDUALLY

apparatus *n*: a preparation for action: a collection or set of materials, instruments, appliances, or machinery designed for a particular use

appear *vb*: to be clear to the mind: be obvious or evident: to reveal itself to an observer or reader: be manifest

appointment *vb*: designation by virtue of a vested power of a person to enjoy an estate or other specific property subject to that power: an arrangement for a meeting: ENGAGEMENT

apportion *vb*: to divide and assign in proportion: divide and distribute proportionately: make an apportionment of: portion out: ALLOT

are BE

arm *n*: POWER, MIGHT: STRENGTH SUPPORT

army *n*: a body of persons organized for the advancement of a cause

arrange *vb*: to put in correct, convenient, or desired order: adjust properly: DISPOSE, PLACE: to put in order beforehand: make preparations for: PLAN: to effect usually by consulting: come to an agreement or understanding about: SETTLE *as* adv: to the same degree or amount: to such an extent: EQUALLY—used to modify an adjective or an adverb: for instance: by way of example: THUS—usually used to introduce illustrative details

as pron: THAT, WHO, WHICH: a fact that: THAT

ascend vb: to go upon upward from a lower level or degree: RISE

assemblage n: a collection of individuals or particular things: ASSEMBLAGE

assemble vb: to bring or summon together into a group, crowd, company, assembly, or unit

assembly n: a company of persons collected together in one place usually for some common purpose

asylum n: a place of refuge and protection (as a temple, altar, or statue of a god or in later times a Christian church) where criminals and debtors found shelter and from which they could not be forcibly taken without sacrilege: SANCTUARY: a place of retreat and security: SHELTER

attain vb: REACH, GAIN, ACHIEVE, ACCOMPLISH: to get at the knowledge of: ASCERTAIN: to come into possession of: OBTAIN: OVERTAKE: get at: CATCH: to reach or come to by progression or motion: arrive at

attendant n: one who attends or accompanies another in order to render a service

B

back *adv.*: to or toward the rear: to or toward a place away from any place regarded as the front, center, or forward position: at the rear or a position be- hind: at a place considered away from the front, center, or forward position: in or into the past: AGO

bar *n*: a piece (as of wood or metal) longer than it is wide and usually having considerable rigidity that is used as a lever, handle, support, or division maker

basin *n*: a great depression in the surface of the lithosphere occupied by an ocean

battle *n*: participation in armed conflict: WARFARE

be *vb*: to equal in meaning: have the same connotation: have a (specified) qualification or characteristic: to exist either absolutely or in relations or under conditions specified: have an objective existence: have reality or actuality: LIVE

bear give birth to young

beautiful *adj*: keenly delighting the senses as approaching perfection or the ideal in form, proportion, arrangement, color, or sound: delighting with a higher, more exalted appeal: calling forth great spiritual, intellectual, and aesthetic appreciation: lofty in effect

because *conj*: SINCE: for the reason that: on account of the cause that—used to introduce dependent clauses: in order that: to the end that

become *vb*: COME, ARRIVE: GO: to come to exist or occur: to emerge as an entity: grow to manifest a certain essence, nature, development, or significance

before *prep*: preceding (a point, turn, or incident in time): earlier than: preceding (something or someone in a chronological series): in the presence of: in sight or notice of: face to face with: CONFRONTING: in defiance of: in firm opposition to: in the estimation of: according to the precepts, doctrines, or views emanating from or associated with: in greater esteem, significance, or value than: more important than: as a result of: in consequence of

beget *vb*: to acquire especially through effort: to procreate as the father: SIRE: to give birth to: BREED: to make (a woman) pregnant: to produce usually as an effect or as a natural outgrowth

begin *vb*: to come into existence: ARISE: originate or be called into being

besides *adv*: in addition: over and above: MOREOVER, FURTHERMORE: OTHERWISE, ELSE

between *prep*: from one to the other of: JOINING, CONNECTING: in common to: in the joint possession, action, or agency of: SEPARATING, DISTINGUISHING: setting apart

bind *vb*: to make secure by tying: to confine with or as if with chains or other bonds so as to deprive of liberty: make captive: to hold in check: keep in place: RESTRAIN

bitter *adj*: marked by intensity or severity: RIGOROUS: accompanied by severe pain or suffering of mind or body: difficult to bear: VEHEMENT, RELENTLESS, DETERMINED: exhibiting intense animosity

blade n: the portion of the tongue immediately behind the tip and lying approximately opposite the teethridge when the tongue is at rest: this portion of the tongue together with the tip: an edged instrument: as: SWORD

blandishment n: speech, action, or device that flatters and tends to coax, or cajole

blunt *vb*: to lessen or destroy the force or effectiveness of: WEAKEN

booty n: PLUNDER, SPOILS: loot taken in war: REWARD, PRIZE, GAIN

bore vb: make a hole in or through: PENETRATE

borrow vb: to receive temporarily from another, implying or expressing the in- tention of returning the thing received or of giving its equivalent to the lender: obtain the temporary use of

both adj: the two: the one and the other

branch n: something that extends from, enters into, or is an offshoot of a main body or source

break vb: to violate or transgress by failure to follow, observe, or act in accordance with: fail to keep

breath n: SPIRIT, ANIMATION, VITALITY, LIFE

brick n: a block

brighten vb: to cause to shine: to make illustrious or more illustrious: to give a brighter hue or color to: to make more cheerful: ENLIVEN

bring vb: to convey, lead, carry, or cause to come along from one place to another, the direction of movement being toward the place from which the action is being regarded

builder n: one that builds

burdensome adj: difficult or distressing to carry or to bear: OPPRESSIVE

burst vb: to pass from one place to another especially with great vigor against obstacles or on release from some restraint: to appear or disappear suddenly or unexpectedly—usually with words expressing direction: to make or undergo an abrupt change: as: to pass from a less to a more vigorous, ardent, or glowing state

but vb: to thrust or push head foremost: strike with the head or horns

C

capacity n: the power or ability to hold, receive, or accommodate

capital adj: of a city: most important: being the seat of government

capture vb: to take, seize, or catch especially as captive or prize by force, surprise, stratagem, craft, or skill: as: to subdue into surrender and loss of independence: to seize and occupy: to get control or secure domination of: WIN, GAIN

care vb: to have a liking, fondness, or taste: have regard or respect

castle n: a retreat or stronghold safe against intrusion or invasion

catch vb: to capture or seize especially after pursuit or attempts to capture: TRAP, ENSNARE, ENTANGLE: DECEIVE

causal adj: expressing or indicating cause: marked by cause and effect

cavalry n: the component of an army mounted on horseback or moving in motor vehicles and having combat missions (as reconnaissance and counter-reconnaissance) that requires great mobility

cease vb: to come to an end: break off or taper off to a stop: to give over or bring to an end an activity or action: DISCONTINUE

certainty n: something that is certain: the quality or state of being certain

chief adj: accorded highest rank, office, or rating: superior in authority,

power, or influence: SALIENT: subordinating other persons, things, items of

the same kind or class

choose vb: to select (as one thing over another) especially with free will and by exercise of judgment

circumspect adj: marked by caution and earnest attention to all significant circumstances and possibly consequences of action

Michelle Lynn

(as action to be under-taken) and usually by prudence and discretion

city n: an inhabited place: HAMLET, VILLAGE

clarify vb: to make clear and bright by lightening the darkness and obscurity of

cleanse vb: to release, deliver, or absolve from sin or guilt: rid of any moral blemish: FREE, ABSOLVE

clear adj: shining brightly: GLEAMING, LUSTROUS: entirely light: UNDIMMED, UNDARKENED, BRIGHT: having the sky free from clouds: having the air free from mist, haze, or dust: giving free passage to light or to the sight

clearly adv: in a clear manner: without doubt or question

close vb: to block out: SCREEN, EXCLUDE

coast n: a region or area especially of the earth: the border or frontier of a country: the land near a border

cohere vb: to become harmoniously united by common interests or sense of social membership or by emotional ties and especially with the cooperative playing down any individual differences or disagreements

colored adj: FEIGNED, PRETENDED

come vb: to move toward or away from something: pass from one point toward another nearer or more central: APPROACH: to approach or reach a condition through or as if through change: to arrive at a particular place, end, result, or conclusion

commander n: one in an official position of command or control

compact n: an agreement, understanding, or covenant between two or more parties

companionship n: the quality or state of being a companion: the fellowship existing among companions *complete* vb: to make whole, entire, or perfect: end after satisfying all demands or requirements: to mark the end of: show attainment to the total or totality of

compute vb: to determine or ascertain especially by mathematical means: arrive at an answer to or sum for

concord n: agreement by stipulation, compact, or covenant: TREATY; especially: one establishing or reestablishing peaceful and amicable relationships between people or nations

condition n: something that exists as an occasion of something else: a circumstance that is essential to the appearance or occurrence of something else: PREREQUISITE

congregation n: an assembly of persons: GATHERING

conjunction n: the act of conjoining or state of being conjoined: UNION, ASSOCIATION, CONBINATION

conquer vb: to procure by effort: ACQUIRE, GET, GAIN: to gain or acquire by force of arms: take possession of by violent means: gain domination over : SUBJUGATE: to overcome by force of arms: VANQUISH: to gain or win by overcoming obstacles or opposition: gain mastery over: to subdue or over- come by mental or moral power: SURMOUNT

consecrate vb: to make or declare sacred or holy: effect the consecration of : set apart, dedicate, devote to the service or worship of God

conspicuous adj: obvious to the eye or mind: plainly visible: MANIFEST: attracting or tending to attract attention by reason of size, brilliance, contrast, station: STRIKING, EMINENT

constant n: marked by firmness, steadfastness, resolution, or faithfulness : not weak, yielding, vacillating, or disloyal

constantly adv: with loyalty: FAITHFULLY

consume vb: to destroy or do away with completely (as if by fire, disease, famine, decomposition): cause to waste away utterly:

Michelle Lynn

to engage or absorb fully the attention, interest, or energy of: ENGROSS

continuance *adv*: a holding on or remaining in a particular state or course of action: permanence especially of action, condition, habits, or abode: PERSEVERANCE: PREOLONGATION, DURATION: a continuing or remaining in some place or condition: ABIDING, STAY

contrivance *n*: the act or faculty of contriving: inventive ability: skill at devising: INGENUITY: the quality or state of being contrived: artificial arrangement or mechanical assembling as opposed to natural or logical development: a thing contrived: ARTIFICE, SCHEME, PLAM: a mechanical device: INVENTION, APPLIANCE

contumely *n*: rude language or treatment arising from haughtiness and contempt: an instance of contumely: INSULT: the suffering of contumely : HUMILIATION

copiousness *n*: PLENTY, RICHNESS, FULLNESS

courageous *adj*: having or characterized by courage: marked by bold resolution in withstanding the dangerous, alarming, or difficult: BRAVE

cover *vb*: to lie over: spread over: be placed on or often over the whole surface of: ENVELOP, FILM, COAT

cross *vb*: to transfer

crowd *n*: a large number of persons especially when collected into a somewhat compact body without order: THRONG: an unorganized aggregate of people temporarily united in response to a common stimulus or situation in which the individuality of the participants is submerged

crunch *vb*: to grind or press with a noise of crushing

cure *vb*: HEAL: to restore to health, soundness, or normality: to bring about recovery from: REMEDY: to treat so as to remove, eliminate, or rectify: to free or relieve (a person) from an objectionable or harmful condition or inclination

Cushite *n {Cush (Kush), an ancient country in the Nile valley adjoining Egypt}*: a native or inhabitant of ancient Cush

cut *vb*: to divide into segments: separate into parts with an action or result suggestive of that of an edged instrument: divide off or up

D

dainty n: something delicious to the taste: DELICACY: something that aroused favor or excites pleasure: something choice or pleasing

dark adj: not readily perceptible: as: not clear to the understanding

daughter n: a human female descended from remote ancestors: female descendant: girl or woman of a given lineage: something derived from it's source or origin as if feminine <the United States is a daughter of Great Britain>: a female in a spiritual kinship analogous to the physical <daughters of the church>

day n: a day set aside for a particular purpose: a date on which some notable event occurred or on which the occurrence of a notable event is celebrated: a particular day that is identified by reference to or that is commonly associated with some unique historical event: the period of the existence or prominence of a person or thing: AGE: the term of one's career, activity, or life: LIFETIME: the time during which ones life continues

decay vb: to decline from a prosperous condition: to pass gradually from a comparatively sound or perfect state to one of unsoundness, imperfection or dissolution

deceive vb: to take unawares especially by craft or trickery: ENSNARE, MISLEAD: to be false to: BETRAY: to disappoint (as an expectation): to deprive especially by fraud or stealth: CHEAT, DEFRAUD: to cause to believe the false: DELUDE

decide vb: to make clear: EXPLAIN, INTERPRET: to make known publicly, formally, or explicitly especially by language: announce, proclaim, or publish especially by a formal statement or official pronouncement: communicate to others: to make evident or give evidence of: serve as a means of revealing: MANIFEST, SHOW

defender n: one that defends: PROTECTOR, ADVOCATE, CHAMPION, VINDICATOR, UPHOLDER

defense n: capability of resisting attack: practice or manner of self protection: means or method of defending: defensive plan, policy, or structure

defense v: to furnish with defenses

deity n: a person or thing that is exalted or revered as supremely good or great: one that holds or wields supreme power or influence in some field

deject vb: to cast down: bend down: OVERTHROW: to lower especially in rank or condition: ABASE, HUMBLE: to reduce especially in force, degree, or quality: WEAKEN, LESSEN

delight n: a high degree of gratification of mind or sense: a high-wrought state of pleasurable feeling: lively pleasure: JOY: extreme satisfaction: something that gives great pleasure or gratification: the power of affording pleasurable emotion or felicity

delight v: to have or take great satisfaction or pleasure: become greatly pleased or rejoiced—used with or in an infinitive: to give keen enjoyment or pleasure

deliverance n: the act of delivering or state of being delivered: as: the act of freeing or state of being freed (as from restraint, captivity, peril): RESCUE, LIBERATION, RELEASE

deluge n: an irresistible rush of something (as overwhelming numbers, quantity, or volume)

descendent n: one that is descended from another or from a common stock: a lineal or collateral blood relative usually of a later generation: something that derives its character directly from a precursor or prototype: especially: an offshoot from an antecedent practice or idea

Michelle Lynn

designation n: the act of indicating or identifying by a mark, letter, or sign or by classification or specification: a distinguishing name: a title earned or awarded

desirable adj: worth seeking or doing as advantageous, beneficial, or wise: ADVISABLE, EXPEDIENT

desist vb: to give over or leave off: refrain from or forbear continuing an action, activity, or endeavor under way—often used with from or in: to cease from: DISCONTINUE

desolate vb: to deprive partially or wholly of inhabitants: DEPOPULATE: to lay waste: RAVAGE: to leave in a ruinous or barren state

despond vb: to feel utter discouragement: undergo deep depression of spirits at vanquishing hope, courage, or confidence

destruction n: the action or process of destroying a material or immaterial object: demolition or complete ruin: killing or annihilation: a bringing to an end: ELIMINATION, ERADICATION: IMPAIRMENT, DISRUPTION, DISINTEGRATION

destructive adj: having the capability, property, or effect of destroying: causing destruction: tending to bring about demolition or devastation: tending to take life or promote death: dangerously injurious to a living being: DEADLY ANNIHILATIVE: tending to impair, damage, or wreck: productive of evil results: DELETERIOUS

devastate vb: to lay waste: RAVAGE: OVERPOWER, OVERCOME, OVERWHELM

devote vb: to set apart by a solemn act of appropriation: dedicate or consecrate especially formally: to provide (something) for use: to give up (as time, money, thought, effort) to the cause, for the benefit, or to the advancement something regarded as deserving support, improvement, or aid: to attach the attention or center the activities of (oneself) on

direction *n*: something that is imposed as authoritative instruction or bidding: an explicit instruction: ORDER, COMMAND: the way of advancement, furtherance, or cultivation: AIM, PURPOSE, OBJECTIVE

disesteem: to consciously lack esteem for: regard with disfavor or slight contempt

disgrace *n*: loss of grace, favor, or honor: the condition of one fallen from grace or honor usually through some indecorous, dishonest, or immoral action

disgusting *adj*: causing disgust: SICKENING, REVOLTING, NAUSEATING, LOATHESOME

disperse *vb*: to cause to break up and go in different ways: send or drive into different places: SCATTER

disquietude *n*: lack of peace or tranquillity: UNEASINESS, AGITATION, ANXIETY

disregard *vb*: to treat without fitting respect or attention: to treat as unworthy of regard or notice: to give no thought to: pay no attention to

dissimulate *vb*: to hide under a false appearance: DISSEMBLE

dissolve *vb*: to cause to disperse or disappear: get rid of: do away with: DESTROY: to separate into component parts: DISINTEGRATE, DECOMPOSE

distinction *n*: a part of a divided whole: CATEGORY, SECTION: the act of separating into parts: PARTITION, DIVISION: CLASS, GRADE, RANK: the act of distinguishing a difference: DISCRIMINATION, DIFFERENTIATION

distinguish *vb*: to perceive as being separate or different: DIFFERENTIATE: to mark as separate or different as one thing from another: make a difference between: DISCRIMINATE: to set above or apart from others: make eminent: give prestige to: to separate or divide into portions or sections: mark (parts) as separate

district n: the territory under a feudal lord's jurisdiction: a territorial division (as of a nation, state, county, or city) marked off or defined for administrative, electoral, judicial, or other purposes

disturb vb: to destroy the rest, tranquillity, or settled state of: stir up: AGITATE, TROUBLE

do vb: CAUSE, MAKE: to bring to pass: carry out: PUT: to perform (as an action) by oneself or before another: EXECUTE: to be the cause of: bring about as a result: EFFECT: to give freely: RENDER, PAY: to bring to an end: COMPLETE, FINISH: to take place: go on: HAPPEN

dominion n: a supremacy in determining and directing the actions of others or in governing politically, socially, or personally: acknowledged ascendancy over human or nonhuman forces such as assures cogency in commanding or restraining and being obeyed: SOVEREIGNTY

drive vb: to subject to effective pressure or compulsion to act in a certain way or to submit to a certain condition

driver n: one that drives something: as: a person in actual physical control of a vehicle (as an automobile)

drought n: a period of dryness especially protracted and causing extensive damage to crops or preventing their successful growth

dry adj: free or relatively free from water or liquid

dull adj: lacking sharpness of edge or point: BLUNT

during prep: throughout the continuance or course of: at some point in the course of

E

earth n: areas of land uncovered by water: the solid footing formed of earth: the solid materials that make up the physical globe: a particular region of the world: COUNTRY, LAND

east n: the general direction of sunrise: the direction toward the right of one facing north

eat vb: to take in in order to obtain some benefit: to submit tamely to (as insult or abuse): accept as ones portion: to accept unquestioningly: believe uncritically

Edom *(Edomite)* n: a member of an ancient people who were descended from Esau and who lived southeast of the Dead Sea *see also map*

effervescence n: inner excitement or turmoil usually finding expression in lively action: the quality or state of being effervescent

egress n: the act or right of going or coming out (as from a place of confinement): a place or means of going: EXIT, OUTLET

Egypt adj: *{from a country in northeastern Africa}*: of or from Egypt: of the kind or style prevalent in Egypt

either—or n: am unavoidable choice or exclusive division between only two alternatives: DICHOTOMY

emit vb: to send out: DISCHARGE, RELEASE: as: to throw out or give off or out (as effluvia, light, heat, gases, or charged particles)

empire n: an extended territory usually comprising a group of nations, states, or peoples under the control or domination of a single sovereign power: supreme or absolute power especially of an emperor: imperial dominion, sway, or sovereignty

encampment n: the place where a body of troops or campers is encamped: CAMP: individuals that make up an encampment

end n: cessation of a course of action, pursuit, or activity

engagement *n*: hostile encounter between military forces: a duel or other single combat

enraged *adj*: INFURIATED, MADDENED

equally *adv*: in an equal manner or way: in equal amounts or shares: with equal treatment for each: JUSTLY, IMPARTIALLY: UNIFORMLY, EVENLY: in the same way: LIKEWISE, SIMILARLY: to an equal degree: ALIKE

escape *vb*: to get or be out of the way of (something one wishes to avoid): miss or succeed in averting (pain or misfortune): AVOID, ELUDE, EVADE: to be unnoticed by or not obvious, apparent, or recallable to

even *adv*: without disagreement: in accord: as well: PRECISELY, JUST, EXACTLY: to a degree that extends: FULLY, QUITE: at the very time that: ALREADY: TRULY, INDEED, NAY

every *adj*: COMPLETE, ENTIRE

examine *vb*: to test by an appropriate method: INVESTIGATE: as: to look over: inspect visually or by use of other senses (as for the determination of accuracy, propriety, or quality): to inspect or test for evidence of disease or abnormality

except *conj*: on any other condition than that: UNLESS

exile *n*: forced removal from one's native country: expulsion from home: BANISHMENT: voluntary absence from one's country

exist *vb*: to have actual or real being whether material or spiritual: have being in space and time: to have being in any specified condition or place or with respect to any understood limitation: to continue to be: maintain being: to have life or the function of vitality: LIVE

expend *vb*: to pay out or distribute: SPEND: to consume by use: use up

explain *vb*: to make manifest: present in detail: EXPOUND, DISCLOSE: to make plain or understandable: clear of complexities or obscurity: INTERPRET, CLARIFY: to give the meaning or significance of: provide an understanding of: to give the reason for or cause of: account for

expose vb: to disclose or reveal the faults, frailties, or unsoundness of: bring to light (as something criminal or shameful): UNMASK

extension n: a carrying forward: LENGTHENING, FURTHERING, DEVELOPING: the action of spreading out (as in area) or state of being spread out: EXPANSION, ENLARGEMENT, AUGMENTATION, INCREASE

extremity n: a culminating point (as of emotion or pain): HEIGHT, APEX, CLIMAX: the fullest possible extent: utmost limit: utmost degree

F

fabricate *vb*: to form by art and labor: MANUFACTURE, PRODUCE: to form into a whole by uniting parts: CONSTRUCT, BUILD: INVENT, FORMULATE: CREATE: to make up with intent to deceive

face *n*: ASSURANCE, CONFIDENCE: DIGNITY, PRESTIGE: outward appearance or aspect: SEMBLANCE: visible or apparent state or condition: outward appearance of dignity or prestige or of freedom from abashment, confusion, anger, or distress: broadly: DISGUISE, PRETENCE

failure *n*: DEFICIENCY, LACK: the fact of being cumulatively inadequate or not matching hopes or expectations: ABSENCE, NONEXISTENCE: marked weakening: the fact of becoming exhausted or enfeebled: DETERIORATION: inability to perform a vital function: a collapsing, fracturing, or giving way under stress

fall *n*: loss of greatness, power, status, influence, or dominion: COLLAPSE, DOWNFALL: the surrender or capture of a besieged fortress or town

fall *v*: to suffer destruction, capture, or total military defeat: COLLAPSE: to suffer ruin, defeat, or failure: fail utterly: to make a hostile move or attack physically or verbally: FELL *fell* *v*: to cut, beat, or knock down or bring down

falter *vb*: to hesitate in purpose or action: WAVER, FLINCH: to lose drive, effectiveness, or momentum in some way: WEAKEN, DECLINE, FAIL

far *adv*: to a great extent: MUCH: by a broad space: WIDELY

fascinate *vb*: to transfix and hold spellbound by or as if by irresistible power: to command the attention or interest of strongly or irresistibly often by the artful, subtle, challenging, strange, or piquant

fasten vb: to focus or direct (as the attention) intently or steadily: place (as one's hopes) strongly: to attach, affix, or associate (oneself) persistently and usually objectionably or with or as if with the intent to annoy or exploit or with the result of limiting the freedom of another

fat adj: well furnished, filled, or stocked: ABUNDANT: PROSPEROUS, WEALTHY: PRODUCTIVE, FERTILE, FRUITFUL

father n: a make ancestor more remote than a parent; FOREFATHER, ANCESTOR: one that originates or institutes: one that first constructs, d designs, or frames: SOURCE, ORIGIN

fatness n: FERTILITY, FRUITFULNESS

fear n: the state or habit of feeling agitation or dismay: a condition between anxiety and terror either natural and well-grounded or unreasoned and blind

feed vb: to move in or as if in supplying something with what it uses or consumes

fertile adj: characterized by production of great quantities: abundant in yield: PRODUCTIVE

festival n: a time of celebration marked by special observances: an occasion observed with religious ceremonies: FEAST

fever n: a state of agitated or intense activity: urgent haste: an abnormal often unstable condition of mind or society

few adj: consisting of or amounting to a small number: not many

filthy adj: covered with, having the appearance of, or containing filth: very dirty: UNDERHANDED, VILE: OBSCENE

find vb: to secure or obtain (something needed or desirable) by effort or management: summon up: PROCURE: to attain to: arrive at: REACH

finished adj: brought to conclusion: ENDED, COMPLETED: possessed of, brought to, or displaying the highest degree of skill, polish, or excellence: marked by the highest quality: CONSUMMATE, PERFECTED

first *adj*: being number one in a countable series: beginning a series: foremost in rank, importance, or worth: CHIEF

firstfruits *n*: the earliest products, effects, or results of any work, endeavor, or process

fix *vb*: to set or place definitely: STATION, SETTLE: to assign precisely: settle on: DETERMINE, DEFINE: ASSIGN, PLACE

flash *n*: SHOW, DISPLAY ; especially: a vulgar ostentatious display: a showy ostentatious person: SWELL, FOP: something or someone that attracts notice (as by gaudiness or excellence)

flattery *n*: the act or practice of flattering: the act of pleasing by artful commendation: ADULATION: something that flatters or is felt flatteringly; often: false, insincere, or excessive praise: a pleasing self-deception

flight *n*: a number of similar beings or things passing through or capable of passing the air together: a swarm of insects

flock *n*: a band or company of people: all Christians in their relation to Christ

foam *vb*: to froth at the mouth in anger: be angry: RAGE

for *conj*: by reason that: for the reason that: BECAUSE: for this reason or on this ground: NAMELY: as indicated or shown by the following circumstance

force *n*: strength or energy especially of an exceptional degree: active power: VIGOR: power or capacity to sway, convince, or impose obligation: VALIDITY, EFFECT: might or greatness especially of a prince or state; often: strength or capacity for waging war

foreign *adj*: born in, belonging to, derived from, intended for, or characteristic of some place or country (or nation) other than the one under consideration: not native or domestic: of, relating to, proceeding from some other person, material thing, or substance than the one under consideration

foreigner n: something originating in another country

foreleg n: either of the anterior pair of legs of a quadruped or multiped: a front leg of a legged inanimate object (as a chair)

forth adv: out especially from a state of concealment, retirement, confinement, or nondevelopment: out into notice or view

fortification n: something that fortifies, defends, or strengthens; especially: works erected to defend a place or position

fortified past of *fortify*

fortify vb: to make strong: STRENGTHEN: as: to strengthen and secure (as a town) by forts or batteries or by surrounding with fortifications: to give physical strength, courage, or endurance to: INVIGORATE, REFRESH

four n: four units in a countable series

fourth n: number four in a countable series

fraud n: an instance or an act of trickery or deceit especially when involving misrepresentation: an act of deluding: DELUSION

from prep: used as a function word to indicate a starting point: used as a function word to indicate the source or original or moving force of something

front n: a sphere or area of conflict or activity

front prep: directly before: before the foremost part of: ahead of

froth vb: VENT, VOICE

fury n: violent anger: extreme wrath: RAGE: extreme impetuosity or violence: unrestrained force

fuse vb: to unite as if by melting together: BLEND, INTEGRATE: to become integrated: UNITE, MERGE

future n: time that is to come: what is going to happen

Michelle Lynn

G

gallop n: a rapid rate or pace

gather vb: to effect the collection of (as tax, tribute, dues, contributions): to prepare (as oneself) by mustering strength or force

gazelle vb: to move in easy leaps suggesting those of a gazelle

gentile n: a person of a non-Jewish nation or of non-Jewish faith; especially: a Christian as distinguished from a Jew: HEATHEN, PAGAN

give vb: to transfer from one's authority, custody, or responsibility: to deliver or deal by some bodily action: to carry out (a movement of or as if of the body): EXECUTE, MAKE: to cause to have or receive: OCCASION

gloomy adj: full of gloom: partially or totally dark: SHADOWY: dimly or murkily glimmering; especially: dismally and depressingly: having an appearance of gloom

go vb: to move on a course: pass from point to point or station to station: proceed by any of several means: to take a certain course or follow a certain procedure: to reach a certain point: ATTAIN, EXTEND

god n: a being of more than human attributes and powers: a person or thing that is honored as a god or deified: something held to be of supreme value

God n: the supreme or ultimate reality: the holy, infinite, and eternal spiritual reality presented in the Bible as the creator, sustainer, judge, righteous sovereign, and redeemer of the universe who acts with power in history in carrying out his purpose

gold n: gold coins: a gold piece: MONEY, RICHES: something resembling gold; especially: something treasured as the essence or finest exemplification of its kind *grandeur* n: greatness of power or position: the quality of being majestic, magnificent, splendid, stately or imposing in an awe-inspiring way especially to the view

grandson n: a son's or daughter's son

grate vb: FRET, IRRITATE, OFFEND

great adj: large in number: NUMEROUS: PREDOMINANT, OVERRULING: considerable or remarkable in magnitude, power, intensity, degree, or effectiveness: LOUD: HEAVY, FORCEFUL: INTENSE: FAR-REACHING: big in scope: EXTREME, MARKED

grow vb: to pass by degrees into a state or condition: come to be: develop by degrees: BECOME

gush vb: to give free reign to a sudden copious flow or issuing forth

H

habitable *adj*: capable of being inhabited: that may be inhabited or dwelt in

halve *vb*: to divide into two equal parts: separate into halves

hand *n*: personal possession: CONTROL, DIRECTION, SUPERVISION: right or privilege in controlling or directioning

harass *vb*: to tire out (as with physical or mental effort): EXHAUST, FATIGUE: to vex, trouble, or annoy continually or chronically (as with anxieties, burdens, or misfortune): PLAGUE, BEDEVIL, BADGER

hasten *vb*: to urge on: HURRY: to speed up: ACCELERATE: to send or bring up quickly *he* *pron*: that male one: that one regarded as masculine (as by personification): that one whose sex is unknown or immaterial—used as a nominative case form in general statements (as in statutes) to include females, fictitious persons (as corporation), and several persons collectively

head *n*: one who stands in relation to others somewhat as the head does to the other members of the body: DIRECTOR, CHIEF

heard *vb*: to be made aware of by the ear: apprehend by the ear: to be informed or gain knowledge of by hearing

heart *n*: the whole personality including intellectual as well as emotional functions or traits: INTELLECT, UNDERSTANDING, OPINION, ATTITUDE, POSTURE: COURAGE, ARDOR, ENTHUSIASM: the central or decisive part of something: CENTRAL: as: an inner central area or region: an essential part: the part that determines the real nature of something or gives significance to the other parts: the determining aspect: the center of activity: a vital part on which continuing activity or existence depends

heat n: the energy associated with the random motions of the molecules, atoms, or smaller structural units of which matter is composed

heathendom n: the part of the world where heathenism prevails

heathenism n: the religious system or rites of heathens: IDOLATRY, PAGANISM

heavy adj: having great weight

help vb: to give assistance or support to: AID: to be of use to: BENEFIT: to further the advancement of: PROMOTE

hidden adj: being out of sight or off the beaten track: CONCEALED: UNEXPLAINED, UNDISCLOSED, OBSCURE, SECRET: obscured by something that makes recognition difficult: covered up

high adj: advanced toward its acme or fullest extent: advanced toward its most active or culminating point; specifically: constituting the late, fully developed, or most creative stage or period (as of an artistic style or career or historical movement)

hinder adj: situated behind or at or in the rear: BACK, HIND

hold back vb: to keep in check: RESTRAIN, CURB: to keep from advancing to the next stage, grade, or level

honor vb: to show high regard or appreciation for: pay tribute to: EXALT, PRAISE: to confer a distinction upon

honorable adj: of great renown: ILLUSTRIOUS

how adv: in what manner or way: by what means or process: to what extent, degree, number, or amount: by what measure or quantity

Michelle Lynn

I

I pron: self

idol n: an image of a divinity: a representation or symbol of a deity or any other being or thing made or used as an object of worship: a false god: a heathen deity: something or someone on which the affections are strongly and often excessively set: an object of passionate devotion:a person or thing greatly loved or adored

idolatrous adj: of or relating to idolatry: as: being or resembling idolatry: given to or practicing idolatry

Idumaea {ancient region south of the Dead Sea in Palestine} Edomite

ignore vb: to be ignorant of: to refuse to take notice of: shut the eyes to: disregard willfully

image n: a reproduction of a person or thing: as: STATUE: DEVICE, EMBLEM: a figure used as a talisman or amulet especially in conjurations (as by a sorcerer in casting spells): PICTURE, PORTRAIT: a sculptured or fabricated object of symbolic value: IDOL: specifically: a holy picture (as an icon): a thing actually or seemingly reproducing another: the optical counterpart of an object produced by a lens, mirror, or other optical system and being the geometric figure make up of the foci corresponding to the points of the object—see REAL IMAGE, VIRTUAL IMAGE: any likeness of an object produced on a photographic material: exact likeness: SEMBLANCE

implied vb: to convey or communicate not by direct forthright statement but by allusion or reference likely to lead to natural inference: suggest or hint at

in prep: used as a function word to indicate location or position in space or in some materially bounded object: within the limits of a space of time expressed or implied: used as a function word to indicate means or instrumentality: used as a function word to indicate consideration of a thing strictly limited to its own essence, nature, or merits, apart from its relations to others

inbred *n*: an individual resulting from the mating of closely related parents: a product of inbreeding

inclose *variation of* **enclose** *vb*: to close in: SURROUND: specifically: to fence off or in (common land) in order to appropriate to an individual use: ENVELOP, ENFOLD: to hem in: CONFINE: subject (a religion or a building or an area) to the rules of enclosure: to seize or grasp securely: HOLD

increase *vb*: to become greater in some respect (as in size, quantity, number, degree, value, intensity, power, authority, reputation, wealth): GROW, ADVANCE, WAX

insolent *adj*: haughty and contemptuous or brutal in behavior or language: OVERBEARING: lacking usual or proper respect for rank or position: presumptuously disrespectful or familiar toward equals or superiors: provokingly free or pert: proceeding from or characterized by insolence: exceeding due bounds: EXCESSIVE, EXTRAVAGANT: of such scope as to give an effect of contemptuous self-assurance: not customary: NOVEL, STRANGE, UNUSUAL

instruction *n*: something that instructs or is imparted in order to instruct: as: LESSON, PRECEPT: INFORMATION, NEWS REPORT: something given by by way of direction or order **instruct** *vb*: to give special knowledge or information to

intelligent *adj*: marked by quick active perception and understanding: showing or having some special knowledge, skill, or aptitude

intention *n*: an intended object: AIM, END: the import or meaning of something: something that is conveyed or intended to be conveyed to the understanding: SIGNIFICANCE

inundate *vb*: to overwhelm by great numbers or superfluity of something: SWAMP

Michelle Lynn

Ionian n: a native or inhabitant of Ionia; especially: one of the Greek people descended from an early group of Hellenic invaders of Greece

ire n: ANGER, WRATH

island n: a tract of land surrounded by water and smaller than a continent: a tract of land cut off on two or more sides by water: PENINSULA: something resembling an island by its isolated, surrounded, or sequestered position

islander n: a native or inhabitant of an island

issue vb: to go out or come out or flow out

it pron: that one—used as neuter pronoun of the third person singular that is the subject or direct object or indirect object of a verb or the object of a preposition and usually used in reference to: a lifeless thing or: a plant or: an insect or an animal whose sex is unknown or disregarded or: an infant or child whose sex is unknown or disregarded or: a group or classification of individuals or things

iteration n: the action of repeating or reiteration: REPETITION, REITERATION

J

Javan {*definition from concordance*}: the name of a son of Joktan {*definition from dictionary*}: a native or inhabitant of Java (an island in Indonesia

join vb: to put or bring into close contact, association, or relationship: ATTACH, UNITE, COUPLE

judgeship n: the jurisdiction or office of a judge

jurisdiction n: authority of a sovereign power to govern or legislate: power or right to exercise authority: the limits or territory within which any particular power may be exercised: sphere of authority: CONTROL

K

king n: one that holds a supreme or preeminent position in a particular sphere or class

Kittite (Chittim) descendants of Javan

knife n: a weapon consisting of or resembling a knife

knife vb: to try to defeat by underhanded means (as a political candidate of one's own party): to work secretly against (one justified in expecting support): UNDERMINE

know vb: to apprehend immediately with the mind or with the senses: perceive directly: have direct unambiguous cognition of: to have perception, cognition, or understanding of especially to an extensive or complete extent: to recognize the quality of: see clearly the character of: DISCERN

L

land *n*: a portion (as a country, estate, farm, or tract) of the earth's solid surface considered by itself or as belonging to an individual or a people: REALM, DOMAIN: any ground, soil, or earth whatsoever regarded as the subject of ownership (as meadows, pastures, woods) and everything annexed to it whether by nature (as trees, water) or by man (as buildings, fences) extending indefinitely vertically upwards and downwards

large *adj*: having more than usual power, capacity, range or scope: COMPREHENSIVE: involving few restrictions: permitting considerable liberty (as of action or conscience)

last *adj*: lowest in rank or degree

last *n*: the last part: CONCLUSION, END

late *adj*: coming or occurring at an advanced stage (as of life or a period)

leader *n*: a person or animal that leads

libation *n*: the act of pouring a liquid (as wine) either on the ground or on a victim in a sacrifice to a deity

Libyan *n* {*Libya, ancient territory variously conceived in northern Africa*}: a member of any of the people's indigenous in historical ancient times to the region immediately west of Egypt

lie *n*: an assertion of something known or believed by the speaker to be untrue: a deliberate misrepresentation of fact with intent to deceive: something that misleads or deceives

life *n*: something resembling animate life: as: continued active existence and development

lift *vb*: to raise from a lower to a higher position: to raise in rank, condition, or position: to take up and remove (as a tent or camp): to put an end to (a blockade or siege) by causing the withdraw of investing forces

Michelle Lynn

lineage *n*: descent in a line from a common progenitor: derivation or source of origin: line of descent or tradition: BACKGROUND

little *n*: something not very extensive (as in amount, quantity): only a small amount or quantity: something far short of everything: something constituting only a tiny fraction of all: practically nothing

lizard *n*: any relatively long-bodied reptile with legs and tapering tail (as crocodile or dinosaur)

lo *interjection*: used to call attention or to express surprise

long *adv*: for the duration of a specified period

loosen *vb*: to set free: release from restraint: let loose: to make looser: free from or lessen the tightness, firmness, or fixedness of: to cause to become less strict: relax the severity of

lots *n*: something that comes to or happens to one upon whom a choice by lot has fallen: SHARE, PART, ALLOTMENT: one's way of life or one's share of worldly reward or privation determined by chance, fate, or divine providence: FORTUNE, DESTINY

M

machine n: a structure or constructed thing whether material or immaterial: ERECTION, HANDIWORK: SHIP, BOAT: CONVEYANCE, VEHICLE: APPLIANCE, DEVICE: a military engine (as a siege tower or catapult): any of various apparatuses formerly used in the production of theatrical stage effects: an assemblage of parts that are usually solid bodies or electricity in conductors and that transmit forces, motion, and energy one to another in some predetermined manner and to some desired end (as for sewing a seam, printing a newspaper, hoisting a load, or maintaining an electric current: an instrument (as a lever) designed to transmit or modify the application of power, force, or motion: a mechanical device of the particular kind relevant or under consideration

magistrate n: a public official entrusted with the administration of the laws

maintain vb: to keep in a state of repair, efficiency, or validity: preserve from failure or decline: to sustain against opposition or danger: back up: DEFEND, UPHOLD: to uphold in argument: contend for: to persevere in: carry on: keep up: CONTINUE: to provide for: bear the expense of: SUPPORT

make vb: BEHAVE, ACT: to seem to begin (an action): BEGIN: to bring about: to cause to happen to or be experienced by someone: to cause to exist, occur, or appear: bring to pass: CREATE, CAUSE: to give rise to: favor the growth or occurrence of: to be or be capable of being changed or fashioned into: to develop into: be or become useful as: serve as

manifest adj: capable of being readily and instantly perceived by the senses and especially by the sight: not hidden or concealed: open to view: capable of being easily understood or recognized at once by the mind: not obscure: OBVIOUS

Michelle Lynn

massing n: the act or an instance of gathering or forming into a mass

means n: resources (as of force or wealth) available for disposal: material resources in such supply as to form the basis for an economically secure and sheltered life

Mediterranean adj: enclosed or nearly enclosed with land *meet* adv: in a suitable manner: FITLY, SUFFICIENTLY

meeting vb: an act or process of coming together: as: DUEL: a chance or planned encounter

midwife n: one that helps to produce or bring forth something

might n: the power, authority, or collective resources wielded by an individual, group, or other entity

mighty adj: having or wielding great power or authority: strong in material resources or social position: POWERFUL

Mitsrajim Egypt

Moab n {an ancient kingdom in Syria}: a member of a people living in Old Testament times east of the Dead Sea, north of the Edomites, and at one period south of the Ammonites *see map*

money n: something generally accepted as a medium of exchange, a measure of value, or a means of payment

more adj: superior in kind or degree: superior in quality or intensity: superior in age: OLDER: ADDITIONAL, FURTHER: of a larger size or extent

mound vb: to gather into a heap: PILE

mound n: an encompassing hedge or fence: a line of demarcation: BOUNDARY: an earthwork used as a fortification: RAMPART

mount vb: to become greater in amount or extent: INCREASE: to reach an ultimate amount or extent: TOTAL: to wing upward: SOAR: to make or appear to make a steep ascent: CLIMB: to become promoted: ADVANCE

mountains n: a region characterized by mountains

much *adj*: that exists or is present in an indicated relative quantity or amount or to an indicated relative extent or degree: MANY

myriad *n*: the number of ten thousand: ten thousand persons or things—used especially in translations from the Greek or Latin: an immense number: an indefinitely large number: a great multitude—usually used with *of* and often used in the plural

N

nation n: a community of people composed of one or more nationalities and possessing a more or less defined territory and government: a particular group or aggregation (as of men or animals)

near adj: closely akin: closely or intimately related or associated: not far distant in time, place, or degree: ADJACENT, NIGH Negeb see map

next prep: nearest or adjacent to (as in place or order)

no adv: NOT: used as a function word to express the negative of an alternative choice or possibility: in no respect or degree: not at all—used in comparisons: not so—used to express negation, dissent, denial, or refusal in answer to a question or request: used with a following adjective to imply a meaning expressed by the opposite positive statement: used as a function word to emphasize a following negative or to introduce a more emphatic, explicit, or comprehensive statement

no adj: not any: hardly any: very little: not a: quite other than a: far from being a—usually used to modify a predicate noun: not any possible: that is absent, lacking, or nonexistent

noise n: loud, confused, or senseless shouting or outcry: din or uproar of persons: general or common talk or discussion: RUMOR: especially: evil or slanderous report

noisy adj: making or given to making noise: CLAMOROUS, VOCIFEROUS: full of or characterized by the presence of noise: tending to attract attention usually by reason or showiness, gaudiness, or brightness of color: LOUD

non-entity n: something that does not exist or exists only in the imagination: the quality or state of not existing: NONEXISTENCE: a person who is totally undistinguished or unimpressive in mind, character, or achievement: one of small or mediocre talents: something of no consequence or significance: something totally lacking in distinction: the condition of being a non-entity

north n: regions or countries lying to the north of a specified or implied point of orientation: something (as people, culture, or institutions) characteristic of the North

nose n: the front or forward end or projection of something: the nose regarded as a symbol of officious or prying concern, interest, or intervention

nostril n: the fleshy lateral wall of the nose

not adv: used as a function word to turn an expression consisting of a word or group of words into an implicitly opposite expression: NO: in no manner or degree: in no way: NOWISE:

now adv: at the present time: at this moment: in the time immediately before the present: very lately: a moment ago: in the time immediately to follow: without delay: FORTHWITH: used with the sense of present time weakened or lost to introduce an important point or indicate a transition from one idea to another

numb adj: devoid of sensation especially due to cold: BENUMBED: devoid of emotion: DESENSITIZED, INDIFFERENT: devoid of skill

number n: an unspecified total: SEVERAL

numerous adj: consisting of great numbers of units: existing in abundance: MANY, PLENTIFUL: consisting of a great number of individuals: LARGE, MULTITUDINOUS

Michelle Lynn

O

obligation n: a bond with a condition annexed and a penalty for non-fulfillment; broadly: a formal and binding agreement or acknowledgment of a liability to pay a specified sum or do a specified thing

observation n: an act or faculty of observing or taking notice: an act of seeing or fixing the mind upon something

obstinate adj: not yielding readily: not easily subdued or removed

occur vb: to be found or met with: APPEAR: to present itself: come to pass: take place: HAPPEN

of prep: used as a function word to indicate the place or thing from which anything moves, comes, goes, or is directed or impelled: used as a function word to indicate an anterior condition from which a transition has been made: at an interval or in a direction with respect to—used to indicate something from which position or reckoning is defined: used as a function word to indicate something from which a person or thing is delivered: from by birth or descent: used as a function word to indicate the cause, motive, or reason by which a person or thing is actuated or impelled: used as a function word to indicate the agent or doer of an act or action, etc.

oil n: any of various substances that typically are unctuous viscous combustible liquids or solids easily liquifiable of warming and are not miscible with water but are soluble in ether, naphtha, and often alcohol and other organic solvents, that leave a greasy not necessarily permanent stain (as on paper or cloth), that may be of animal, vegetable, mineral, or other synthetic origin, and that are used according to their typed chiefly as lubricants, fuels, and illuminants as food, in soap and candles, and in perfumes and flavoring materials: PETROLEUM

older *comparative of* **old** *adj*: dating from the remote past: ANCIENT: persisting from an earlier time: CHRONIC: of long standing: having a status strengthened by the passage of time

one *adj*: being a single unit or entire being or thing and no more: existing alone in a specified sphere: constituting a unified entity made up of or formed from or produced by two or more components or sources: that is so united to or merged with something else as to form a single harmonious whole with it: that is at one: that is in agreement: UNITED

only *adv*: as a single solitary fact or instance or occurrence: as just the one simple thing and nothing more or different: SIMPLY, MERELY, JUST: EXCLUSIVELY, SOLELY: at the very least: without going any further than necessary: by that much indeed: all the more as a matter of fact: in the final outcome: at last: as a final result: with nevertheless the final outcome or result: as recently as: in the immediate past

opening *vb*: to move (as a door or lid) from its shut position

oracle *n*: a revelation received from the God of Judaism and Christianity: a divine revelation

order *vb*: to arrange or dispose according to some plan or with reference to some end: put in a particular order: arrange in a series or sequence

other *pron*: a different one

out *prep*: used as a function word to indicate direction from the inside to the outside: used as a function word to indicate movement or change of position from the inside to the outside: used as a function word to indicate movement or direction away from the center

over *prep*: used as a function word to indicate position higher up than and usually directly above another object: used as a function word to indicate the possession or enjoyment of authority, power, or jurisdiction in regard to some thing or person: used as a function word to indicate a relation of superiority, advantage, or preference to another

overhead *adj*: operating or situated above or overhead

P

palace n: the official residence of a sovereign

pale adj: deficient in chroma: deficient in vividness of hue or luster but of high brilliance

palpitate vb: to beat rapidly and strongly: THROB: bound with emotion or exertion: pulsate violently

parallel n: something equal or similar in all essential details: COUNTERPART: agreement in many or all essential details: RESEMBLANCE, SIMILARITY, ANALOGUE

part n: one of the equal or unequal portions into which something is or is regarded as divided: something less than a whole: a unit (as a number, quantity, or mass) held to constitute with one or more other units something larger: CONSTITUENT, FRACTION, FRAGMENT, MEMBER, PIECE: an essential portion or integral element of something

pass vb: to move on: PROCEED: to proceed to a specified place or destination: to proceed along a specified route: take a particular course

pavilion n: a large often sumptuous tent: something resembling a canopy or tent

paw n: the foot of a quadruped (as the lion, dog, or cat) having claws; broadly: the foot of an animal

payment n: the act of paying or giving compensation: the discharge of a debt or an obligation

people n: human beings making up a group or assembly: persons linked by a common factor: as: the members of a geographically distinct community: persons who share in common a point of origin or residence, etc.

perish vb: to become destroyed or ruined: come to an especially violent or untimely end: pass away completely (as by

Michelle Lynn

disintegration): DIE: to suffer spiritual or moral death: become spiritually lost: to deteriorate or decay to the point of being unserviceable or useless: SPOIL

permit *vb*: to consent to expressly or formally: grant leave for or the privilege of: ALLOW, TOLERATE: to give (a person) leave: AUTHORIZE

Persia (Persian) *n*: one of the people of Persia: as: one of the ancient Iranian Caucasians who under Cyrus and his successors became the dominant Asiatic race: a member of one of the peoples forming the modern Iranian nationality

person *n*: an individual human being: PERSONAGE: a human being as distinguished from an animal or thing

pieces *n*: a part of a whole: FRAGMENT, PORTION: MAN—usually used disparagingly: GIRL, WOMAN, BAGGAGE

pierced *vb*: to make a way into or through something as a pointed instrument does: break through: ENTER, PENETRATE

place *n*: a building or locality used for a special purpose

plait *vb*: to unite by or as if by interweaving

plan *n*: a method of achieving something: a way of carrying out a design: DEVICE: a method of doing something: PROCEDURE, WAY: a proposed undertaking or goal: AIM, INTENTION

plant *vb*: to establish or institute in a particular place or region

play *vb*: to perform on a musical instrument

plot *vb*: to plan or contrive (as something evil or unlawful) especially secret

point *vb*: to cause to have a sharp point: SHARPEN: to give added force, emphasis, or piquancy to: give more point to

poison *n*: a substance (as a drug) that in suitable quantities has properties harmful or fatal to an organism when it is brought into contact with or absorbed by the organism: a substance that through its chemical action usually kills, injures, or impairs an organism: something destructive or harmful to the success, prosperity, or happiness of something else

polluted adj: made unclean or impure: morally corrupt or defiled: physically tainted

positiveness n: the quality or state of being positive; especially: dogmatic assertiveness

post n: the place at which a body of troops is stationed

posterity n: the offspring of one progenitor to the furthest generation: DESCENDENTS: all succeeding generations: future time

poured vb: to cause or allow to flow: emit in a steady stream: DIFFUSE, DISCHARGE: to dispense from a container: to supply copiously: convey as if through a sluice: CHANNEL, SPOUT: to produce in abundance: to apply in liberal amounts (as for coercion or to supply motive power): to expend wholly: to give full expression to or a detailed account of: SPILL, VENT

power n: a position of ascendancy: ability to compel obedience: CONTROL, DOMINION: a military force or its equipment: ability to wage war: a large number or quantity: MULTITUDE, ABUNDANCE, HEAP

powerful adj: having great force or potency: STRONG, COMPELLING: having great prestige or effect: INFLUENTIAL, STIMULATING

praise vb: to express approbation of: EXTOL, COMMENT, APPLAUD: to glorify (a god or a saint) by homage and ascription of perfection especially in song: LAUD, MAGNIFY: to determine the worth of: APPRAISE: to hold in esteem: VALUE, PRIZE

predict vb: to declare in advance: PROPHESY

prepare vb: to make ready beforehand for some purpose: put into condition for a particular use, application, or disposition

present adj: being in one place and not elsewhere: being within reach, sight, or call or within contemplated limits: being in view

Michelle Lynn

or at hand: being before, beside, with or in the same place as someone or something

price n: the cost at which something is obtained

prince n: a person at the head of a class or profession: one very outstanding in a specified respect

produce n: something that is brought forth or yielded either naturally or as a result of effort or work

profane vb: to violate or treat with abuse, irreverence, obloquy, or contempt (something sacred): treat as not sacred: DESECRATE, POSSUTE: to debase by a wrong, unworthy, or vulgar use: ABUSE, DEFILE, VULGARIZE

property n: something that is or may be owned or possessed: WEALTH, GOODS: specifically: a piece of real estate: the exclusive right to possess, enjoy, and dispose of a thing: a valuable right or interest primarily a source or element of wealth: OWNERSHIP

protect vb: to cover or shield from that which would injure, destroy, or detrimentally affect: secure or preserve usually against attack, disintegration, encroachment, or harm: GUARD

pudenda n: the external genital organs of a human being and especially of a woman

punishment n: retributive suffering, pain, or loss: PENALTY

push vb: to exert physical force upon so as to cause or tend to cause motion away from the force: to cause to move or tend to move away or ahead by steady pressure in contact: to butt or thrust against with the head or horns: to force to go (as if by driving or displacing): CROWD: to make, effect, or accomplish by forcing aside obstacles or opposition: to promote or carry out with vigor: urge or press the advancement, adoption, or practice of: to press forward against obstacles or opposition or with energy: advance persistently or courageously *put* *vb*: to place or cause to be placed in a specified direction or into or out of a specified place: to bring into or establish in a specified state or condition: to bring into the power or under the protection or care of someone: to establish or cause to take effect (a limit or restraint)

Q

quality *n*: peculiar and essential character: NATURE, KIND: a distinctive, inherent feature: PROPERTY, VIRTUE

R

raise vb: to lift or restore to or set in an erect position: set upright: cause or help to stand: to rouse or incite to action or effort: summon to resist or repel injury: call to war, struggle, or conflict: to cause to increase in height, level, bulk, size, amount, or value

rampart n: something that fortifies, defends, or secures against attack or intrusion: a protective barrier: BULWARK

range n: a series or chain of mountain peaks considered as forming one connected system: a ridge of mountains: mountainous country

recognition n: the action of recognizing or state of being recognized: as: discernment of the character, status, or class of something: special notice or attention

red adj: tinged with red: REDDISH

redness n: the quality or state of being red

refine vb: to reduce to a fine, unmixed, or pure state: separate from extraneous matter: free from dross or alloy: free or cleanse from impurities: to free (as the mind or soul) from moral imperfection, grossness, dullness, earthiness: SPIRITUALIZE, ELEVATE

regard vb: to pay attention to: notice or remark particularly: to look after: take care or for: to treat (a thing) as something of peculiar value, sanctity, or worth: to have care for: heed in conduct or practice: have respect for (as a person): show respect or consideration for

region n: REALM, KINGDOM: a particular part of the world or universe

regular adj: formed, built, arranged, or ordered according to some established rule, law, principle, or type: harmonious in form, structure or arrangement

reject vb: to refuse to acknowledge, adopt, believe, acquiesce in, receive, or submit to: decline to accept: REFUSE: to cast off (a person): FORSAKE

release vb: to loosen or remove the force or effect of: ALLEVIATE: to set free from restraint, confinement, or servitude: set at liberty: let go

relinquish vb: FORSAKE: to withdraw or retreat from: ABANDON: to desist from: leave off: cease from considering, practicing, exercising, or cherishing

remain vb: to stay in the same place or with the same person or group: RESIDE, DWELL: to continue unchanged in form, condition, status, or quantity: continue to be: STAND

repair vb: to restore by replacing a part or putting together what is torn or broken: FIX, MEND: to restore to a sound or healthy state: RENEW, REVIVIFY: to make good: REMEDY

repeatedly adv: renewed or recurring again and again: CONSTANT, FREQUENT: said, done, or presented again

repose vb: to lie at rest: to lie dead: to remain still or concealed: lie quiet or hidden: to take rest: cease from activity, exertion, or movement

rescue vb: to free from confinement, violence, danger, or evil: liberate from actual restraint: SAVE, DELIVER

resign vb: to give over or consign (as to the care or possession of another): let go into anothers possession or control, often submissively or confidingly: RELEGATE, COMMIT: to give (oneself) over unresistingly, typically, to the effects of an indicated dominance, control, or influence with stoic acceptance, calm resignation, or confidence

respect n: an act of noticing with attention: the giving of particular attention to: CONSIDERATION: HEED, CARE, CIRCUMSPECTION:

high or special regard: deferential regard (as from a servant to his master): ESTEEM

restrain vb: to hold (as a person) back from some action, procedure, or course: prevent from doing something (as by physical or moral force or social pressure): to limit or restrict to or in respect to a particular action or course: keep within bounds or under control

retreat n: an act of retiring or withdrawing (as from what is difficult, dangerous, or disagreeable or as into privacy from business, public life, or society): the process of receding

retreat vb: to make a retreat: retire from a position or place: WITHDRAW

return vb: to go back or come back again (as to a place, person, or condition)

revelation n: an act of revealing or communicating divine truth; especially: God's disclosure or manifestation of himself or of his will to man: something that is revealed by God to man

revere vb: to regard with reverence or profound respect and affection: practice an affectionate deference toward: show love and honor to

revolution n: the completion of a course (as of years)

rich adj: possessed of great temporal power: MIGHTY: possessing or controlling great wealth: WEALTHY

rider n: one that rides a vehicle

rise vb: to assume an upright or standing position: to go to war: take up arms: launch an attack: make insurrection: to attain a higher level: gain in vigor, clarity, grace, or effectiveness: to advance in rank, position, or esteem

river n: a natural surface stream of water of considerable volume and permanent or seasonal flow: CREEK: WATERCOURSE: ESTUARY, TIDAL RIVER: INLET, STRAIT: something resembling a river

robust *adj*: having or exhibiting strength or vigorous health: POWERFUL, MUSCULAR: firm and assured in purpose, opinion, or outlook

root *n*: a race, family, or progenitor that is the source or beginning of a group or line of descendants: a descendant or offshoot of a line or family: SCION

ruin *v*: to lay waste: reduce to wreckage: DEVASTATE, OVERTHROW: to damage or destroy irredeemably: inflict irreparable injury on

rule *n*: a generally prevailing condition, quality, state or mode of activity or behavior: the exercise of authority or control: DOMINION, GOVERNMENT, SWAY: a period during which a specified ruler or government exercises control

rule *vb*: to control, direct, or influence the mind, character, or actions of: to exercise authority or power over: GOVERN

ruler *n*: one that exercises authority, command, or dominating influence

S

sacred *adj*: CONSECRATED: dedicated or set apart (as to honor or veneration of a deity, group, or person): devoted exclusively to the service or use (as of a particular person, purpose, or group): holy or hallowed especially by association with the divine or consecrated: worthy of religious veneration: entitled to reverence and respect: VENERABLE

same *pron*: something that has previously been defined or described

sanctity *n*: holiness of life and character: SAINTLINESS, GODLINESS: the quality or state of being holy or sacred: a religious binding force: INVIOLABILITY, SACREDNESS

sanctuary *n*: a sacred and inviolable asylum: a place of refuge and protection: immunity from law by entering such a place: the right or privilege of conferring such immunity: a place or resort for those who seek relief: a refuge from turmoil and strife: HAVEN

scrutinize *vb*: to subject to scrutiny: examine closely: INSPECT

sea *n*: the great body of salty water that covers much of the earth's surface: the oceans of the world with their dependent saline water; broadly: the waters of the earth as distinguished from the land and air

seclude *vb*: to exclude or debar from a privilege, rank, or dignity: expel or bat from a membership or office: to exclude from consideration: to keep out from a place or society: to separate by or as if by a barrier: keep apart or distinct

security *n*: the quality or state of being secure: as: freedom from danger: SAFETY: carefree or cocky overconfidence: freedom from fear, anxiety, or care: freedom from uncertainty or doubt: CONFIDENCE, ASSURANCE: sureness of technique: basis

Michelle Lynn

for confidence: GUARANTEE: FIRMNESS: DEPENDABILITY, STABILITY

seeing *n*: the act of using ones sense of sight: the faculty or power of sight or insight: VISION

seize *vb*: to possess or take by force: CAPTURE: to take prisoner: ARREST

select *adj*: chosen from a number or group by fitness or preference

select *vb*: to choose from a number or group usually by fitness, excellence, or other distinguishing features

self *pron*: MYSELF: HIMSELF, HERSELF

send away *vb*: DISPATCH: to banish from a place

send for *vb*: to request by message to come or be brought: SUMMON, ORDER

send out *vb*: ISSUE: to dispatch (as an order, or shipment) from a store or similar establishment

separate *vb*: to make a distinction between: DISCRIMINATE, DISTINGUISH

separation *n*: an act or instance of dividing: DETACHMENT, DISPERSAL

severe *adj*: absolute or rigorous in restraint, punishment, or requirement: INFLEXIBLE, STRINGENT, RESTRICTIVE

she *pron*: that female one: that one regarded as feminine (as by personification)

ship *n*: any large vessel

shiver *vb*: to undergo trembling (as from cold, fear, or the application of physical force): SHAKE, QUIVER, VIBRATE

shoot *n*: a growth from a main stem or stock: OFFSHOOT

show *vb*: to make evident or apparent: serve as the means to reveal or make visible

sight *n*: faculty of mental or spiritual perception resembling vision

signal *n*: an act, event, or watchword that has been agreed upon as the occasion of concerted action

silver *n*: coin make of silver: silver money: MONEY

sky *n*: the expanse of space surrounding the earth: the upper atmosphere

slipperiness *n*: the quality or state of being slippery **slippery** *adj*: not to be trusted: SHIFTY, TRICKY: marked by evasion, deceit, or trickery

smooth *adj*: avoiding or minimizing what is harsh or unpleasant or objectionable: plausibly flattering: INGRATIATING

smoothness *n*: the quality, state, or fact of being smooth: absence of irregularities of surface, movement, or functioning

soil *n*: firm land: EARTH: COUNTRY, LAND

soil *vb*: to stain or defile morally: CORRUPT, POLLUTE

son *n*: the male offspring of human beings: a male descendant

south *n*: regions or countries lying to the south of a specified or implied point of orientation

speak *vb*: to give expression to thoughts, opinions, or feelings by other than verbal means: to communicate by signals: SIGNAL: to communicate by being interesting or attractive: APPEAL: to give proof or evidence of: INDICATE, SUGGEST

spill *vb*: to give forth in an overflowing manner: pour freely

spirit *n*: the immaterial intelligent or sentient part of a person: the vital principle in man coming as a gift from God and providing ones personality with its inward structure, dynamic drive, and creative response to the demands it encounters in the process of becoming

splendor *n*: great brightness: brilliant luster: BRILLIANCY: sumptuous display, ornament, or ceremonial: gorgeous show: MAGNIFICENCE, POMP, GLORY: BEAUTY: EXCELLENCE, VALUE, WORTH

Michelle Lynn

split n: to affect as if by cleaving or forcing apart

spread vb: to become known more widely: CIRCULATE: to increase in range, incidence, or influence

stability n: steadiness or firmness of character, resolution, or purpose: CONSTANCY, STEADFASTNESS

stand vb: to take up or maintain a (specified) posture: to hold one's ground: maintain one's position ; resist attack: to be in a particular state or situation

stand n: a defensive effort of some duration or degree of success: a place or port where one stands: STATION, POSITION

steed n: HORSE; especially: a spirited horse for state or war

step n: pace with or as if with another

still adv: to or at a greater distance: FARTHER: in addition: beyond this: to a greater extent

stone n: a concretion of earthy or mineral matter of igneous, sedimentary, or metamorphic origin: such a concretion mined, quarried, or shaped in a definite form or size for a specified function: as: a building block

storm vb: to blow with violence: to attack, take, or win over by storm

stout adj: FIERCE, MENACING: displaying insolent conceit: ARROGANT, HAUGHTY: resistant to stress or pressure: TOUGH, RIGID

straight adj: exhibiting no deviation from what is established or accepted as usual, normal, or proper: as: making no exceptions or deviations in one's support of something accepted as right (as a principle, policy, or party)

strange adj: discouraging familiarities: RESERVED, DISTANT, COLD

strength n: moral courage: FORTITUDE, INTEGRITY: physical force or vigor: BRAWN, VITALITY: ability to produce an effect: INFLUENCE: a source of power or influence: military might

strengthen *vb*: to give added strength or vigor to: to increase in power or amount: improve in effectiveness: AUGMENT, INTENSIFY

stretched *vb*: to reach out: hold out: put forth: EXTEND

strike in *vb*: to enter into competition: TRY: to associate as a confederate or collaborator: to fall into or express agreement

strike out *vb*: to create or form with apparent ease: produce as if by a stroke: to enter vigorously and suddenly on

strong *adj*: having great muscular power: capable of exerting great bodily force: accomplished or supported by marked physical power: able to bear or endure: ROBUST, RUGGED: able to withstand stress or violence: not easily broken or injured: having or exhibiting moral or intellectual force, endurance, or vigor: having great resources of wealth

stumble *vb*: to fall into sin, error, or waywardness: ERR: to falter through lack of knowledge or experience: BLUNDER: to proceed, speak, or act in a hesitant or faltering manner

stun *vb*: to cause to lose consciousness (as by a blow or concussion): to bewilder or daze with noise, clamor or din: BENUMB: to shock or paralyze with strong emotional impression: STUPEFY: to overcome with astonishment or disbelief: CONFOUND, PERPLEX: to overcome with pleasure or beauty

stupefy *vb*: to make physically stupid, dull, or insensible: BENUMB: to numb or deaden the faculties of perception and understanding of

subdue *vb*: to conquer by force or by superior power and bring into subjection: VANQUISH, CRUSH: to bring (as a person) into subjection or order by or as if by persuasion, intimidation, or threat of punishment: to reduce the intensity or degree of: make less prominent: tone down

subject *n*: one that is placed under the authority, dominion, control, or influence of someone or something

sunrise *n*: the apparent rising of the sun above the horizon: atmospheric effects that accompany the sun's appearance: the time the sun appears whether in fair or cloudy weather

surround *vb*: to constitute part of the determining environment or accustomed condition of: ENVIRON: to form a ring around

sword *n*: an instrument of destruction: a military force: coercive power or jurisdiction

T

table *n*: a flat slab (as of wood or stone): TABLET: a set of laws inscribed on tablets: TABLET: an indelible record

tax *vb*: to make subject to the payment of a tax: levy a charge on; especially: to exact money from for the support of the government: to place under onerous and rigorous demands

team *n*: a wagon, carriage, or other drawn vehicle

tear away *vb*: to remove (as oneself) reluctantly

tent *n*: ABODE, DWELLING, HABITATION

texture *n*: something composed of closely interwoven elements: the essential part of something: SUBSTANCE, NATURE: the size and organization of small constituent parts of a body or substance

that *pron*: at which: in which: on which: by which: with which: to which: the person who: persons who

these *plural of* **this**

they *pron*: those ones: he or she: THOSE: PEOPLE: unspecified persons and especially those responsible for a particular act, practice, or decision

think *vb*: to exercise the powers of judgment, conception, or inference as distinguished from simple sense perception: to exercise the powers of thought with regard to a particular matter: to call an idea (as of a possible solution or a device) to mind by mental effort: to have a thought in the mind: have a thought come into the mind: to have or form a particular idea: REGARD

third *adj*: number three in a countable series

this *pron*: the person, thing, or idea that is present or near in place, time, or thought, or that has just been mentioned: the present time: this time

those *plural of* **that**

though adv: HOWEVER, NEVERTHELESS—used at the end or in the middle of a sentence

three adj: being one more than two in number

thrice adv: three times

time n: a period during which something (as an action, process, or condition) exists or continues: an interval comprising a limited and continuous action, condition, or state of being: measured or measurable duration: a point or period when something occurs: the moment of an event, process, or condition: OCCASION

to adv: used as a function word to indicate direction toward: in favor of: PRO

top adj: of, relating to, or at the top: HIGHEST, TOPMOST, UPPERMOST: foremost in order, rank, achievement, value, or precedence: CHIEF, HEAD, PREEMINENT

totter vb: to be indecisive: WAVER: to oscillate or lean dizzily: SHIMMY, SWAY: to become unstable: threaten to collapse: to move unsteadily: STAGGER, WOBBLE

toward prep: in the direction of: to a point approaching: TO: along a course leading to: with a view to gaining: to the end or purpose of

transition n: a passage or movement from one state, condition, or place to another: CHANGE

treacherous n: characterized by or manifesting treachery: marked by ready disposition to betray confidence or faith pledged: violating or capable of violating allegiance: DISLOYAL, FALSE, PERFIDOUS, TRAITOROUS: likely to betray confidence or trust: UNRELIABLE, UNTRUSTWORTHY: characterized by usually hidden dangers, hazards, or perils

tremble vb: to fear exceedingly: shudder at

tribal adj: resembling a tribe in possessing a sense of identification with and loyalty to the habits, traits, and values characteristic of a close-knit familistic, sociocultural, occupational, or political group or in ceremonial or ritualistic activity

tribe *n*: a social group comprising numerous families, clans, or generations together with slaves, dependents, or adopted strangers

trickle *vb*: to run or fall in drops: flow in a thin gentle stream

troop *n*: a flock of animals or birds

trustworthy *(ness) adj*: worthy of confidence: DEPENDABLE

truth *n*: the quality or state of being faithful: FIDELITY, CONSTANCY: sincerity in character, action, and speech: genuineness in expressing feeling or belief: TRUTHFULNESS, HONESTY

tumult *n*: a disorderly and violent movement, agitation, or milling about, of a crowd accompanied usually with great uproar and confusion of voices: COMMOTION, TURMOIL: a noisy and turbulent popular uprising: DISTURBANCE, RIOT

turn *vb*: to set in another especially contrary direction: to cause to have or take another path or direction: bend or change the course of: to reverse the course or direction of: make go back: to cause to retreat: to direct one's course: to reverse a course or direction: go backward or in the opposite direction: become reversed: to have a reactive usually adverse effect on: RECOIL: to change one's course: take a different course or direction: to become changed, altered, or transformed (as in nature, character, or appearance): pass from one state to another: CHANGE

twine *vb*: INTERLACE

twist *vb*: to wrest the meaning or sense of: PERVERT, TORTURE

two *adj*: being more than one in number

twofold *adj*: having two parts or aspects: DOUBLE, DUAL

tyrannize *vb*: to act the tyrant: exercise arbitrary power: rule or act with unjust and oppressive severity *tyrant* n: a person in a position of control who exercises unlawful or improper authority or lawful and proper authority in an arbitrary or oppressive manner: one who by unfair or unreasonable demands or rigorous exploitation imposes burdens and hardships on those under his control

U

understand *vb*: to grasp the meaning of: COMPREHEND

unit *n*: a single thing or person or group that is a constituent and isolable member of some more inclusive whole

unite *vb*: to become one or as of one

united *adj*: make one: COMBINED: relating to or produced by joint action: CONJOINT: formed by or resulting from union: being or living in agreement: HARMONIOUS

unknown *adj*: not known: as: STRANGE, UNFAMILIAR: not apprehended: not ascertained: INCALCULABLE, INEXPRESSIBLE: lacking an established or normal status: having no formal recognition

unless *prep*: except possibly: EXCEPT

unsubstantial *(ity) adj*: not substantial: as: lacking a basis in fact: not having matter or substance: VISIONARY, UNREAL: lacking firmness or strength in construction: WEAK, UNSTABLE

until *conj*: up to the time that: till such time as: before the time that: to the point or degree that: so long or so far that

unto *prep*: used as a function word to indicate direction and completion of movement toward a place, destination, or object

upon *prep*: having a powerful influence on: lying heavily on: on the occasion of: at the time of

upper *adj*: higher in rank or order: superior in position

upward *adv*: toward a higher position: in a direction from a lower to a higher place: in the upper parts especially of the body: toward the head: toward a greater amount or higher number, degree, or rate

upward *adj*: marked by an increase: RISING

V

valiant *adj*: FIRM, STRONG, ROBUST: possessing or acting with bravery or boldness: COURAGEOUS, INTREPID, STOUTHEARTED: marked by, exhibiting, or carried out with courage, persistence, or determination: HEROIC

valor *n*: the quality or state of mind with which a person faces danger or hardship boldly or firmly: BRAVERY, COURAGE

valuable *adj*: having or exhibiting desirable or esteemed characteristics or qualities especially of an intrinsic nature: VALUED: characterized by usefulness, worth, or serviceableness usually for a specified purpose

value *n*: relative worth, utility, or importance: degree of excellence: status in as scale of preferences

value *vb*: to show concern for: HEED

vehement *(ence) adj*: immoderate in strength or degree: INTENSITY, SEVERITY

vehicle *n*: a means of carrying or transporting something: CONVEYANCE

very *adv*: to a high degree: to a considerable extent: EXTREMELY, EXCEEDINGLY

vigor *n*: active strength or force of body or mind: capacity for physical, intellectual, or moral exertion: effective energy or power: intensity of action or effect: FORCE, ENERGY

violate *vb*: to fail to keep: BREAK, DISREGARD: to do harm to the person or especially the chastity of; specifically: to commit rape on: to fail to show the requisite respect for: treat or handle in a disrespectful or high-handed manner: PROFANE, DESECRATE: to damage or destroy especially by violence

violent *adj*: characterized by extreme force: marked by abnormally sudden physical activity and intensity: extremely or intensely vivid or loud: unusually intense: unnaturally strong: produced or effected by force: UNNATURAL

virtue *n*: moral practice or action: conformity to a standard of right (as divine law or the highest good): moral excellence: integrity of character: up- rightness of conduct: RECTITUDE, MORALITY: an active quality or power whether of physical or of moral nature: the capacity or power adequate to the production of a given effect: ENERGY, POTENCE, STRENGTH

W

wages n: RECOMPENSE, REQUITAL, REWARD

wake vb: to rouse from sleep: AWAKEN: to bring to motion, action, or life: STIR, EXCITE: to arouse consciousness or interest in: ALERT

waking vb: to remain awake on watch or guard especially over a sick person or a corpse

war vb: to make or wage war: carry on armed hostilities: to be in active or vigorous conflict or contention especially during an extended period

war n: a state of usually open and declared armed hostile conflict between political units (as states or nations)

warfare n: military operations between enemies: armed contest: HOSTILITIES, WAR; broadly: activity undertaken by a political unit (as a state or nation) to weaken or destroy another: the process of struggle between competing entities: CONFLICT

warm adj: sending or giving out heat usually to a comfortable or beneficial degree: producing sensations of heat

warrior n: a man engaged or experienced in warfare and especially in primitive warfare or the close combat typical of ancient or medieval times: an advocate or war

waver vb: to falter in battle: hesitate as if about to give way: CHECK

wealth n: WEAL, WELFARE, GOOD, HAPPINESS: large possessions: abundance of things that are objects of human desire: abundance of worldly estate: AFFLUENCE, RICHED: abundant supply: large accumulation

weave vb: to produce by elaborately combining available materials or elements: CONTRIVE

weight n: the relatively great importance or authority accorded something: measurable influence especially in determining the act of others

weighty adj: having much importance or consequence: MOMENTOUS: expressing or characterized by seriousness or gravity: EARNEST, SOLEMN

west n: regions or countries lying to the west of a specified point or implied point of orientation

western adj: situated in or lying toward the west: coming from the west

what n: STUFF, MATTER, SUBSTANCE: THING, OBJECT: the thing or things involved or meant or referred to: the identity or nature of something: all that may be known or stated about an individual thing: the complex of qualities that constitute the character of a thing

when adv: at that time: in what period: how long ago: in what circumstances: at which time: and then: WHEREUPON: at, in, or during which

where n: LOCATION, PLACE; especially: the place in which something mentioned is or occurs

which n: what one or ones out of a group

while conj: during the time that: until the end of the time that: as long as: during which time: and during the same time: and meanwhile: UNTIL

white adj: free from spot or blemish: as: free from moral stain or impurity: outstandingly righteous: INNOCENT

who n: the person or persons involved or meant or referred to

whole adj: constituting the total sum or undiminished entirety of: INTEGRAL: each of or all of the

wickedness n: the quality or state of being wicked: EVIL, SINFULNESS: wicked character or conduct: VICE

wind n: a destructive force or influence: a force or agency that carries along or influences: TENDENCY, TREND

with prep: in opposition to: AGAINST—used as a function word to indicate one that shares in an action, transaction, or arrangement: by means of: by the use or agency of: THROUGH: as a result of: in consequence of: because of—used as a function word to indicate manner of action—used as a function word to indicate a related or supplementary fact or circumstance: immediately consequent upon: at the moment or time of: used as a function word to indicate accompaniment or companionship

without adv: with a lack of something: so as to be deprived

woman n: one possessing in high degree the qualities considered distinctive of womanhood

wound vb: to inflict a wound upon: CUT, STAB, PIERCE, LACERATE: to hurt or damage as if by a wound: INJURE

wrong adj: deviating from what is just and good: lacking in moral rectitude and integrity: not up to the mark: not quite right: AMISS, UNSATISFACTORY

Y

yea *adv*: more than this: not only so but—used to mark addition or substitution of a more explicit or emphatic phrase and thus interchangeable with nay

year *n*: a time or era marked in some special way: a period taken as a unit notable for a particular characteristic: 12 months that constitute a measure of age or duration

yellow *n*: something that is yellow or is chiefly distinguished by a yellow color

Michelle Lynn

ENDNOTES

11:1

1   *Darius the Mede.* The Columbia Encyclopedia, Sixth Edition 2006

2   **"Cyrus II."***Encyclopædia Britannica* from Encyclopædia Britannica 2006 CD. [Accessed October 30, 2007].

11:2

3   H. G Wells, *The Outline of History* (Garden City, New York: International Collectors Library, 1971), p. 265

4   Ibid, p. 271

5   **"Xerxes I."***Encyclopædia Britannica* from Encyclopædia Britannica 2006 CD.[Accessed October 30, 2007].

11:3

6   J.M. Roberts, *History of the World* (New York: Oxford University Press, 1993), p. 170

7   *The Last Two Million Years* (London: The Readers Digest Association, 1974), p. 103

8   **"Alexander the Great."***Encyclopædia Britannica* from Encyclopædia Britannica 2006 CD. [Accessed October 30, 2007].

11:4

9   Roberts, *History of the World*, p.

10 Donald Dudley, *The Civilization of Rome* (New York: New American Library, 1960)

11 Roberts, *History of the World*, p. 189

12 Ibid, p. 186

13 **"Roman Republic and Empire."***Encyclopædia Britannica* from Encyclopædia Britannica 2006 CD. [Accessed October 30, 2007].

11:5

14 Roberts, *History of the World*, p. 173

15 Ibid, p. 175

16 **"Ptolemy I Soter."***Encyclopædia Britannica* from Encyclopædia Britannica 2006 CD. [Accessed October 30, 2007].

11:6

17 *Cleopatra.* Encyclopedia Britannica Online http://members.eb.com/bol/topic?eu=24721&sctn=1#s_top (1 June 2001)

18 Wells, *The Outline of History*, p. 397

19 *Cleopatra.* Encyclopedia Britannica Online

20 Wells, *The Outline of History*, p. 397

21 Ibid, p. 398

22 **"Cleopatra."***Encyclopædia Britannica* from Encyclopædia Britannica 2006 CD. [Accessed October 30, 2007].

11:7

23 Roberts, *History of the World*, p. 229

24 Ibid, p. 232

25 *Byzantine empire.* Encyclopedia Britannica Online http://members.eb.com/bol/topic?eu=108723&sctn=1#85278 [1 June 2001]

26 Wells, *The Outline of History*, p. 436

27 **"Byzantine Empire."***Encyclopædia Britannica* from Encyclopædia Britannica 2006 CD. [Accessed October 30, 2007].

11:8

28 *The Last Two Million Years*, p. 71
29 Roberts, *History of the World*, p. 228
30 Ibid., p. 233
31 **"Egypt."***Encyclopædia Britannica* from Encyclopædia Britannica 2006 CD. [Accessed October 30, 2007].

11:9

32 Roberts, *History of the World*, p. 260
33 The Last Two Million Years, p. 150
34 **"Muhammad."***Encyclopædia Britannica* from Encyclopædia Britannica 2006 CD. [Accessed October 30, 2007].

11:10

35 The Last Two Million Years, p. 150
36 Ibid., p.148
37 Wells, *The Outline of History*, p.559
38 Old World Contacts / Department of History / The University of Calgary

11:11

39 Roberts, History of the World, p. 297
40 Coliers Encyclopedia, s.v. "crusades"
41 Old World Contacts / Department of History / The University of Calgary
42 http://www.fanaticus.org/DBA/armies/Variants/Peoplescrusade.html

11:12

43 Wells, *The Outline of History*, p.563

44 The Last Two Million Years, p. 220

45 http://www.fanaticus.org/DBA/armies/Variants/Peoplescrusade.html

46 http://crusades.boisestate.edu/1st/

11:13

47 Coliers Encyclopedia, s.v. "crusades"

48 The Last Two Million Years, p. 220-1

49 Coliers Encyclopedia, s.v. "crusades"

50 **"Crusades."**Encyclopædia Britannica from Encyclopædia Britannica 2006 CD. [Accessed November 2, 2007].

11:14

51 Roberts, History of the World, p. 420 (chart)

52 Wells, The Outline of History, p. 564

53 Roberts, History of the World, p. 417

54 Wells, The Outline of History, p. 566

55 http://www.infoplease.com/ce6/history/A0857644.html

11:15

56 National Geographic Atlas of World History, p. 132-133

57 The Last Two Million Years, p. 221

58 National Geographic Atlas of World History, p. 111

59 The Last Two Million Years, p. 223

60 "Jews," Microsoft® Encarta® Online Encyclopedia 2004 http://encarta. msn.com ©1997-2004 Microsoft Corporation. All Rights Reserved.

61 http://www.eng-h.gov.uk%252Fmpp%252Fmcd%252Fmbc.htm

62 http://www.bow.k12.nh.us/CyberBUS/castle%20and%20castle%20 items/castles.htm

63 "Jews," Microsoft®Encarta®Online Encyclopedia 2004 http://encarta. msn.com ©1997-2004 Microsoft Corporation. All Rights Reserved.

11:16

64 Roberts, History of the World, p. 395

65 Ibid.

66 Ibid., p.396

67 The Last Two Million Years, p. 224

68 Roberts, History of the World, p. 395

69 http://www.uh.edu/engines/epi1530.htm—The Engines of Our Ingenuity is Copyright © 1988-2000 by John H. Lienhard

11:17

70 Roberts, History of the World, p. 396

71 Wells, The Outline of History, p. 576-7

72 The Last Two Million Years, p. 291

73 Webster's New International Dictionary, 3d ed., s.v. "dogma"

74 Wells, The Outline of History, p. 577

75 "Inquisition," Microsoft® Encarta® Online Encyclopedia 2005 http://encarta.msn.com © 1997-2005 Microsoft Corporation. All Rights Reserved. © 1993-2005 Microsoft Corporation. All Rights Reserved.

11:18

76 Atlas of World History, p.150

77 Roberts, History of the World, p. 398

78 The World's Great Religions, p. 200

79 Wells, The Outline of History, p. 577

80 Ibid. p. 643

81 The World's Great Religions, p. 200

82 http://www.emayzine.com/lectures/decline_church.htm

11:19

83 The Last Two Million Years, p. 226

84 Wells, The Outline of History, p. 643-4

85 Roberts, *History of the World*, p.415

86 Wells, *The Outline of History*, p. 581

87 Roberts, *History of the World*, p. 401

88 http://www.emayzine.com/lectures/decline_church.htm

11:20

89 *People And The Earth: An Environmental Atlas : Medieval Times*, Andrea Due, vol.3 (Dansbury: Grolier Educational) p.17

90 *The Last Two Million Years*, p. 226

91 Roberts, *History of the World*, p. 402

92 http://www.brown.edu/Departments/Italian_Studies/dweb/society/structure/merchant_cult.shtml

93 http://www.digitaltermpapers.com/a11931.htm

11:21

94 Wells, *The Outline of History*, p.625

95 Roberts, *History of the World*, p.413

96 Wells, *The Outline of History*, p.625-6

97 *Medieval Times*, p.29

98 *What Life Was Like in the Age of Chivalry* (Alexandria, Virginia: Time Life Books, 1997), p.129

99 *The Last Two Million Years*, p.230

100 http://www.insecta-inspecta.com/fleas/bdeath/Europe.html

101 http://www.shsu.edu/~eng_wpf/history/johnball.html

102 http://www.castles-of-britain.com/castle32.htm

11:22

103 *The Old World Past and Present*, p.252-3

104 *The Last Two Million Years*, p.226 (Inset)

105 http://www.public.iastate.edu/~gbetcher/373/guilds.htm

11:23

106 *The Last Two Million Years*, p.228 (Inset)

107 Campbell, Webb, Nida, *The Old World: Past and Present*, p.307

108 *The Last Two Million Years*, p.230

109 Ibid., p.231(Inset)

110 Ibid., p.230

111 *The Last Two Million Years*, p.231(Inset)

112 http://www.shsu.edu/~his_ncp/Renn.html ([Excerpted from Philip Van Ness Myers, *Mediæval and Modern History* (Boston: Ginn and Company, 1905), pp. 251-274]

11:24

113 Campbell, Webb, Nida, *The Old World: Past and Present.*, p.258

114 Ibid., p.259

115 *What Life Was Like in the Age of Chivalry*, p.143

116 *The Last Two Million Years*, p. 230

117 http://www.inside.iskl.edu.my/i-bay/academics/ms/grade8renaissance/banking/Banking.htm

11:25

118 *The Last Two Million Years*, p.155

119 *The End of Europe's Middle Ages*, The Applied History Research Group (Department of History/ The University of Calgary: 1998)p.2-3 wysiwyg://5/http://www.ucalgary.ca/HIST/tutor/indmiddle/ottoman.html

120 Wells, *The Outline of History*, p.601

121 Noel Grove, *National Geographic Atlas of World History* (Washington DC: National Geographic Society: 1997)

122 http://www.ucalgary.ca/applied_history/tutor/endmiddle/FRAMES/ottoframe.html

11:26

123 *humanism.* Encyclopedia Britannica Online http://members.eb.com/bol/topic?eu=109244&sctn+1

124 Grove, *National Geographic Atlas of World History*, p.161

125 http://www.historyguide.org/intellect/humanism.html *copyright* © *2000 Steven Kreis*

11:27

126 Ibid., p.164

127 Groves, *National Geographic Atlas of World History*, p.165

128 Ibid., p.202

129 http://www.newgenevacenter.org/west/reformation.htm

130 http://www.ucalgary.ca/applied_history/tutor/endmiddle/FRAMES/ottoframe.html

131 http://www.globalspecialoperations.com/clash.html

11:28

132 Grove, *The National Geographic Atlas of World History*, p.166

133 Wells, *The Outline of History*, p.650

134 http://www.mariner.org/educationalad/ageofex/portuguese_exp.php

135 www.historycooperative.org/proceedings/seascapes/casale.html
Copyright © 2003 by the American Historical Association. Compiled by Debbi Ann Doyle and Brandon Schneider. Format by Chris Hale.

11:29

136 Wells, *The Outline of History*, p.614

137 Ibid., p.233

138 Wells, *The Outline of History*, p.658

139 **"Columbus, Christopher."** *Encyclopædia Britannica* from Encyclopædia Britannica 2006 CD. [Accessed February 28, 2008].

11:30

140 Grove, *The National Geographic Atlas of World History*, p.170

141 *The Last Two Million Years*, p.197

142 Grove, *The National Geographic Atlas of World History*, p.170

143 *The Last Two Million Years*, p.337

144 Ibid., p.338

145 Ibid., p.236

146 Ibid., p.237

147 http://www.u-s-history.com/pages/h1031.html © 2002-2005 Online Highways™

148 http://www.millersv.edu/~columbus/data/art/GILES-01.ART

149 http://www.britannia.com/history/monarchs/mon41.html

11:31

150 *The Last Two Million Years*, p.233 (inset)

151 James Strong, LL.D., S.T.D., *The New Strong's Exhaustive Concordance of the Bible* (Nashville: Thomas Nelson Publishers, 1990), Greek Dictionary #3126

11:33

152 http://www.wsu.edu/~dee/REFORM/WARS.HTM

153 http://www.zum.de/whkmla/period/renaissance/rendef.html

154 http://www.themayflowersociety.com/history.htm

155 http://www.learner.org/exhibits/renaissance/middleages_sub.html

11:36

156 *The Last Two Million Years*, p.239

157 Ibid., p.240

158 Wells, *The Outline of History*, p.690

159 *The Last Two Million Years*, p.240

160 Ibid., p.239

161 http://www.louis-xiv.de/louisold/louisxiv.html

162 http://www.wsu.edu/~dee/ENLIGHT/PRE.HTM

11:37

163 *The Last Two Million Years*, p.242-3

164 Wells, *The Outline of History*, p.690-1

165 *The Last Two Million Years*, p.250

166 *The Last Two Million Years*, p.248 (Inset)

167 Wells, *The Outline of History*, p.714

168 http://www.wsu.edu/~dee/ENLIGHT/ENLIGHT.HTM

169 http://www.wsu.edu/~dee/ENLIGHT/PHIL.HTM

11:38

170 *The Last Two Million Years*, p.250

171 Campbell, Webb, Nida, *The Old World : Past and Present*, p.347-8

172 http://www.wsu.edu/~dee/ENLIGHT/ROUSSEAU.HTM

173 http://www.ushistory.org/declaration/document/index.htm

174 http://chnm.gmu.edu/revolution/searchfr.php?function=find&keywor d=&topEurope=1&sourceText=1&Find=Find#

11:39

175 *The Last Two Million Years*, p.257

176 http://www.wsu.edu/~dee/ENLIGHT/INDUSTRY.HTM

11:40

177 Grove, *National Geographic Atlas of World History*, p.318

178 Ibid.

179 *mechanized warfare*. Encyclopedia.com http://www.encyclopedia. com/articles/08268.html

180 *tank*. Encyclopedia.com http://www.encyclopedia.com/articles/12625. html

181 Grove, *National Geographic Atlas of World History*, p.318

182 **"World War I."***Encyclopædia Britannica* from Encyclopædia Britannica 2006 CD. [Accessed February 28, 2008].

11:41

183 Grove, *National Geographic Atlas of World History*, p.318

184 *world war I aftermath and reckoning.* Encyclopedia.com http://www. encyclopedia.com/articles/14006aftermathandreckoning.html

185 *Lands and Peoples*, Volume 2 (Danbury, Connecticut: Grolier Incorporated, 1993), p.120

186 *Lands and Peoples*, p.121

187 **"Jordan."***Encyclopædia Britannica* from Encyclopædia Britannica 2006 CD. [Accessed February 28, 2008].

11:42

188 *The Last Two Million Years*, p. 262

189 Ibid., p.381-2

190 http://www.touregypt.net/hbritish.htm

11:43

191 *The Last Two Million Years*, p.417

192 Ibid., p.443

193 Ibid., p444

194 http://en.wikipedia.org/wiki/Suez_Canal

195 **"Libya."***Encyclopædia Britannica* from Encyclopædia Britannica 2006 CD. [Accessed February 28, 2008].

196 **"Sudan, The."***Encyclopædia Britannica* from Encyclopædia Britannica 2006 CD. [Accessed February 28, 2008].

11:44

197 Groves, *National Geographic Atlas of World History*, p.332-3

[198] Ibid., p.334

[199] Groves, *The National Geographic Atlas of World History*, p.336-7

[200] Wells, *The Outline of History*, p.991

[201] http://en.wikipedia.org/wiki/World_War_II

11:45

[202] *The Last Two Million Years*, p.264

[203] Ibid., p.354

[204] *The Story of America* (Pleasantville, New York: The Readers Digest Association, Inc., 1975), p.8

[205] *The Story of America*, p.90

[206] *The Last Two Million Years*, p.264

[207] http://www.aptnlibrary.com/ctca_how_we_lived.html